How to Use Advertising to Build Strong Brands

How to Use Advertising to Build Strong Brands

EDITED BY

JOHN PHILIP JONES

SAGE Publications
International Educational and Professional Publisher
Thousand Oaks   London   New Delhi

For information:

SAGE Publications, Inc.
2455 Teller Road
Thousand Oaks, California 91320
E-mail: order@sagepub.com

SAGE Publications Ltd.
6 Bonhill Street
London EC2A 4PU
United Kingdom

SAGE Publications India Pvt. Ltd.
M-32 Market
Greater Kailash I
New Delhi 110 048 India

Printed in the United States of America

Library of Congress Cataloging-in-Publication Data

Main entry under title:

How to use advertising to build strong brands / edited by
John Philip Jones.
    p. cm.
  Includes bibliographical references and index.
  ISBN 0-7619-1242-8 (cloth: acid-free paper)
  ISBN 0-7619-1243-6 (pbk.: acid-free paper)
  1. Advertising—Brand name products. 2. Brand name products.
I. Jones, John Philip.
  HF6161.B4 H69 1999
  659.1—dc21   99-6165

This book is printed on acid-free paper.

99 00 01 02 03 10 9 8 7 6 5 4 3 2 1

Acquiring Editor:	Harry Briggs
Editorial Assistant:	Mary Ann Vail
Production Editor:	Astrid Virding
Editorial Assistant:	Stephanie Allen
Designer/Typesetter:	Janelle LeMaster
Cover Designer:	Ravi Balasuriya

This series of handbooks is dedicated to David Ogilvy.

Every advertisement should be thought of as a contribution to the complex symbol which is the brand image. If you take that long view, a great many day-to-day problems solve themselves.

—David Ogilvy, 1963
Confessions of an Advertising Man

Contents

Part II

New and Growing Brands   **119**

Part III

Part IV

Part V

Developing an Understanding of Brands   335

Introduction

John Philip Jones

This handbook is the third in a series of five. The individual volumes are following one another off the press with minimal delays between them. The titles of the five volumes are as follows:

1. *How Advertising Works: The Role of Research*
2. *The Advertising Business: Operations, Creativity, Media Planning, Integrated Communications*
3. *How to Use Advertising to Build Strong Brands*
4. *International Advertising: Realities and Myths*
5. *Advertising Organizations and Publications: A Resource Guide*

Volume 3, like its predecessors, is the work of a number of authors—21 in all. Of these, 15 are North American and 6 are British; 11 are practitioners and 10 are academics. They are all specialists in their fields, and a number of them are at the leading edge of professional knowledge and expertise.

Advertising's greatest single contribution to business is its ability to build brands. The brand concept is described in detail in this book, especially in Chapter 2, which is devoted to the important topic of added values.

A brand is a product or service used by consumers. These consumers are mostly members of the general public, but on occasion the consumers of a brand can be industrial or business users. In all events, if a brand is to be successful it must be functionally efficient; indeed, it must be superior—or be perceived as superior—to competitive brands in the qualities most valued by its users. (These qualities may be quite different from the qualities required by users of other brands.) But a brand is more than just a product with functional properties, even superior ones. A successful brand will build a preference—a psychological predilection—in the minds of its users that encourages them to buy the brand repeatedly. This is why brands are the basic source of a manufacturer's long-term profitability. The consumer's preference for a brand is built substantially by what have become known as added values.

The brand concept had become an established tool of business before the end of the 19th century. However, until well into the 20th century the use of brands was confined largely to repeat-purchase packaged goods. This category (or group of categories) of merchandise still accounts for a third of the top 100 brand names. However, the extension of the concept—the development of brands in new fields—has been a most important characteristic of marketing practice during the past 50 years. This extension will shortly be illustrated, but the field where brands originated—repeat-purchase packaged goods—must first be described.

Repeat-Purchase Packaged Goods

The term *repeat-purchase packaged goods*—in Europe, *fast-moving consumer goods* (fmcg)—describes a large field. The important individual categories within it are packaged, canned, and frozen foods; over-the-counter drugs; tobacco products; toiletries and cosmetics; wine, beer, and liquor; soaps and cleaners; gum and candy; and soft drinks. This mixed collection of categories has considerable homogeneity from a marketing standpoint. All of the categories have six common general characteristics, and in most of these they differ at least in degree from other categories of products and services (such as automotive, travel, retail, direct response, financial, and entertainment).

1. Women are the most important group of buyers.

Repeat-purchase packaged goods are sold predominantly in supermarkets, drugstores, and mass merchandisers. In the large majority of cases, the buyers are women, although such goods are of course used by all members of the family in addition to the homemaker. There have been changes in the individual roles of women and men in many homes; 20% of households now have a male homemaker, and on a third of all shopping occasions a man is present, either buying alone or accompanying the lady of the house. Nevertheless, many if not most manufacturers of packaged goods continue to refer to their target consumer as *she*. The only other advertising category in which a female target group is comparably important is the retail one.

2. Buyers buy repeatedly and have repertoires of brands.

Brands are bought not once but repeatedly, in many cases in predictably regular patterns; hence the truth of the saying that when we build brands we are making customers and not just sales. In marketing jargon, we are building a long-term franchise.

In virtually every category examined empirically, it has been found that two-thirds of buyers normally buy (with varying degrees of irregularity) more than one brand. This introduces the extremely important concept of the repertoire of brands: the collection the homemaker buys in varying proportions, often (again) in predictably regular patterns.

The uniformity of such patterns will be a surprise to some readers. This element of constancy—or the inertia of habit—in most markets for repeat-purchase goods partly explains the manifest difficulty of breaking into such markets with new brands. It also suggests the large role for advertising aimed at reinforcement and protection for the majority of established brands. Indeed, much advertising is addressed to existing regular and irregular users of such brands. We advertise to these people in order to hold as well as to increase our market share. We talk to them with the intention of reinforcing their loyalty to our brand, to compliment them on their wisdom in using it so that they will remain friendly with us, and to encourage them to use it more than before. If we look upon advertising in this way, our approach becomes different from what conventional wisdom suggests, which is that advertising is a means of converting people, persuading them to switch from Brand A to Brand B. There is much evidence that brand advertising, as it is practiced in the real world, is based substantially on continuity and not on conversion.

Because of the large role of habit in the purchase decision, such decision making is often described as "low involvement," a concept first developed by the well-known researcher Herbert E. Krugman.

These factors of repetition and multibrand purchasing are generally more important with packaged goods than with most other categories because of characteristics endemic to such markets, notably the high rate of product use. The importance of repeat purchase means that in advertising repeat-purchase packaged goods, it is not only ethical but also good business to be truthful, because if the advertising overpromises, the customer will punish the manufacturer by not buying the brand again.

3. Competitive brands differ from one another in functional terms.

Many readers will be stopped by this statement. It may disturb a deep-seated and rather remarkable belief held by numerous people—especially journalists and academics—that competitive brands in any market are indistinguishable from one another in functional terms. The widespread prevalence of this belief has caused products in such markets to be referred to as "parity products" or "homogeneous package goods," and product improvements in them to be described as "cosmetic changes" or "induced product differentiation" created by advertising.

Most consumer goods markets are oligopolies dominated by a small number of large competitive manufacturers. It is substantially true that the nature of oligopolistic competition and the relative ease with which functional improvements can be copied are forces that cause functional innovations in new and restaged brands to be widely and sometimes rapidly diffused through markets. It is, however, both wrong and dangerous to infer from the force and characteristics of oligopolistic competition that all brands are functionally interchangeable. It is wrong because it flies in the face of the facts, and it is dangerous because such a line of thinking can persuade marketers to introduce new brands that offer a mere functional parity with their competitors, with a subsequent rate of failure that is in most cases only too easily and disheartyingly predictable.

The statements of researchers, advertisers, and workers in advertising agencies—people who have day-to-day operational knowledge of brands—

make it quite clear that competing brands in any category tend to be functionally different from one another. Their evidence of differences between brands in functional terms comes mainly from blind product tests, in which the names of the brands being compared are not disclosed, in order to focus exclusive attention on their functional properties.

Although product tests normally provide fairly clear-cut results, it is not always wise to interpret them in an equally clear-cut way. Brands with a "minority appeal" should not always be rejected by manufacturers, because these are often able to attract small groups of users interested in specific attributes, on which such brands might score well. In fact, in most markets there is a "tail" of profitable brands with individual market shares of less than 5%, all of which sell steadily to relatively small numbers of consumers.

What have knowledgeable practitioners got to say about functional product differences? Here are the views of five of them.[1] James O. Peckham, Sr., a researcher with 40 years of experience with the A. C. Nielsen Company, has written:

> Based on a composite trend of eight new and/or improved brands marketed nationally prior to the start of our study, we see that consumer purchases of these new brands are up 51% in the two-year period. If we examine the individual brands making up this fine sales trend, we find that they all had a "consumer plus" readily demonstrable to the consumer.

Again:

> The board chairman of one of the leading manufacturers of a household product recently stated in a speech before the National Industrial Conference Board that the company's top brand had had 55 product improvements in the 29 years of its existence.

And again:

> On a blind product test of your new brand versus leading brands already on the market, you should not ordinarily consider trying to build a consumer franchise unless you have a 60-40 preference—and 65-35 would be preferable.

J. Hugh Davidson, a senior executive in a major international marketing company, published an empirical examination of successful and unsuccessful new products in which he concluded that fully 74% of the successes I studied offered the consumer better performance at the same or higher price. . . . My study revealed a close correlation between a brand's success and its distinctiveness.

David Ogilvy, one of the most distinguished practitioners in the advertising agency field, referred to statements by the former chairman of Procter & Gamble (P&G):

Says Harness, "The key to successful marketing is superior product performance. . . . If the consumer does not perceive any real benefits in the brand, then no amount of ingenious advertising and selling can save it."

To which Ogilvy responded:

The best of all ways to beat P&G is, of course, to market a better product. Bell Brand potato chips defeated P&G's Pringles because they tasted better. And Rave overtook Lilt in less than a year because, not containing ammonia, it is a better product.

Bill Bernbach, who, like Ogilvy, was one of the luminaries of the postwar advertising scene, was equally clear on the importance of functionality:

I think the most important element in success in ad writing is the product itself. I can't say that often enough. Or emphasize it enough. Because I think a great ad campaign will make a bad product fail faster. It will get more people to know it's bad. And it's the product itself that's all important and that's why we, as an agency, work so closely with the client on his product—looking for improvements, looking for ways to make people want it, looking for additions to the product, looking for changes in the product. Because when you have that, you are giving the people something that they can't get elsewhere. And that is fundamentally what sells.

Rosser Reeves, as well-known a figure in the field as Ogilvy and Bernbach, observed:

The agency can induce the client to change his product, improve his product. We have done this on numerous occasions. . . . A great advertising man of three decades ago once said: "A gifted product is mightier than a gifted pen." How right he was! This is not a secondary road. It is often the first, and the best road, to travel.

4. Brands are enriched with added values.

In addition to the functional rewards that consumers get from using brands, there are further benefits to the consumer that are substantially psychic: added values, which are built by consumers' experience of using brands and by the advertising and the packaging. Added values are important to all products and services, especially to repeat-purchase packaged goods, but their importance relative to functional benefits varies according to product category; for instance, added values are relatively more important for toiletries than for food products. Packaged goods include those categories in which added values are of the most substantial importance.

The result of added values is that successful brands are preferred to their competitors in named product tests by a higher margin than in blind product tests, because the latter screen out added values and force respondents to react exclusively to functional performance. But it is important to appreciate that added values are added on top of functional performance and do not substitute for it. A misconception of this point is the main reason unsuccessful marketers have sacrificed fortunes in new brand ventures.

This matter is exceptionally important in the discussion of advertising. Here there is a real role for intuition and imagination, which are regarded by many people as predominantly feminine qualities, as well as for the logic, precision, and drive sometimes seen as predominantly masculine virtues. The reader will note how the feminine association of intuition and imagination is generally consistent with the first characteristic of repeat-purchase packaged goods in the present analysis: the importance of women as target consumers.

5. The field is relatively advertising-intensive.

This means that a brand's advertising, when expressed as a proportion of the value of its sales, is a relatively high figure. Data in the journal *Advertising Age* (which are published annually on a company and not a brand basis) show a median figure in most of the categories of repeat-purchase packaged goods above 4% and substantially higher in certain categories. The comparable figures in categories other than packaged goods are mostly much lower. For instance, those for the automotive, airline, and retail categories are all about 2%.

The obvious inference from the information in the preceding paragraph is that advertising is a relatively important sales-generating activity in packaged goods marketing, or rather that it is perceived as such by the manufacturers, whose expenditures measured in real terms are relatively constant year by year. This consistency suggests that companies have experience-based guidelines for the marketplace effectiveness of certain levels of advertising pressure.

6. The field is very large.

Advertising investments in the various categories of repeat-purchase goods are consistently extremely large, accounting for probably a third of advertising of all types in the United States. The size of the total category and its special importance to large advertisers have significant additional related effects. For instance, television is the most important advertising medium for the largest advertisers (except those in the tobacco and hard liquor industries, owing to government prohibition), and it is no coincidence that it is with packaged goods that television has developed its ability both to show the functional characteristics of brands by demonstrating them and generate nonfunctional added values largely through the communication of mood and emotion.

Manufacturers of repeat-purchase packaged goods also have become the most important clients of the largest and most sophisticated advertising agencies. Improvements in the techniques and skills of writing and scheduling advertisements almost invariably take place with packaged goods, and we are accustomed to associating most of the advances in the marketing field with names such as Procter & Gamble, Philip Morris/Kraft General Foods, RJR Nabisco, Unilever, Johnson & Johnson, Warner-Lambert, Coca-Cola, and Anheuser-Busch, along with the advertising agencies employed by such companies.

Extensions of the Brand Concept

Every year, *Advertising Age* lists the top brand names in the United States, ranked by their measured advertising expenditures. These "Top 100 Megabrands" in 1997 fell into the categories listed in Table 1.1. Repeat-purchase packaged goods and related fields account for 32 out of the top 100 names. Although they represent a very substantial proportion (28%) of the aggregate advertising expenditure of the 100 leaders, this proportion is much less than it once was. During the early 1960s the comparable figure was approximately 70%, and during the early 1980s it was about 60%.[2]

TABLE 1.1 Distribution of Top 100 Brands, 1997

Repeat-purchase packaged goods	21
Quasi repeat-purchase packaged goods (fast food, photographic film, greeting cards, agricultural commodities)	11
Automotive	26
Retail	14
Communications services	7
Electronic equipment	7
Financial services	7
Others (entertainment, collectibles, etc.)	8

SOURCE: Derived from data published in the July 13, 1998, issue of *Advertising Age*. Copyright Crain Communications Inc., 1998.

The decline in the proportion of total advertising expenditure accounted for by repeat-purchase packaged goods does not mean that the manufacturers of these goods have suffered a catastrophic long-term loss of business. The most important change affecting them directly has been the growth in the strength and bargaining power of the retail trade, which has clipped manufacturers' wings to a noticeable although not disastrous extent by reducing manufacturers' margins. Some of these margins have gone indirectly into retailers' own advertising. There are 14 large retailers included in Table 1.1. An even more weighty factor is the increase in the importance of store brands in the food and drug fields. But most such brands come from local and regional retailers, which are individually too small to come up on the list of the "Top 100 Megabrands."

The major reason the leading manufacturers' brands of repeat-purchase packaged goods now account for a slowly but continuously diminishing share of total advertising is that the aggregate growth in the field has for some years been driven by the other categories shown in Table 1.1: automotive (e.g., Chevrolet), retail (e.g., Sears), communications services (e.g., AT&T), electronic equipment (e.g., IBM), financial services (e.g., American Express), entertainment (e.g., HBO), and collectibles (e.g., Franklin Mint). These all represent a vast outward expansion of brands.

This has by no means come to a halt. In fact, there are no obvious limits to the extension of the brand concept into new territory. With this in mind, I have devoted the five chapters in Part IV of this volume to branding's frontiers—the employment of the brand concept in what until relatively recently were rather unexpected fields.

What Brands Contribute to Manufacturers' Business

The alternative to manufacturers' pursuing branding strategies is for them to be in commodity businesses, such as growing and preparing bulk vegetables, constructing components for machinery, manufacturing building supplies, or making generic drugs. Manufacturers of commodities compete on price. There is no differentiation of products within segments or even within categories—the ruling price in the market is the lowest one, and the ruling manufacturer's margin is also the lowest. There is no place in such markets for added values.

Branding offers manufacturers three incomparable advantages: Brands encourage customer loyalty, brands generate higher profits than do unbranded commodities, and brands can become (within limits) extendable assets.

1. Brands encourage customer loyalty.

By definition, all successful brands of repeat-purchase packaged goods are bought with varying degree of repetition. The same is true, mutatis mutandis, for brands in other fields. Even with durables (e.g., automobiles), although repurchase is infrequent, it is an important objective for a manufacturer.

Successful brands encourage repurchase through consumers' satisfaction with their functional properties, working in harmony with added values created and built by the advertising. The advertising works to reinforce consumers' satisfaction with the brand.

A brand's franchise—its consumer base—is polarized in terms of volume usage. As a general rule, the 20% of heaviest buyers account for more than half total volume, and the 80% of lightest buyers account for the remainder. This is demonstrated in Table 1.2.[3]

The 20% of heaviest users of any brand are an especially important group for its manufacturer. These people must be kept faithful because of the loss of business that would ensue if their loyalty were to erode. And because these consumers already regard the brand favorably, it is often easier to encourage extra purchases from them than from light users.

The obvious reason so much business is concentrated on heavy users is that their rate of purchase is higher than that of light users. The rate of purchase for all users in a category and all users of a brand can easily be averaged. This produces the mean number of purchase occasions per annum. This rate of

TABLE 1.2 Volume Accounted for by 20% of Heaviest Buyers

Product Type	%
Packaged detergents	53
Liquid detergents	54
Bar soaps	50
Shampoo	53
Toilet tissue	46
Ice cream	58
Mayonnaise	52
Peanut butter	55
Ground coffee	55
Diet carbonated soft drinks	67
Breakfast cereals	52
Analgesics	59

usage contains an important internal bias, which is demonstrated in Table 1.3. In the right-hand column, the figures are indexed on the average for all buyers of all brands in the category. The data are ranked by brand quintiles—that is, the brands are clustered into five equal-size groups and ranked by the size of the brands in each quintile, from the smallest to the largest.[4]

It is clear from Table 1.3 that as a brand grows larger and more successful, its users will use it more often. The big breakthrough comes with brands whose share of market exceeds about 15%. In earlier writings I have coined the term *penetration supercharge* to describe this phenomenon, which is at the heart of, and the most demonstrable manifestation of, branding.[5] It is the main engine propelling the manufacturers of successful brands toward future prosperity.

2. Brands generate higher profits than do unbranded commodities.

The extra profitability of successful brands comes from three sources. First is the tendency, described in the preceding paragraph, for users of larger brands to buy them with greater-than-average frequency. Second—a related point—is that when measured per percentage point of market share, the advertising expenditure needed to support large brands is significantly lower than that needed to support small ones. In other words, larger brands are more advertising-efficient; they use their advertising budgets more economically than small brands can. There is a widely published regression called the

TABLE 1.3   Average Purchase Frequency (Indexed), Brands Ranked by Quintiles

	Average Share of Market (%)	Average Purchase Frequency (index, average = 100)
First quintile	1.8	84
Second quintile	2.8	94
Third quintile	3.9	92
Fourth quintile	6.8	97
Fifth quintile	18.7	125

advertising-intensiveness curve that demonstrates clearly this difference between large and small brands. It is described in Chapter 11 of this volume.

The third aspect of the profitability of brands is the most direct one. Brands can command higher prices than can unbranded commodities. The truth of this statement is evident from a visit to any supermarket, such as the one described in my book *What's in a Name?*[6] In a more recent examination of the average prices of 78 different and typical brands, I calculated their category averages, with each brand's price indexed on this average. Ranking the brands by size, I found that brands numbered among the largest 20 averaged an index of 112—that is, their prices were 12% above the average. Brands numbered 59 through 68 averaged 107; those numbered 69 through 78 (i.e., the very largest) averaged 117. Big brands command above-average prices, and the biggest brands command the highest prices of all.[7]

3. Brands can become (within limits) extendable assets.

Brand stretching, sometimes known as line extension, has been one of the most striking characteristics of marketing practice during the 1980s and 1990s. There are a number of hidden reasons behind it, but it is basically derived from the theory that the equity of a brand in one product category can be partially transferred to other brands in that category (liquid Tide based on powder Tide) or to brands in different categories (Ivory shampoo based on Ivory toilet soap) by the simple means of using the same name and package design.

There have been many successful examples of line extension, but there have also been many failures. The failures have mainly been caused by manufacturers' underspending on the launch of the new brands, in the erroneous belief that the name itself will provide all the brand equity that a new brand will need. As described in Chapter 11 in this volume, all new brands require advertising investments determined by the volumes of advertising in their product categories. The transferable equity does not amount to much in the short term unless it is supported by advertising.

However, taking a long view, the policy of marketing different brands under the same umbrella name undoubtedly carries some synergy, and manufacturers as disparate as Kraft, Kellogg's, Cadbury's, Ford, the Franklin Mint, and L. L. Bean can attest to its value. This can be manifested in a strengthening of the manufacturer's position vis-à-vis the consumer; for example, it becomes easier for a manufacturer to persuade a consumer to sample a brand with an established name than a brand with a new one. In the food and drug fields, there is a second and perhaps more important aspect of synergy, one concerned with the retail trade. This use of a common brand name generally strengthens the manufacturer's presence—notably its in-store display—and does much to augment sales personnel's confidence, "clout," and bargaining ability in their negotiations with their retail customers.

Brands and Their Owners

Branding for the mass market calls for talent and large resources. The size of the investment required tends to make it the exclusive domain of large companies. Small start-ups based on brains and drive but not much capital sometimes—but only too rarely—succeed, and when they do so they operate almost invariably in rapidly growing product categories—Macintosh in personal computers, Microsoft in software, Yahoo! in search engines for the Internet. In a country like the United States, the large majority of product categories are not growing. Market maturity means not only a deceleration of category expansion, but also domination by a handful of large oligopolists. Small new competitors are almost never able to break in.

The difficulties and expense of branding are of three main types:

- The failure rate of new brand introductions is discouragingly high (as discussed in Chapter 13 of this volume). Only large firms have sufficient resources to absorb such losses. Success or failure may not be apparent for a period of many months—perhaps years—after the launch, a long enough time for rival manufacturers to develop their responses to an initially successful newcomer. Slice and Lever 2000 are good examples to illustrate this point. Despite strikingly successful launches, these brands did not manage to sustain their original momentum. After 2 or 3 years, established competitors came out with product variants that took back much of the business initially gained by the newcomers.

- Closely related to the high failure rate of new brand introductions is their high initial cost in terms of research and development, production capacity, sales force resources, and—not least—advertising and sales promotions. As explained in Chapters 11 and 13, it is rare for a new brand to make money within its first 2 or 3 years of existence. Only large companies have the resources to sustain the necessary investment.

- The successful progress of an ongoing brand also calls for high expenditures, to pay for improving the formula and design to keep the brand in its (often leading) position in the marketplace and for regular advertising restages. However, as Sir David Orr, a prominent advertiser, has pointed out, "Provided that [a brand] is kept up-to-date as a product, by technical innovation and updating, and that its communication is kept relevant, it can be sustained for decades or more." [8]

The essential reason major companies in consumer goods fields persist without flagging or discouragement in new brand ventures, despite the high failure rate, and the reason they often (but not always) devote the most painstaking attention to protecting their geese that lay the golden eggs, is that brands are their business. This phrase has an emphatically positive connotation, with brands seen as manufacturers' source of protection and growth. Besides other qualities, brand innovation invariably calls for aggressiveness. Unless manufacturers strive to be first with new brand ideas, at the same time building walls around their existing properties, they will lose both opportunities and business to rich and talented competitors—and in most product categories there is no shortage of these.

Notes

1. All as quoted in John Philip Jones, *What's in a Name? Advertising and the Concept of Brands* (New York: Simon & Schuster-Lexington, 1986), 4-6.

2. Ibid., 248.

3. See John Philip Jones, *When Ads Work: New Proof That Advertising Triggers Sales* (New York: Simon & Schuster-Lexington, 1995), chap. 12.

4. Ibid.

5. Jones, *What's in a Name?* 114, 126.

6. Ibid., 18-21.

7. Jones, *When Ads Work.*

8. Sir David Orr, "Foreword," in John Philip Jones, *Does It Pay to Advertise? Cases Illustrating Successful Brand Advertising* (New York: Simon & Schuster-Lexington, 1989), xx.

P a r t   I

Brands: Added Values and Brand Equity

Brands and Added Values

John Philip Jones

A Historical Perspective

The concept of the brand is centrally important to an understanding of advertising's long-term effects. It is advertising that transforms a product that provides functional benefits and no more into a brand that offers the consumer psychological rewards in addition to the functional ones. However, brands—which in many cases originated a hundred or more years ago—were developed for a different set of purposes altogether.[1]

The first purpose of branding was to confirm the legal protection afforded by the inventor's patent, and the second was to guarantee quality and homogeneity after sellers and buyers had lost face-to-face contact. This was a result of the growth of industrialization, with manufacture in large factories distant from where most consumers lived. The majority of consumer goods markets today are oligopolies; that is, they are dominated by a small number of manufacturers whose brands are in close competition with one another. A third purpose of branding stemmed directly from oligopolists' need to differentiate their products. They quite correctly saw branding as a device that would enable them to control their markets better, by preventing other people's products from being substituted for theirs.

Generally speaking, oligopolists will compete on price, normally by means of active and continuous price promotions. But competition among them is not confined to price. The strength of oligopolists' brands and in particular the added values that enrich them move the field of competition from price reduction to product and brand improvement, progress in the latter tending to reduce the need for the former (although it is never eliminated). Margins are at least maintained, but not all are put into profit, because building brands costs a great deal of money.

Manufacturers will do everything possible to make their brands distinctive. They will aim to persuade users that their brands are unique, thereby protecting the brands from the direct competition of other brands. A strong brand suppresses or at least reduces substitution.

Economists describe this blocking of substitution as a reduction in the price elasticity of demand. The demand curve—the geometrical description used in price analysis—becomes more vertical (see Figure 2.1). A brand with an elastic demand curve—which is relatively horizontal—has many substitutes, and an increase in price will lead to a substantial loss of sales. A brand with an inelastic demand curve—which is relatively vertical—has few substitutes, and an increase in price will lead to little loss of business.[2]

Using as illustrations the demand curves in Figure 2.1, the purpose of advertising is twofold:

1. It boosts demand in toto. If the demand curve before advertising is D1, then the curve after advertising, D2, shows that at every level of price, the quantity sold is higher than before.
2. It also reduces substitution and makes the demand curve less elastic, tilting it in the vertical direction (D3). This means that the manufacturer will not lose much business from a price increase. In other words, it enables the manufacturer to maintain better control of the pricing process.

The Role of Added Values

In this important process of increasing a manufacturer's control of pricing, the key ingredient is the distinction between a product and a brand. A product

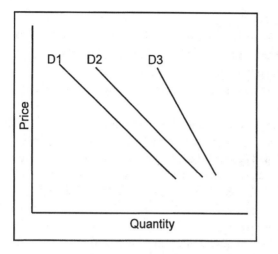

Figure 2.1. The Effect of Advertising on Demand

is something with merely a functional purpose. A brand offers something in addition to its functional purpose. All brands are products (including brands, such as Hertz and American Airlines, that are services) in that they serve a functional purpose. But not all products are brands. Thus the definition of a brand should be as follows: *A brand is a product that provides functional benefits plus added values that some consumers value enough to buy.*

Added values form the most important part of the definition of a brand. By way of introduction, two general points must be made. First, the strongest brands are often the most distinctive. In their distinctiveness, however, they are also generally well balanced between motivating benefits (those generally functional benefits that prompt the consumer to use any brand in the product field) and discriminating benefits (those that prompt the consumer to buy one brand rather than another). All brands are different from others in the obvious sense that their names and packaging are different, but distinctiveness generally goes beyond these elements. However, when a brand and its advertising are based so much on discriminators that they neglect motivators, this is a recipe for a weak brand.

The second point I want to make concerns the emphasis that should be placed on *some consumers* in the above definition. Tastes differ so widely that no brand can be all things to all people. Moreover, a manufacturer who strives to cover too wide a field will produce a brand that is number two or number three over a wide range of attributes, rather than number one over a limited range of qualities (which might enable it to become first choice to a limited group of consumers—the normal route to success). Most marketing professionals contend that it is more attractive to go for a limited part of the market rather than to move head-on against the entrenched competition in the largest sector.

We now come to the matter of added values, a subject that has caused some of the greatest controversies embracing the techniques, economics, and ethics of advertising. There is no doubt whatsoever that added values play a role in almost all purchasing decisions. These values are over and beyond the functional benefits for which the brand or product is bought. The idea of added values is not a new one—it was described succinctly by James Webb Young in a book titled *How to Become an Advertising Man,* which was based on his teaching at the University of Chicago some 50 years ago (although the book was first published only in 1963): "the use of advertising to add a subjective value to the tangible values of the product, for subjective values are no less real than the tangible ones." [3]

Young describes a simple five-part model of how advertising works:

- By familiarizing
- By reminding
- By spreading news
- By overcoming inertia
- By adding a value not in the product

Young implies, although he does not make the point explicitly, that advertising's most important role is the last of the five—adding values. This is of course a matter of prime importance with established brands, because it enables them to maintain their distinctiveness (i.e., reducing competitive brands' ability to substitute, as explained).

What are these added values and where do they come from? Some marketing professionals claim that every factor from a brand's early history to the distribution of its competitors has a bearing on them, but although this is not completely untrue, some factors are clearly more important than others. All the most important added values are nonfunctional, although I would include as an added value the unexpected functional uses we sometimes find for some brands (such as the way Arm & Hammer baking soda can be used to sweeten a swimming pool or deodorize a refrigerator). But this is by and large an exception. Most brands have a known and restricted range of functions, and added values are the *nonfunctional benefits over and beyond them.*

By *known and restricted range of functions,* I mean for an automobile its ability to move us from place to place safely, reliably, and economically; for a suit of clothes, its warmth and appearance; for a packet of cornflakes, its taste and nutrition; for a bottle of perfume, its smell; and for a power drill, its ability to produce holes of a range of uniform sizes reliably, safely, and quickly. Beyond these functional qualities, the most important added values are as follows:

1. Those that come from *experience of the brand:* These include familiarity, known reliability, and reduction of risks. A brand becomes an old friend. This introduces the centrally important notion of brand personality, which can on occasion be interpreted as the voice of the manufacturer (e.g., Betty Crocker or the Jolly Green Giant). But it is much more frequently interpreted as the personality of the brand itself—its functional and nonfunctional features as they might be described in quasi-human terms, a device used by some advertising agencies to map a brand's position in relation to its competition.

2. Those that come from *the sorts of people who use the brand* (rich or snobbish or young or glamorous or masculine or feminine): The reader can find many examples of brands that have these user-associations, most of which are fostered by the advertising.

3. Those that come from *a belief that the brand is effective:* This is related to the way in which some medicines, even placebos, work on people's beliefs and sometimes even make them do their job. There is good evidence that the branding of proprietary drugs affects the mind's influence over bodily processes: "Double-blind trials demonstrated that branding accounts for a quarter to a third of the pain relief. That is to say, branding works like an ingredient of its own interacting with the pharmacological active ingredients to produce something more powerful than an unbranded tablet." [4] Belief in effectiveness also plays an important role in cosmetics, in their ability to make their users feel more beautiful, with generally beneficial results.

4. Those that come from *the appearance of the brand:* This is the prime role of packaging. And lest it be thought that this matters only for brands sold to impressionable adolescents, I refer the reader to Theodore Levitt's well-known essay "The Morality (?) of Advertising," in which, as part of a well-reasoned discussion of added values, he recounts the following anecdote: "A few years ago, an electronics laboratory offered a $700 testing device for sale. The company ordered two different front panels to be designed, one by the engineers who developed the equipment and one by professional industrial designers. When the two models were shown to a sample of laboratory directors with Ph.D.'s, the professional design attracted twice the purchase intentions that the

engineers' design did. Obviously the laboratory director who had been baptized
into science at M.I.T. is quite as responsive to the blandishments of packaging
as the Boston matron." [5]

The reader may be surprised that I have omitted from this list the added
values that come from a manufacturer's name and reputation. I have done so
for three reasons. First, consumers do not know who manufactures many of
the brands they use. (Try to think of who makes the leading brands of laundry
detergent, bar soap, or shampoo.) Second, brand names are sometimes used as
"umbrella" devices to help launch new but related brands (like Ivory shampoo,
which follows Ivory soap), and in examining such strategy, Nielsen has found
evidence that the umbrella name has little direct influence on the success of
the new brand.[6] Third, a familiar brand name is no longer needed as a guarantee
of a new product's homogeneity and quality. All branded goods are known to
be homogeneous and to perform their functions reasonably well. It is doubtful
whether flagrant deceit was ever common, and it is rare indeed today for no
better reason than the legal penalties attached to deception in advertising.

The contribution of added values to consumer choice is easily demonstrated
through the commonly used technique of matched product tests. In these tests,
members of one sample of consumers use and judge different brands blind
(i.e., in coded but unnamed packages) and members of a second and similar
sample of consumers use and judge those same brands in their normal containers. The general pattern is that the preferences among identified brands are
quite different from preferences among those same brands in coded but
unidentified containers. A leading breakfast cereal was preferred to two
competitors in blind test in the ratios of 47:27:26. When the test was repeated
with identified packages, the preferences changed to 59:26:15. The proportion
of people preferring the leading brand was therefore 47% blind and 59%
named, a difference of one-fourth (12 percentage points on a base of 47), which
can only have come from the added values in the brand that were not in the
product alone.

Added values arise mainly from people's use and experience of the brand,
from the advertising, and from the packaging. It follows that added values are
not immediately available to a manufacturer of a new brand; rather, they are
built over time. A brand enters the world naked and must rely almost solely
on its functional properties for its initial survival. There is good empirical
support for this belief. The majority of the large number of new brands that do
not succeed fail because of their functional weaknesses. It also follows that
old and successful brands build up a large stock of added values in the goodwill

of their users, so that a new brand whose manufacturer has ambitions to overtake them must start off with a generous margin of functional superiority if the new brand is to make any progress.

The role of advertising in building added values is undeniable. But what type of advertising is most effective? I believe that the best brand-building advertising is self-effacing. The impression left on the viewer/reader should be of the brand and not of the advertising per se. This point is illustrated forcefully in a parable told by Alfred Politz, which I paraphrase as follows:

> There were once three rooms, all opening on the same beautiful view. However, when a person entered any of the rooms, he or she could not see the view directly; it was possible to see only a mirror in which the view was reflected. In the first room, the mirror was cracked; in the second, the mirror was a lovely 18th-century artifact; in the third, the whole wall was a plate glass mirror.
>
> A man entered the first room and saw a beautiful view reflected in a cracked mirror. A man entered the second room and saw a beautiful view reflected in an antique mirror. A man entered the third room and saw only a beautiful view.

For *view,* read *brand.* For *mirror,* read *advertising.* Politz inhabits the third room. And so do I.[7]

Young & Rubicam Brand Asset Valuator

The measurement of added values has always been a difficult task. One of the more interesting approaches employing quantitative consumer research is the Brand Asset Valuator (BAV), developed by the leading advertising agency Young & Rubicam (Y&R) and published in 1994. The BAV classifies the strength of a brand as a totality—as an amalgam of functional properties and added values.

The BAV is the end product of information collected from interviews with 30,000 people in 19 countries. It is built from two variables, each following a continuum: *brand vitality,* based on a brand's relevance and differentiation; and *brand stature,* based on a brand's esteem and familiarity.

Specific brands are plotted on a scatter diagram, which is divided into four quadrants. These cluster the brands according to four combinations (see Figure 2.2). Moving clockwise from the bottom left-hand quadrant, the brands are classified as follows: (a) low vitality–low stature, (b) high vitality–low stature, (c) high vitality–high stature, and (d) low vitality–high stature.

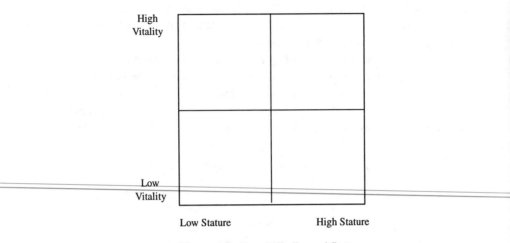

High
Vitality

Low
Vitality

Low Stature   High Stature

Figure 2.2. Brand Vitality and Stature

The BAV is a diagnostic tool that may be used to help direct a brand's (and a manufacturer's) strategy. It has obvious "hands-on" value. Y&R has published the names of typical brands that score high in various countries in relevance, differentiation, esteem, and familiarity. The classification is well-founded, but there are few surprises in the positioning of specific brands.

Notes

1. John Philip Jones, *What's in a Name? Advertising and the Concept of Brands* (New York: Simon & Schuster-Lexington, 1986), chap. 2.

2. John Philip Jones, *How Much Is Enough? Getting the Most From Your Advertising Dollar* (New York: Simon & Schuster-Lexington, 1992), app. A.

3. James Webb Young, *How to Become an Advertising Man* (Chicago: Crain, 1979[1963]), 73.

4. Judie Lannon and Peter Cooper, "Humanistic Advertising: A Holistic Cultural Perspective," *International Journal of Advertising,* July/September 1983, 206.

5. Theodore Levitt, "The Morality (?) of Advertising," *Harvard Business Review,* July/August 1970, 89.

6. James O. Peckham, Sr., *The Wheel of Marketing,* 2nd ed. (privately published, 1981; available through A. C. Nielsen, New York), 89-91.

7. Hugh S. Hardy (ed.), *The Politz Papers* (Chicago: American Marketing Association, 1990), 40.

Brand Ideas and Their Importance

"When Do You Tell the Agency What the Brand Means?"

Harold F. Clark, Jr.

A t a recent gathering of marketing directors and product managers from Central European countries, the group facilitator carefully explained the basics of brand planning: target groups, competitive framework, benefit(s), reasons, brand positioning, brand character, and, finally, in a comprehensive summary at the end of the second day, the components of a brand briefing to the advertising agency. "Any questions?" he asked, confident there would be few. "Yes, one," replied a bright marketing director from Hungary. "When do you tell the agency what the brand means?"

Behind this telling question are two critical assumptions:

1. The brand should have a meaning.
2. Everyone involved in the brand should know what that meaning is.

Neither of these assumptions is automatically true. Not every brand has a broadly understood and agreed-upon meaning. Frequently, there is no clear, articulated statement of what the brand does (or even should) stand for. And if you were to ask each person working on a brand what it stands for, you would be unlikely to get consistent responses.

Yet consumers know what a brand means. A favorite research technique to determine brand personality asks consumers, "If this brand came to life, who would it be?" Agencies expect people to answer this question—and they can. They express a meaning that supersedes brand positioning, brand character, the competitive framework, and even target group. For them, what the brand stands for summarizes its quality and superiority (or inferiority). Marketers manage the components of branding; consumers perceive brands holistically. They know what a brand means; for them, it is the essence of the brand, or what we call the *brand idea*.

The Brand Idea

A brand is more than an object; it is a relationship between the brand-as-object and the consuming public, a relationship that derives from a unique combination of associations attached to a product (name, package, history, advertising, promotion, and so on) by which consumers differentiate one product from another. Neither the product nor the brand is a static entity. Products change all the time. Kodak in 1932 described the benefits of its film in precisely the same language that is used today. Obviously, in that period of time, the physical film product has changed dramatically. Products change as market conditions change, as research and development departments discover new formulations, as retail distribution or pricing changes, as consumers' needs and perceptions change.

What endures is the sense of the brand. What Kodak meant to parents photographing their baby with a Kodak Brownie in 1932 is what Kodak means to parents today. People, then as now, trust Kodak to preserve their memories. As their needs have changed, their brand, "Kodak," has remained consistent and relevant. It has never let them down. The result is a strong bond between consumers and the Kodak brand.

Such a strong brand relationship develops when a product continues to meet people's needs with product performance that is better than or different from other alternatives people could find to meet those needs. People cling long and hard to their conviction that "their" brands are somehow superior to all others in the category.

The goal of any brand marketer is to develop as many of these relationships as possible—the more relationships, the bigger the brand. The stronger the relationships, the greater the brand loyalty—the brand equity that brand has with the consuming public. For the brands with which they have the strongest relationships, consumers have the clearest sense of what those brands stand for, of what those brands mean to them.

The *brand idea* is the expression, or phrase, that summarizes this meaning. It is not an advertising slogan; indeed, it may never even appear in advertising. Rather, it is the set of words that defines what the greatest number of people would say if asked to tell the first thing they think of when the brand is mentioned.

To determine the characteristics of a brand idea, informal research has been conducted among different groups of people who have been asked what various brands mean to them. From the analysis of these brand response surveys, it is possible to define some of the characteristics that the strongest brand ideas have in common: reality, a proprietary nature, uniqueness, longevity, and consistency.

Real, Positive, and True

A brand idea is a real idea for consumers and nonconsumers alike. It stands for a genuine feeling. The strength of consumers' relationships to a brand lies in their conviction that what they believe is true. "Perception is reality" is more than an advertising cliché; advertising can be said to work only if it is able to influence perceptions positively.

As long as consumer perceptions are positive and match what the marketers wish their brand to stand for, advertising communications can work to re-inforce those perceptions or possibly to modify them slightly. It is very difficult to change a negative perception or correct a misperception. In the early 1970s, the Miller Brewing Company waited 28 months before its new "Miller Time" campaign showed any positive results in the brand attitude tracking studies. Schlitz was never able to erase the negative image it inadvertently created with its campaign that claimed the brewery had shortened the 28-day brewing process to 14 days.

Paradoxically, it is easy to destroy a positive perception. One brand response research showed that more than 50% of the responses to Exxon related to the *Valdez* oil spill; all the mentions of power, energy, transportation, research, exploration, and the "tiger in the tank" together did not equal the strength of that oil spill. It will take far longer to rebuild a positive brand idea for Exxon than the short time it took to destroy it.

Proprietary

The brand idea must belong to one brand and to no other. A cowboy sitting on a horse at the top of a particularly scenic canyon beneath snow-capped mountains evokes only one brand. A boot company that wanted to use such a photograph discovered that even with the boot manufacturer's logo prominent at the bottom of the advertisement, the vast majority of respondents thought Marlboro was the advertiser.

A brand idea can become proprietary through usage. The source of a brand idea is frequently, but not necessarily, a particularly penetrating and effective advertising idea that so aptly fits a brand that consumers increasingly relate it to that brand and no other. Marlboro did not "own" cowboys until it began to use cowboys in an advertising campaign developed by Leo Burnett in the late 1950s.

For a brand idea to work, it must "fit" the brand—that is, make sense to a large enough number of people who feel it is appropriate and relevant. If people believe a brand is trying to "put them on" or be something that it is not and cannot become, they will reject it.

People discriminate between brands by means of brand ideas. The stronger the brand idea, the greater the likelihood that customers will be able to identify that brand unmistakably, to recall its name, and to ask for it with security. That degree of strength depends on an idea that comfortably fits that brand and no other.

Unique

A strong brand idea cannot be confused with any other. It is fresh and original. It always stands out.

In the early 1990s, long-distance telephone services became one of the most heavily advertised categories in the U.S. marketplace. Each of three major marketers vied to establish its brand idea: AT&T, "powerful, ubiquitous, reliable, and strong"; MCI, "low price"; and Sprint, "pin-drop clarity." In 1993-1994, the advertising for AT&T began to attack MCI on price, and MCI introduced a series of striking image commercials about the Internet. According to subsequent brand response research, the brand ideas for both these carriers became muddied. Neither stood for much that was unique. Sprint, on the other hand, stood for pin-drop clarity in more than 55% of the responses and, because of Candice Bergen, for classy irreverence in an additional 26% of the responses. Sprint took a unique demonstration and a distinctive personality and appropriated them in ways that gave Sprint the clearest brand identity, even though it is the smallest spender of the three.

Long-Lasting

A strong brand idea will last a long time, through generations of consuming groups. Johnson & Johnson's "No More Tears" baby shampoo is recognized as a compelling, discriminating brand idea that belongs to the J&J brand even though competitors have used the phrase "no tears" and J&J itself has changed advertising and promotional expressions for the brand.

In the early 1970s, BBDO developed the "Have It Your Way" campaign for Burger King. The line contributed to the important brand idea for the number-two fast-food hamburger restaurant: flame-broiled burgers customized just for you. Over the years, the corporation has changed advertising executions almost annually, but personalized service with good, fresh food has persisted as the core of the brand idea. Today, many people can still hum the "Hold-the-pickles-hold-the-lettuce-special-orders-don't-upset-us" theme even though they haven't heard it for 20 years. Possibly you hummed it yourself, just now.

In the late 1960s, one of the lemon-lime soft drinks introduced an advertising idea that quickly became its defining brand idea: the "un-cola" for 7-Up.

Later, the brand abandoned this idea when the company changed advertising agencies in the 1970s. Recently, it has reappeared in some of its advertising because, 20 years later, it remains a compelling, discriminating brand idea.

Another aspect of longevity is the time it takes to develop a strong brand idea. It is not something that exists, full blown, as a brand is being introduced. Because it depends on understanding how customers define their relationships to the brand, enough of those relationships have to be developed and sustained over a period of time for the brand idea to become adequately defined. The advertiser may control the stimulus that evokes the relationship between the customer and brand, but finally what matters is how the customer defines that relationship.

One brand response survey found that Chevrolet enjoys one of the clearest brand ideas the survey uncovered: 81.8% of the responses positioned Chevrolet as "America's car." This response dates back to an advertising campaign from the 1950s, "See the USA in Your Chevrolet," and continues through to the "Heartbeat of America." No campaign has aggressively claimed the "America's car" brand idea overtly. Rather, it has been the careful accumulation of many stimuli over many, many years.

Consistent

The most difficult task in managing a brand idea is that of maintaining its consistency. As we have seen, a brand idea can be powerful and long-lasting. Sometimes, as in the case of Burger King or 7-Up, it will last in consumers' minds despite the advertiser's best efforts to erase it. Chevrolet enjoys a discriminating identity as a result of its consistent imagery over decades.

Regardless of various marketing attempts to change or modify a brand's position or personality, the loyal consumer continues to think of it in terms of all the familiar triggers: its packaging, logo, distinctive coloring, name, advertising/promotion symbols, and so on. People do not "see" change or define brands in terms of what is different. They recognize and adhere to the familiar—what they know, what they are comfortable with. Therefore, if a product enjoys a clear, compelling, and easy-to-communicate brand idea, marketing management should have the courage to stay with it.

This kind of courage faces many obstacles. New product managers invariably want to change elements of the brand and put their own imprint on it. Agencies look for new and better "breakthrough" advertising executions. And most deadly of all, well-meaning people place greater emphasis on advertising executions because, it is generally believed, there is no difference between the brand idea and the advertising idea.

Advertising Ideas and the Brand Idea

The brand idea is what the company wants the brand to stand for in the minds of consumers—over time. Longevity and consistency contribute to its effectiveness.

An advertising idea is the translation of the brand idea into advertising communication, at a specific time, to a specific target group, to solve a specific problem.

At a given moment, because of pressures connected with product or market or competition or consumer needs, an advertising campaign is developed for a specific medium to reach a well-defined target group. It has important, concrete, short-term objectives—generally a problem to be solved or an opportunity to be grasped. After it has achieved those objectives, a different campaign to solve a different problem will follow. Both should support and reflect the common brand idea, yet both are distinct from the brand idea.

An advertising idea is just one isolated expression of the brand idea. Another campaign, in another medium, may be a different expression of the same brand idea. A premium beer runs different executions during prime network time from those run during a midnight station break on *Saturday Night Live*. Executions will differ; the brand idea should be consistent and coherent.

The issue becomes complex because advertising ideas have certain characteristics of their own that are similar to brand idea characteristics:

- *Proprietary:* A good advertising idea should be a strong stimulus that evokes only one brand and no one else's.
- *Unique:* A successful advertising idea should be something no one else is doing—or has done.
- *Fresh, original, unexpected:* An effective advertising idea will provide an element of newness, or surprise, to the viewer/reader. If there is nothing new, no reason for a person to stop and pay attention, then that person will "tune out" or "turn the page" and an opportunity will be lost. Originality helps capture attention and reward the viewer/reader. Ideally, this element should relate to the brand idea and should neither contradict nor overwhelm it.
- *Extendable:* The best advertising ideas are capable of being developed and extended over a long period of time. Genuine, long-lasting advertising ideas

differ from one-off advertising executions in that they can be extended in relevant, surprising and engaging ways. Consider the engaging inventiveness of the Absolut Vodka print campaign for the last 18 years. Many brands have single attention-getting advertisements, but if they are not capable of evolving into further expressions of an underlying idea, they probably do not contain an advertising idea at all.

Although brand ideas and advertising ideas involve many similar elements, the two should not be confused. A summary comparison is useful here:

Brand Idea	Advertising Idea
A definable expression	A definable expression
What one wants the brand to stand for in the minds of consumers	How the brand idea is communicated to a specific target group at a specific time to solve a specific problem
The relationship of the brand to the consumer	A stimulus designed to evoke a specific response that addresses a problem
Means the same thing for all people, users as well as nonusers	Can be different for different target groups
Endures: difficult to change; takes years to develop	Changes as product, market, competitive framework, or consumer needs change
Lasts as long as the brand lasts	Temporary, short-term, completed when the schedule is run
Uniquely ours	Uniquely ours
Sustainable for the long term	Meets strategic objectives in the short term
Fresh, stimulating	Fresh, stimulating

The basis for both is obviously an idea: a fundamental meaning that is clear, communicable, and understood by all. Unless one can articulate the idea intelligibly, there may not be a clear idea there at all.

In terms of creating effective advertising, the clearer the brand idea in the minds of the people who create the advertising, the greater the likelihood that they will be able to develop fresh, stimulating advertising ideas that work.

There are many examples of brand ideas that have been translated variously into many different advertising executions. In the summer of 1993, *Sports Illustrated* ran a major article about Nike in which it was clear that Nike's brand idea is "the life force of sport." Nike wishes to own the category of sports superheroes. This global brand idea is supported by dozens (probably hundreds) of different commercials around the world, covering all kinds of sports and sporting figures—professional, amateur, backyard, and street athletes. The executions are uniquely Nike's—they could not be anyone else's. They are strategically relevant because every one of them supports the fundamental Nike brand idea.

Why the Concept of Brand Idea Is Important

The concept of the brand idea serves many purposes: It forms the platform for all communication about the brand, helps in the evaluation of new advertising, establishes continuity for the brand, protects the long-term heritage of the brand and the brand personality, and becomes the "rallying cry" that unites those who work on the brand, those to whom the brand appeals, and the brand's communication plan.

Forms the Platform for All Communication

The concept of the brand idea helps to define the roles for communication channels. Just as different media all have different roles to play in the marketing mix, so do different communication channels. Increasingly, advertisers and agencies recognize the need for all media and all communication vehicles to reflect and support a single, consistent, and coherent brand idea.

Many marketing departments use one firm to develop sales promotions, another to create consumer advertising, a third for point of sale, and possibly a fourth or fifth for product publicity or direct response or interactive. Seldom are all these firms briefed at one time, yet each needs to develop materials that operate synergistically with those developed by the others. Providing each producer with the same brand idea and holding each accountable to develop materials that support that idea helps to assure consistent and coherent through-the-line communications.

Internal communications are equally important. Senior management, production engineers, sales force personnel, technical services, purchasing, packaging, the legal department—many people have roles to play in the successful production and marketing of a brand. Working from the same brand idea is vital for all of them, even those for whom the details of the marketing planning may seem like a foreign language. A clear, simple brand idea helps provide a common base for easily understood and accepted internal communication.

Aids Evaluation

Evaluation of new advertising or promotional recommendations is difficult. If an idea is genuinely new, it is apt to make people uncomfortable (as a
result of its very newness). Like consumers, marketers tend to gravitate toward
the familiar and comfortable. A well-defined brand idea makes it easier to
evaluate and support change: How well does the recommended idea support,
extend, or intensify the brand idea? A positive answer to this question
diminishes the chance that good ideas will be discarded just because they are
new. The brand idea is the anchor that allows new ideas a chance to work.

A thorough understanding of a brand idea can prevent marketers from
making fundamental mistakes. In cola drinks, both Coca-Cola and Pepsi-Cola
have clear brand ideas: Coke is the real, original, genuine, all-American cola
drink. Pepsi is the rebel. In one brand response survey, more than one-third
of the respondents mentioned Coke product attributes (taste or refreshment),
and none of them mentioned target groups. When the same people talked about
Pepsi, nearly 30% mentioned target groups ("Pepsi generation" or "youth"),
and less than 10% talked about taste or refreshment. Knowing the importance
of product attributes within the Coke brand idea would have made it more
difficult for Coca-Cola to approve the product change to "new Coke" in the
mid-1980s.

Critics maintain that it is possible to switch brands in commercials from
competing firms and achieve the same performance scores. Because of their
unmistakable brand ideas, Pepsi and Coke are not interchangeable. The most
distinctive Pepsi commercials reinforce the rebel brand idea (the "archaeolo-
gist" in 2031 who finds a Coke bottle and doesn't know what it is; the delivery
truck that sends the Pepsi to the old people's home and the Coke to the
fraternity; the choice of, and situations selected for, the major testimonial
stars). Conversely, it would not be believable for Pepsi to run a "Coke Anthem"
spot. This thesis is currently being tested. In some recent series of commercials, Coke has been consciously trying to usurp some of Pepsi's traditional
ground of youth and rebellion.

Establishes Continuity

One extraneous problem facing many brands is the relatively constant
turnover in those people who are responsible for the care and nurture of the
brands. A strong, well-articulated brand idea can provide a guideline that

assures continuity and a consistent approach to the market. The brand idea not only provides unity across advertising media and sales promotion, it also provides unity through time.

Protects Long-Term Heritage and Brand Personality

The best examples of a strong brand idea always contain the essence of the brand promise and brand personality. In this way, the heritage and character of the brand are both preserved and nurtured by the brand idea. A strong advertising expression of the idea helps replenish the brand idea, keeping it fresh and relevant for all target groups.

It is important not to take a brand idea for granted—it needs to be supported. One phase of recent brand response research showed that more than 50% of respondents did not recognize the name "S. C. Johnson," and an additional 13.6% misidentified it, confusing it with J&J. A different phase of the same research showed significantly higher awareness of "Johnson's Wax," but even then there was no clear brand idea attached to that recognition.

Becomes the Rallying Cry

The brand idea is the common element that unites people within the marketing organizations working on the brand, the various target groups to whom the brand appeals, and the various executional expressions of the brand's communications plan. It becomes the banner behind which everyone can give support and endorsement. It is the emblem of brand leadership.

Global Brand Ideas

One final word on the usefulness of brand ideas. In the pursuit of global brands, large amounts of time, effort, and money have been expended in attempts to create "global advertising campaigns." The value and strength of a global brand does not lie in a single worldwide execution of the same advertising campaign. Advertising is only a stimulus.

The response is the brand idea. The goal of the international marketer should be the creation of a single brand idea in all markets. The brand should stand for the same thing in the minds of all related consumer groups everywhere. The advertising ideas required to establish that single brand idea will vary from market to market. Indeed, they should vary. They should express all the local flavor and individuality that will serve to make the brand relevant and appropriate in that local market. So long as the final result is a common brand idea, the variety of local expressions is unimportant.

One of the great examples of a brand idea successfully built throughout the world is Lux Toilet Soap: "the toilet soap of the stars." This brand idea has been the basis of the brand's success for 70 years. It began in print in the United States and England and grew through radio and television, featuring film stars: Hollywood stars, television stars, and local cinema stars whose names would not be recognized beyond the borders of their own countries. Countless individual, local executions (plus some major multinational blockbuster executions) have helped Unilever manage a brand that appears both local and intimate (because it uses locally recognizable stars) and world-powerful (because it uses stars of international stature like Sophia Loren and Michelle Pfeiffer). The goal was not to create a single pool of worldwide commercials; rather, it was to create a world-class brand and brand idea. Lux toilet soap continues to be a leading toilet soap brand throughout the world.

A strong brand idea is the basis of a successful brand that endures. At a time when it is more and more costly to establish any new brand or to sustain an existing brand with no perceptible product advantage in a stagnant market segment, a compelling brand idea is critical. Every brand has a meaning; marketers need to know what that meaning is, how to preserve its relevance and potency, and how to stimulate the agency to create advertising that contains a genuine advertising idea that nourishes the brand idea.

So the answer to the Hungarian marketing director's question, "When do you tell an agency what the brand means?" is clear:

Now.

4

Brands and Their Symbols

Judie Lannon

It is probably not too much of an exaggeration to say that everything that human beings do carries symbolic value of some kind or another. We choose to buy products, services, and brands for myriad complex reasons—some rational, others not. In advanced consumer societies, our needs could be satisfied much more cheaply than they are; we spend our money on what we want, not just on what we need, and what we want will always be a blend of functional and emotional values and meanings (even if that meaning is "no nonsense, good value"). Nothing is value-free.

This chapter explores four questions:

1. Why do people want or, indeed, need symbols?
2. How do meanings and symbols get into brands?
3. How do we understand what particular meanings and symbols a brand carries?
4. How should brand owners and their advertising agencies manage brand symbolism effectively and competitively over time?

Why Do People Want or Need Symbols?

Product Versus Brand

The core principle and starting point of this discussion is the important distinction between the product and the brand. One way of making the distinction clear is to think of products as things made in factories: compositions of ingredients, materials, and workmanship, but no more than that. Products are what manufacturers make.

The brand, however, is what consumers buy, and by the time it gets to the consumer it will have acquired many layers of meaning. It will be packaged in something that has appropriate shape and design; the surface colors and design will have been chosen to convey something about the product inside; it will carry a price; it will be available in certain shops and not others; it will have been promoted through advertising or other media in a particular way; and over time, it will be known to be bought by certain sorts of people rather than by other sorts of people. These "layers" added to the naked product build a patina, contributing meaning and symbolism to it so that what the consumer finally chooses is a whole bundle of meanings. In a coherent, well-managed brand, these layers will all relate to each other, with the end objective of interpreting the properties of the physical product aesthetically and psychologically in such a way as to add value for the consumer.

The original function of branding was legal protection, at a time when brands were much more functionally differentiated than they are today. As the transfer of technology speeded up and competitors (and, more recently, retailers) became able to copy technological advances very quickly, the competitive advantage shifted gradually to psychological rewards—what could be called the brand's *added values*. Therefore, for the brand owner, endowing the brand with appropriate psychological nuances and rewards was a way of creating an additional reason for consumers to want that brand over the brands offered by competitors.

Creative advertising people have always done this intuitively, as is evident from some of the available collections of great advertisements over the years. What is new is that the competitiveness of the modern marketplace requires all brands to understand symbolic values in a more systematic way.

How Do People Make Choices?

The subject of how people make choices is one that was originally dominated by economists. However, because economic thought tends to be restricted to fairly sterile theories based on utility maximization, it is more fruitful to turn to anthropology, psychology, and sociology, which can offer richer explanations and insights.

One of the characteristics of life in advanced consumer societies is the vast, almost paralyzing, proliferation of choice, seen at its most spectacularly daunting in the modern American supermarket. Strategies for emerging from the supermarket with sanity intact involve a complex mixture of habit and impulse. Why choose Maxwell House rather than Nescafé or Folgers, or why choose Coke instead of Pepsi? Why Revlon rather than Max Factor, or Crest rather than Colgate? Why reach for Budweiser rather than Miller? Certainly with these examples of relatively cheap packaged goods, functional product differences as measured in blind product tests are minimal, and when they do exist they are seldom on the same scale as brand share differences.

Or—even more baffling—why do some people pay very high prices for brands when there are plenty of cheaper equivalents? Russian teenagers have been known to pay a month's salary for a pair of Levi's, and Russian taxi drivers treat Marlboro cigarettes as negotiable currency. An American teenager, quite literally, killed for a pair of Nike running shoes. Or, if you are prepared to spend more than $40,000 on a car, why choose a Mercedes rather than a BMW or a Cadillac or a Jaguar? Clearly something else is happening.

The first and most important consideration is that people find symbolic values helpful in making choices. An unpublished study by a U.S. advertising agency illustrated that people find it easier to discriminate between products where the differences are largely emotional than between products in categories where the differences are functional. Symbols are easy to buy because they can discriminate between brands vividly, in contrast to rational product evaluation, which is hard work and time-consuming. Therefore people actively cooperate and collude in endowing products with symbolic and metaphoric meanings, because these meanings are useful in helping them to form habits. Thus favorite, trusted brands become signposts through the clutter of media messages and supermarket facings. But this is only the most superficial utility of symbols, important though it is for many categories of ordinary repeat-purchase packaged goods.

Different Sorts of Meaning and Self-Expression

At a deeper and much more complex level, brand symbolism becomes a part of the individual's efforts to construct and maintain identity: What we buy can say things about who we are, where we are going, who we are not. The symbolic and metaphoric meaning is a way of helping us communicate with each other. Think of brands we choose for family use versus what we serve to guests; of gifts appropriate for baby-sitters or neighbors in contrast to those appropriate for loved ones; of clothes appropriate for casual situations versus those for making an impression—and what kind of impression—and on and on. All activities in which physical things (or services) figure will involve choices about what is or is not appropriate to how we feel, how we wish others to see us, how we think it is right to behave.

Traditionally, anthropologists have looked at the meanings in culture that are carried by products that people choose to own, and so the meanings that brands carry are a natural extension of this line of inquiry. Max Weber, the German sociologist, described culture as "man living in a web of meanings that he himself has chosen," and given that consumption is the preeminent choice activity, the meanings we choose through the individual brands we buy constitute the ultimate study of culture.

We are used to such "status symbols" as Rolex watches and Porsche cars or, at a more mundane level, Johnny Walker Black Label, Baccarat crystal, and Krug champagne—all traditional prestige goods. These goods are bought consciously and deliberately to convey a message of elitism, refinement, and taste—of membership in a rarefied and discerning class. Yet this is only the most obvious kind of symbolism.

Rites and Rituals

Individuals in every society and social subgroup shape their lives around complex structures of rites and rituals. Brands and products often figure in these rites and rituals, and an examination of the brand imagery of the category leader often reveals a set of meanings that mark that link between the brand and the ritual. For instance, Hallmark greeting cards and Chivas Regal identify themselves with the ritual of gift giving.

The most dramatic example, of course, is the diamond engagement ring to mark this particularly important rite of passage. De Beers has advertised "A diamond is forever" for decades in a wide variety of countries, resulting in the diamond engagement ring's becoming culturally prescribed behavior.

Tribes

Separate from the way status in the society or the culture is allocated is a proliferation of subgroups to which people belong. This sort of belonging may have deep or shallow roots. These subgroups or "tribes" may be rooted in social class (e.g., "Sloane Rangers" in the United Kingdom or "Valley girls" in the United States), in the transitory fashions of teenagers (punks, skinheads, rappers, and so on), or in lifestyle (e.g., yuppies). Complex and fluid societies such as the United States contain many such tribes and other groupings of varying stability and varying inclusiveness. Alcoholic drinks are often best understood by this approach: beer as adolescent male bonding, bourbon associated with "good ole boys," brands of single-malt whisky and imported vodkas associated with sophisticated East Coast styles.

Other kinds of meanings also bond people into what could be thought of as metaphoric tribes: Apple computer owners, Filofax owners, Nike wearers, and other groups for whom certain brands have taken on a kind of cult significance.

Myths, Heroes, and Archetypes

We can also look at symbolism at a more mythical level by examining the heroes, archetypes, and legends that people venerate and respect. The study of cultural archetypes and icons is fundamental to an understanding of the success of global advertising, especially the success of brands that have self-expressive dimensions, such as perfumes, drinks, cigarettes, fashions, cosmetics, and some toiletries.

Claude Degrese, a French anthropologist, has described a pantheon of male and female archetypes and uses this typology in work with perfumes, cosmetics, and toiletries. She has established that the archetypes exist in all cultures, but may have slightly different expressions, and the numbers of each archetype will vary from culture to culture. Advertising for the mold-breaking brand Poison from Christian Dior drew from this work in presenting the fragrance as the embodiment of the "sorceress" myth.

Charismatic macho myths are embodied in Levi's 501 jeans (in Europe), Nike and Reebok trainers, and Rolex watches. Lux toilet soap, with its

70-year-old history of using film stars in advertising, draws on the Helen of Troy myth. The David and Goliath myth was seen originally in the advertising of Avis Rent A Car (with Hertz in the role of Goliath); more recently it is evident in ads featuring Apple versus IBM and Virgin Atlantic versus British Airways.

Ideals and Values

Another source of brand symbolism is in the ideals, values, and beliefs that certain groups of people hold and acknowledge as important. A particularly vivid example here is Benetton's "United Colors of Benetton" campaign, which uses a theme that appropriates the values of multiculturalism with its multicolored range of sweaters. Anita Roddick's Body Shop, the ecologically sound, politically correct totality, is the most vivid example of a total idealistic philosophy appropriated by a retail chain. In Britain, the laundry detergent Persil has appropriated the ideal of maternal caring to emphasize softness combined with strength; the Volvo station wagon represents the safety-conscious father; Coke represents "the real thing"—authenticity in a counterfeit world—wrapped around with imagery drawn from the pool of cultural meanings known both within and outside the United States as the "American Dream."

How Do Meanings Get Into Brands?

How meanings get into brands is, of course, the crux of the issue. We need to examine other frames of reference from marketing to understand fully how this works.

First, it is unnecessarily limiting to confine this discussion to advertising alone. A brand is a totality to which many factors contribute. The main factors are as follows:

- *The actual physical product:* What exactly does it do, or not do? Is this special or unique in any way? Are there specific ingredients that are special or unique?
- *Who makes it:* Companies have reputations that come from their other brands or activities. What does the company reputation add to (or subtract from) this particular brand? Traditionally, this dimension has related only to the company's history and skills at manufacturing; in our more socially aware times, the employment practices, ethical standards, and ecological consciousness of the

company might also be considered as part of the reputation that affects the personality of a particular brand.

In small companies it will add to the credibility of the company's products if the president, or better yet the whole family, is dedicated to producing quality products (e.g., the Gucci, Hermès, and Ferragamo families in luxury goods; the Heineken family and the Budweiser dynasty in beer). In larger corporations beliefs are more diffuse, but companies that have particular areas or sources of authority may often have an advantage (if only in marketing efficiencies) over corporations that market goods in many fields. Kellogg's breakfast cereals, Kraft cheese, and Hershey chocolates are household names, and each functions as a potent source of authority in its own category.

- *The brand's price:* Price is the single most important positioning clue in many product fields, not just in conventional prestige categories. Pricing, however, is relative and a function of context; consumers understand the "rules" of marketing and make judgments according to outlet. So normal supermarkets, discount stores, convenience stores, and airline duty-free outlets all carry different expectations. Given that price is a statement of the manufacturer's belief in the value of the brand, it is not surprising that the practice of discounting is damaging to a brand's reputation over time.

- *Where it is seen or sold:* This factor refers to the strategic value of where a brand is bought. For instance, expensive cosmetic houses carefully vet drugstores, and some (e.g., Estée Lauder) rarely if ever are sold outside the more exclusive atmosphere of the department store. Ensuring that a particular brand of chocolates is offered at quality restaurants or that a particular brand of mineral water is associated with good food are ways in which the context may be manipulated to enhance a brand's reputation. The whole burgeoning area of sponsorship does much the same job.

- *Who is believed to use or not use the brand:* With some categories of personal display items—clothing, cars, home furnishings—the kinds of people (in terms of taste, class, education, interest) who are believed to use the product are clues to its desirability.

- *The advertising, packaging, and other related promotional efforts:* These are the most direct sources of knowledge of what the brand is. The job of advertising for new brands is to convey as compellingly as possible that the brand exists, what it is for, in what context is it used, and what sort of people use it.

We now look more closely at the process of constructing advertising to understand its contribution.

The Role of Advertising

The construction of the content of an advertising campaign is a highly complex business. Traditionally, all advertising was seen as the mass-media substitute for the salesman in the living room. So the repetition of a persuasive argument, listing the functional merits of the brand, was seen as the way to do it. However, this one-sided concentration on what is in the product misses the point of what additional rewards people could get from the brand and what may be an important competitive edge. So sophisticated advertising has the double challenge of ensuring that a product story is central to the advertisement and that this is done in such a way as to add levels of meaning and symbolism to the basic product.

A useful concept in thinking about brands and their advertising is that of the brand metaphor. A metaphor is a word or phrase literally denoting one type of object that is used in place of another to suggest a likeness or analogy between them. Everyday speech is full of metaphors—"She is a shrinking violet," "He has a screw loose," "She was a tower of strength"—and they invariably have a figurative dimension. We can easily visualize them.[1]

Advertising makes full and free use of metaphors, often to convey quite "hard" product characteristics. A readily recognized, vivid metaphor has many virtues as an advertising device because it is in the nature of metaphor to carry a number of meanings simultaneously. Advertising metaphors can be used to convey four different kinds of information: (a) the superior functional performance of the brand, (b) the psychological rewards of the brand, (c) the kinds of people who use the brand, and/or (d) the social milieu in which the brand features. For instance, a commercial in Europe for Levi's 501 jeans features a girl and boy whose car has broken down in the desert; they use the boy's jeans as a tow rope. This ad employs a rich mix of symbols to communicate functional product information (sturdiness), the psychological rewards of owning/wearing the product (the boy has saved the girl from an obvious creep), and the social milieu in which the brand features (the setting is 1950s America, which evokes for European teenagers the rebellious teenager movies of the period and James Dean in particular as a cultural icon).

Another vivid example is a commercial for the Volvo 850 that aired when the car was launched in the United Kingdom. As the car is driven, it turns into a galloping horse, and the horse and rider represent the driving experience. The image is supported by the line "It drives like it's alive." Not only does this kind of visual metaphor represent the car—its speed, its handling, its responsiveness—but by tapping into the cowboy archetype, it also stands for the relationship of car to driver, his self-image, and what he wants from this sort of car.

Signs and symbols used as brand metaphors are potent carriers of meaning because they are so concentrated and economical. This is why package design and other graphics are so important to brands. Company symbols such as the "good hands" of Allstate, the "rock" of Prudential, and the "stage coach" of Wells Fargo Bank serve as metaphoric logotypes for what the companies represent. Merrill Lynch's long-time use of its bull to symbolize optimism with overtones of strength and machismo is a good example of a brand metaphor that began as a kind of logotype and developed into advertising. Interestingly, during the 1970s the campaign was modified; the advertising went from showing a herd to showing a single bull, to create a symbol more in keeping with the independent self-image of the target investor.

Symbols, however, are not necessarily metaphors—the Michelin Man, for instance is associated with the tires from long use, but says nothing in particular about the excellence of the tires. In contrast, the Exxon tiger is both a symbol and a metaphor for power. Here, too, we see the metaphor evolving in line with social trends—in the United Kingdom the tiger has become a husband and father with cubs, and he is concerned about the environment.

Familiar packaged goods brands such as Pepperidge Farm, Green Giant vegetables, Timotei shampoo, and Lux toilet soap use metaphors either explicitly or implicitly in their advertising to condense the brands' meanings into a concise form. Pepperidge Farm's Titus Moody and his bakery wagon suggest old-fashioned goodness in baked goods. The Jolly Green Giant anthropomorphically symbolizes goodness, wholesomeness, and farm fresh-ness in canned and frozen vegetables. Timotei shampoo's virginal girl/child represents purity, naturalness, and gentleness. Lux employs film stars in a campaign that is some 70 years old and running in 40-plus markets (more than half the countries in which the brand is sold). The stars seem to work as metaphors for "the most beautiful women in the world"—an idea that in turn works through an evocation of the Helen of Troy myth.

Such meanings get into brands and become part of them partially as a result of repetition and a kind of conditioning, and partially because the meanings and the products themselves go together so naturally that people willingly put them together. An idea in which meanings are embedded can strike a particu-larly strong chord that will reverberate in people's minds for a very long time. For example, the "1984" commercial for Apple computer, in which a regi-mented population was liberated by a young woman and which carried just one word—Macintosh—was shown only once on American television. Yet so powerful was the metaphor that the commercial and the meanings that it carries for Apple (the liberator) versus IBM (the regimented corporate giant) were significant in the appeal that Apple originally engendered and the fanatic loyalty and zeal that its users have shown to the company/brand.

From these examples it is possible to establish principles that help to explain how visual metaphors endow brands with symbolic values and thus serve as effective advertising vehicles:

1. Visual metaphors may enhance effectiveness by moving out of the world of rational persuasive argument (which encourages counterargument) into a world of exaggeration that is acceptable because viewers are not asked to take metaphors literally.

2. Visual metaphors can contain several different kinds of information and thus do not require much in the way of supporting text. Unlike verbal claims, metaphors can package several meanings simultaneously and thus are an economical way of communicating.

3. Visual metaphors require a certain amount of mental processing. At some point they must make the link between image and product; this link should be made quickly and should flow easily and naturally from the juxtaposition of metaphor and physical product or service.

4. Visual metaphors are helpful for defining brands' "territories." Metaphors can help to map out the emotional boundaries for product extensions. If Levi Strauss, for example, had been more conscious of its territory, it never would have made the disastrous move some years ago into men's slacks and leisure wear, with their boring and middle-aged associations.

5. Visual metaphors lend themselves to abbreviation and to adaptation to other media. They can be translated to logos, packaging, and the semipermanent media of corporate identity.

How Do We Understand What Particular Meanings a Brand Carries?

Drawing from the social sciences, a rich and varied range of techniques has been devised by commercial researchers to uncover the meanings people attach to brands. Because anthropology looks at the social context of consumption, the meanings that any kind of consumption ritual and its accompanying brands carry form perhaps the core discipline in understanding brand symbolism. Ironically, however, most market research practitioners are much more likely to come from other disciplines—usually psychology or sociology.

Enabling and Projective Techniques

Quite frequently, straightforward questioning will elicit answers, but because the point of symbolism is its ability to carry considerable emotional content, people often find it difficult to put their ideas satisfactorily into words. So "enabling" and "projective" techniques are used—questions and devices that help people express their motives or thoughts or impressions by going at it indirectly.

Peter Cooper, chairman of the British market research organization CRAM, uses the following basic model in talking about how to research different layers of consciousness:

Factors Being Studied	Technique
Conscious factors	Accessible to structured questionnaire
Private feelings and language	Needs sympathetic interview structure
Intuitive associations	Nonverbal play; the inner world of consumers, brands, and advertising
Unconscious factors	Projective interviewing, and observation deduction; uncensored reactions[2]

Some of the techniques that Cooper and others employ are described below. The use of any particular technique or set of techniques depends very much on the issue being researched, and the ultimate value of any technique is highly dependent on skilled interpretation. However, these methods all share a common feature, which is a kind of "play" quality, in which a range of nonverbal approaches become pathways to emotional ideas through the engagement and stretching of the imagination.

- *Sentence completion and picture completion:* In the latter, people typically are presented with cartoon drawings and are asked to describe a conversation between a brand's user and a nonuser, or to describe what someone might say in a situation, in contrast to what she might be thinking.

- *Personalizing the brand or drawing analogies:* Asking people what sort of a person a brand might be if it were alive, calls up a range of human characteristics that illuminate a brand's image. Similarly, asking, for example, "If a Ford car were an airline, what kind of an airline would it be?" helps extend the imagination and taps into another set of images. An extension of this thought has been developed by the research organization Research International for use with service companies. Respondents are asked not only what they think of the company but what they feel the company thinks of them. Answers like "a special customer" versus "a number" say a great deal about how a company conducts its business.

- *Role playing, psychodrawing, and modeling:* These are more participatory techniques for encouraging people to "act out" or express their feelings through drawing or clay modeling. What does it feel like to be garments washed by one brand of detergent versus another? Draw white bread versus brown bread. How does it feel to fly on one airline compared with another?

- *Collages, montages, picture sorts:* A large collection of pictures (cut from newspapers, magazines, and advertisements) depicting various people, places, moods, possessions (cars, houses, clothes, interiors), and so on is presented to respondents, who are asked to sort them into categories or to combine them in ways that best express different brands.

Techniques like these are typically incorporated into group discussions lasting 2 hours or more among samples of people selected on particular criteria related to known marketplace behavior. For instance, for a brand whose share is declining or failing to grow as anticipated, researchers would interview one sample of regular users of the brand, another of lapsed users, and perhaps a sample of nonusers. Each sample would be investigated with these techniques to identify what it is about the brand, its advertising, its competitors, or other factors in the marketing environment that could account for the problem. Brands new to the marketplace are thoroughly researched to ensure that all elements of the brand mix—product, packaging, and advertising theme—are working coherently together and that the entire bundle of meanings is attractive to prospective buyers.

How Should Brand Owners and Agencies Manage Brand Symbolism?

I have discussed above the uses that people make of symbols and their meanings and how the research practitioner can help companies to understand the meanings of their brands. We now turn to how companies can use this information most efficiently. To do so, we must see how brand symbolism fits into marketing principles and practice.

Companies are, after all, in business to make profits, and their profits will be better secured with larger margins over the cost of production and distribution than with smaller ones. The source of these margins is essentially the brand's added values, which result in more people over time paying higher prices than for the competition, because the values delivered are important to them.

The first point that must be made, however, is that no amount of symbolism will make up for an inadequate product: Brand values are additions, not substitutions. Brands that have been leaders in their categories for decades are mostly owned by aggressive marketers who have fanatical dedication to product quality: Mars, Procter & Gamble, Colgate, and Kellogg's maintain their leadership positions because over time consumers have judged their brands to be of significant intrinsic value.

The second point that must be made is that it is a mistake to oversimplify the relationship between personality types and brands. Although a great deal of work has been done to try to match brand usage to the personality types of lifestyle groups, this work has been curiously disappointing in its applicability to day-to-day marketing and advertising. There are a number of reasons, ranging from the fairly crude research tools used to a too-simplistic model of human behavior. However, another reason is that a single-disciplinary explanation of something as complex as consumer marketing is bound to be inadequate. A psychological description of the marketing process vastly oversimplifies and ignores such critical activities as distribution, media exposure, and pricing policy. These hard, structural marketing disciplines and what are almost lawlike relationships to repeat-buying behavior mean that the student of brand marketing must master the elements of all of them rather than isolate one as more important than others.

Because meanings can change as cultures evolve, as social trends develop, as influences in fashion and media themselves evolve, brand symbolism is not static. When a brand becomes attached to rituals that have ceased to be relevant for one reason or another, it is time to reinterpret the brand's meaning. A good example comes from Britain, which, like all European countries, is rather more ritualized in general than the United States. SmithKline Beecham's Lucozade, a glucose-based drink, was associated for decades with convalescence. As the general health of the population improved and thus Lucozade was needed less and less frequently for invalids, it had to find another set of meanings that could equally stem from the glucose ingredients and association with lost energy. The answer was in sports drinks. With new packaging (moving from a tall, thin bottle to a can) and, most important, new advertising (using celebrity sports heroes), the brand made a successful comeback.

The more common situation, however, is the need to keep the brand continually refreshed, so that its core meaning remains the same but it is regularly reinterpreted according to changing social trends. Here again, Britain provides a number of excellent examples. Persil detergent, marketed by Lever Brothers, used the idea of maternal love and caring as its basic advertising proposition. Early advertising presented mothers in what by today's standards look like oppressive and claustrophobic situations. But social change has not eliminated mothers, it has merely meant that mothers behave differently. Many go out to work; the father now often adopts a quasi-maternal role.

As brands become more and more similar in product function, and differentiating between them becomes harder and harder, the skills of the advertising creative person become increasingly critical. As I have described in this chapter, these skills must include the ability to interpret brands in vivid and compelling ways that endow them with symbolism that adds value to the physical offering and engineers strong synergy.[3]

Notes

1. See Alexander L. Biel and Judie Lannon, "Steel Bullet in a Velvet Glove? The Use of Metaphor in Advertising," *Admap,* April 1993.

2. See Peter Cooper, *The New Qualitative Technology,* ESOMAR Marketing Research Monograph 2 (Amsterdam: European Society for Opinion and Marketing Research, 1987). See also Judie Lannon and Peter Cooper, "Humanistic Advertising: A Holistic Cultural Perspective," *International Journal of Advertising,* vol. 2, July/September 1983.

3. Together, the following two articles provide an extensive bibliography of books and papers related to the topic addressed in this chapter: Judie Lannon, "Mosaics of Meaning," *Journal of Brand Management,* vol. 2, no. 3, December 1994; Judie Lannon, "What Is Postmodernism and What Does It Have to Do With Brands?" *Journal of Brand Management,* vol. 4, no. 2, October 1996.

5

Gestalt

How Brands Are Influenced by Multiple Communications

John Philip Jones

The consumer can respond to an advertisement as an isolated stimulus, and different communications vehicles enable the manufacturer to focus communication in a tailor-made way for each medium and even for each vehicle. However, the consumer's response is also affected by a gestalt, the sum of many communications about the brand—for example, by what he or she knows of it, where it is sold, who uses it, and how it is promoted to the trade and the consumer. Most important, there is an implicit communication about the brand in the advertising company it keeps, in the media and media vehicles in which it appears; to a large extent, the medium is indeed the message. Yet dissonance of all types is only too common in the real world.

An automobile advertisement tries to persuade us that the brand is now better built and more reliable than ever before; at the same time, the advertisement offers a massive price rebate, as if to demonstrate that the manufacturer does not believe its own quality claims. Another car advertisement, for an exceedingly traditional make of automobile with dated styling, tries to persuade younger buyers that the car is now for them—simply by saying that it is now for them. A highly exclusive brand focused on the upper end of its market runs advertisements on prime-time network television, shoulder to shoulder with the most undiscriminating mass-market brands. A highly sophisticated product concept is promoted in advertisements of stupefying banality. These instances are in no way exceptional. We can see these and similarly disheartening examples on television virtually every evening.

When consumers are asked to describe the personalities of well-known banks and gasoline companies, these impressions turn out to be uniformly negative. The implicit—but of course unintended—communications about these organizations (e.g., unfavorable mentions in the media) clearly influence consumers more than do the explicit, planned communications.

During the 1970s, a parable was circulated widely within the J. Walter Thompson agency and presented engagingly by Jeremy Bullmore, then head of the agency's London office—a parable that illustrates vividly the meaning of communications gestalt.

There were once two farmhouses, with a field in front of each. In the field belonging to the first farm there was a crude black wooden sign, and on it the words "Fresh Eggs" were painted. The lettering was the work of an unskilled sign painter, probably the farmer's wife, and although the message was readable, it would have won no prizes in a graphic arts competition. The letters were crooked, the spacing uneven. In the field in front of the second farm was a sign also reading "Fresh Eggs," but this one was clearly the work of an expert designer and a disciple of the Bauhaus. It was a highly polished piece of work and would not have been out of place in an annual publication devoted to examples of graphic excellence.

It was very clear to visitors that the first farm sold the fresher eggs. Even if the eggs were not in fact fresher, they seemed so to people who looked at the two signs.

It would be equally instructive to repeat the exercise, but with a message that reads "Flying Lessons." There is little doubt that the farm that sells the fresher eggs would not offer the safer flying lessons! In a literal sense, the flying lessons are no more connected with the "Flying Lessons" sign than the eggs are with the "Fresh Eggs" sign. Yet this is not so obvious to consumers, to whom any brand projects a total impression to which all communications about the brand make their contributions. When some of these contributions are negative and others—perhaps the majority—are positive, it is perhaps not surprising that the negative ones make the stronger impression.

The general principle of communication gestalt is important to everyone who develops and manages brands. It is especially of value to market researchers, who should evaluate brands on the basis of consumers' responses to the brands as a whole. Researchers should therefore avoid focusing on discrete bits of the communication by asking questions such as the following: Do you think that red is a good color for the packaging? Do you like a fresh scent or a sweet scent? What parts of the advertising can you remember? Do you like the models in the commercials?

6

Brands and Advertising

Roderick White

The vast majority of advertising is about brands—so much so that it might seem otiose to write at length about the relationship between the two. The past few years, however, have seen a variety of issues developing that increase the importance of that relationship and raise questions about precisely what the relationship is. So in this chapter I will look briefly at what a brand is and how this appears to depend on advertising, lay out the key issues, and attempt to draw some relevant conclusions from a debate that has become crowded and confusing.

What Is a Brand?

A brand is the means by which a company differentiates its products from competition and—if successful—protects its position in the market, profit-

NOTE: This chapter was first published as "What Advertising Can Really Do for Brands," *International Journal of Advertising,* vol. 18, no. 1, February 1999. © 1999 by NTC Publications Ltd. Reprinted by permission.

ably, over time. For this to happen, a brand has to achieve a rapport with its consumers; if a brand is not somehow "in the mind" of its target market, it can only be a random purchase, at best.

How should we understand this? Judie Lannon has graphically described a brand, drawing on anthropological analyses, as consisting of a "mosaic of meaning." She describes branding as the mechanism that creates and sustains "consumption myths and consumption rituals, involving products and services endowed with symbolic meanings." [1] If this looks complex, it has the merit of focusing on the reality that a brand exists within society and in the minds of consumers; it is a construct of its inbuilt physical characteristics and functional features, combined with intangible values and associations. If the brand has been carefully developed and marketed, this creates a powerful competitive advantage in the marketplace, which may be able to sustain a premium price (or at least reduce price elasticity), support a stable or growing market share, and enable the brand owner to achieve economies of scale in marketing expenditure.

As Stephen King, J. Walter Thompson London's pioneer of account planning in the 1960s, has put it: "A product is something that is made in a factory: a brand is something that is bought by customers. A product can be copied by a competitor: a brand is unique. A product can be quickly outdated: a successful brand is timeless." [2]

A successful brand draws its unique character from the combination of elements in the marketing mix (including its functional characteristics) and their effects in the minds of consumers. What is more, although it is difficult to have a successful brand that does not deliver excellent functional performance, most successful brands are powerful because their appeal is emotional as well as rational. In fact, a brand that fails to build a strong emotional tie with its users is vulnerable; as competitors match or surpass it on the key functional indicators of performance—as they surely will, over time—an emotional bond can provide the breathing space for management to take action to restore the brand's competitive performance.

All of this points strongly to the importance of marketing communications in creating the brand and developing its strengths. What turns a product (or service) into a brand is the way in which it is presented and communicated in the market: its packaging, point-of-sale support, sales literature, public relations, advertising, and sponsorship, as well as its pricing policy and distribution channels. Any or all of these can contribute to the rounded picture that a brand's buyers (in particular) will, over time, develop of what the brand has to offer—both the functional, physical benefits it delivers and the emotional satisfactions associated with it.

Imaginative marketing will plan these benefits and satisfactions into the brand from the start and integrate the marketing mix so as to ensure that the market takes them on board. How to do this is the theme of many books on the subject of branding, of which perhaps the most satisfactory recent example is Aaker's book on brand equity.[3] A key element in the planning process is brand positioning, for which Ries and Trout provide the "bible." [4]

Clearly, within all this, advertising, as the most intrusive and visible form of marketing communication, has a key role to play. Advertising cannot turn a sow's ear into a silk purse, but, given a good or—ideally—superior product, it can help to build it into a strong brand.

The Role of Advertising

The role of advertising, specifically, has been seen traditionally as one of aiding sales. This it does in four main ways:

1. by creating awareness;
2. by providing essential information;
3. by helping to build a relevant brand image; and, once the brand has become more or less established,
4. by acting as a regular reminder to try, buy, or use the brand.

Although advertising's primary role for a new product launch is to announce and provide information, it has a role in communicating the desired positioning for the brand from the start; once the brand is established, the advertising is much more concerned with ensuring that the positioning becomes fully part of the target audience's mental furniture, with appropriate imagery and associations.

Advertising strategies, therefore, need to be designed with the consumer's responses and reactions in mind, and they need to recognize that there is more to a brand than its physical characteristics. Indeed, in many repeat-purchase packaged goods (fast-moving consumer goods, or fmcg) markets, in particular, where brand "choice" is a barely conscious process as the shopper passes down a supermarket aisle, brands are liable to be bought (or not) on the basis of habits, feelings, and associations just as much as, or more than, on the basis of rational comparison.

It is perfectly possible to build a brand without massive advertising expenditures, though this is most commonly found in service markets such as retailing. Two classic U.K. retail examples are Marks & Spencer, which rarely advertised before the mid-1980s and still spends far less than other chains of comparable size, and John Lewis, a department store group that never had an advertising agency until 2 years ago, but is known all over the country for its founder's powerful statement "Never knowingly undersold." Both firms, of course, have successfully used their stores, rather than the media, as their advertisements. In the same way, most restaurants rely on word of mouth and public relations to attract customers.

What Does Advertising Do for the Brand?

"Advertising sells brands." Yes, but the crucial task for anyone involved in planning or evaluating advertising is to determine precisely how this happens—without this knowledge, we are condemned to floundering and guesswork.

The question of how advertising works has exercised marketing thinkers for more than 100 years: AIDA (Attention–Interest–Desire–Action), the first of the so-called hierarchy-of-effects models, has its origins in 1898.[5] This and similar models of advertising continue to dominate much thinking about what advertising does, although they are clearly a gross, misleading, and mistaken oversimplification. This is a problem because how we believe advertising should work influences how we set out to measure the effects, either in pretesting or in campaign evaluation.

Early models of how advertising works were all based on the idea that advertisers could use ads to get people to do things: to go out and buy Brand X, to switch from Brand Y to Brand Z, and so on. In particular, there was a very straightforward view that good advertising could persuade a consumer (usually by the force of rational argument) to switch—completely—from one brand to another. It was not until the 1960s that it began to be recognized that what mattered was how people responded to an advertisement—and that, therefore, it made sense to set advertising objectives at least in part in terms of consumer response to the advertisement. A further development was the recognition that advertisements do not use people, people use advertisements—if they want to.[6]

Vakratsas and Ambler examined a number of models of advertising, and their key conclusion was that any analysis of advertising needs to recognize that experience, affect, and cognition all have roles to play in how advertising works.[7] Ambler has stressed that it is common to ignore the importance of consumers' prior experience of the brand, whereas most discussions (and research techniques) concentrate primarily on cognition while underrating affect.[8]

Ambler points out that advertising has to operate through *immediate* effects —there is an inevitable gap between exposure to the ad and a purchase (except in the special case of direct response). This requires the laying down of appropriate memory traces that can be retrieved at the point of purchase. How these traces are laid down has been discussed in some detail by Du Plessis, who shows that this is a learning process—whether this is achieved by deliberate, active rehearsal of information or in the informal, accidental way in which, for example, one learns how a room in one's house looks.[9]

Du Plessis points out, too, that modern psychology has come to emphasize the importance of emotions or feelings both in the way in which memories are laid down and in decision making.[10] This helps to explain the results of the 1991 Advertising Research Foundation (ARF) project, which surprised the U.S. advertising research community by finding that liking for an advertisement is the best predictor of marketplace success.[11]

In the United Kingdom, researchers have concluded that it is most unlikely that all advertisements work in the same way (and that, therefore, it makes no sense to try to test them or evaluate them all using a single tightly drawn methodology). Hall and his colleagues carried out research among agency strategists and client personnel responsible for advertising and identified four "frameworks" within which advertising is planned.[12] Basically, what Hall and his followers found is that advertising may aim simply to create sales (mainly direct response), to persuade (an essentially rational approach), to involve (basically emotional), and to achieve salience (to create a sense of something happening). These aims are not, necessarily, mutually exclusive; an advertisement may perform several (or all four) of the tasks outlined, but it will usually be biased one way or the other. Clearly, the way that the advertising is or should be planned, in these terms, will depend on the brand's market situation.

Coming full circle, there are two key elements in modern thinking about campaign evaluation that shed light on what advertising is seen as being able to achieve for a brand. Gordon Brown of Millward Brown emphasized the importance of memory, but stressed the unimportance of detailed recall of the advertisement itself; his agency's key measure is "advertising awareness," which is defined as awareness that the brand has been advertising (e.g., on television) recently.[13] This is essentially a measure of the salience of the advertising. At the same time, two or three research agencies, including Millward Brown, have developed models of consumer relationships with brands that can be tied in with advertising tracking studies. These models aim to assess the degree to which a consumer is committed to a particular brand.[14]

Clearly, advertisers and their agencies are accustomed to seeing advertising as a means by which consumers' attitudes toward a brand can be substantially influenced—usually over time—so as to build up and strengthen the brand's market position. Implicit in this thinking is the evident belief that advertising is quite a powerful force for change—a belief that no one in the agency business would wish to discourage, even though it has provided plenty of fuel for the critics of advertising, from Vance Packard and Ralph Nader onward.

The Developing Debate

During the 1970s and 1980s, a rather different view of both the power of advertising and the nature of successful brands was quietly developing, and this view has become much more open and well-known in the late 1990s. It has two strands to it: a view of brands as being simply large or small, rather than strong or weak; and a view that advertising is essentially a weak force in the marketplace—that is, its ability to achieve significant change in sales, market shares, or brand attitudes is distinctly limited.

Advertising as Weak Force

Econometricians have long had difficulty in identifying the long-term effects of advertising—or even in agreeing how long the effects of an advertisement (or burst of advertisements) might last. This mathematical difficulty has been matched by the frequency with which brand attitude measures on tracking studies have remained stubbornly static or have moved after, rather than before, changes in market share. In other words, it is often brand experience that drives attitude change, not attitude change that drives brand growth.

It has also been extensively argued, by Ehrenberg and his colleagues, that brand attitudes are to all intents and purposes an artifact of brand size, with larger brands tending to have more favorable attitudes (as well as apparently higher brand loyalty) as a result of the by now well-known phenomenon of double jeopardy.[15]

Ehrenberg, working primarily on "steady-state," established markets, for the most part in fmcg sectors, has developed a cogent series of arguments, set out in full in the eight papers of the JOAB (Justifying Our Advertising Budgets) project,[16] that advertising acts primarily as a reminder and has little influence on purchasing behavior beyond ensuring that a brand remains in a consumer's repertoire of purchased brands. Advertising, in Ehrenberg's terms, exists primarily to create "salience" for the brand—to call attention to it. This it does best by being "creative" in the way in which it does so, but we should not expect to see any significant alteration to consumer attitudes toward the brand as a result.[17]

Ehrenberg argues, in fact, that most brands are not differentiated in physical terms and that most advertising does not even try to differentiate them either.[18] (This view of advertising seems to be a very narrow one, and based on an almost perversely literal reading of the text or script. It is not at all clear from Ehrenberg's writings what an advertisement would have to do, short of a direct and detailed competitive comparison, to be admitted to be "differentiating.")

The "weak force" argument has been supported by Jones, but only up to a point; in a recent article he argues, on the basis of the analysis in his book *When Ads Work,* that advertising can act as something much nearer to the conventionally accepted strong force in the short term.[19] This effect, however, is rarely detectable in the long term, because the sometimes dramatic short-term results are nullified by competitive pressures and the limitations of the brand's own budget in the long term.

Weak or Strong Brands

Ehrenberg's view of brands stems from his analysis of purchasing patterns, which show great consistency of consumer behavior. This is common to most markets, and allows easy prediction of brand interrelationships. He extends this analysis to argue, on the basis of material from usage and attitudes (U&A) studies in a number of markets, that attitudinal data neither enable us to distinguish adequately between brands nor provide any great stability over time. From this he concludes that there are no strong brands, only big and small brands.

Values and Attitudes

It should be noted, however, that Ehrenberg's view of consumers' attitudes toward brands is determinedly rationalist. If he were a philosopher, he would be a logical positivist, and his psychology is distinctly Skinnerian.[20] Further, the range of "attitudes" quoted in Ehrenberg's publications on the subject seems distinctly limited. Almost without exception, the attitudes are of a more or less banal, functional character: "tastes nice," "easy to digest," and so on. Although Ehrenberg argues, rightly, that the apparent differences in brand attitudes on a typical U&A survey can be attributed almost entirely to differing levels of usage, and that brand users' attitudes are normally very different from those of nonusers, the material quoted in his various publications looks very thin in terms of emotional, as opposed to functional, attitude statements.

This seems to reflect the unwillingness of marketers (or researchers?) to attempt to quantify systematically and routinely the distinctive and consistent personalities that are attributed to brands in qualitative research (i.e., research involving focus groups or in-depth interviews). These brand personalities are built up, over time, by the combination of positioning and consistent advertising with the brand's physical characteristics. Even in tightly competitive fmcg markets, such as detergent or instant coffee, individual brands can be and are clearly differentiated by consumers on these nontangible dimensions.

Ehrenberg argues that, given the repertoire buying behavior of most consumers in these markets, the values (or whatever we may call them) that attach to brands cannot be very meaningful, or why would a British detergent buyer purchase, on one occasion, "practical, no-nonsense, efficient" Ariel and on another, "caring, motherly, sensible" Persil?

This is a curious argument, given that the rest of his analysis of marketing phenomena recognizes the fickleness of consumers and the irregular nature of purchase of most—even very large—brands. As qualitative researchers such as Wendy Gordon in the United Kingdom have amply shown, brand buying is subject to varying consumer attitudes and mind-sets—what Gordon calls "need states," which may apply as much within a product category as between categories.[21] Although a consumer may usually be sympathetic to the personality/values/associations of Brand X, this by no means prevents her or him from being, from time to time, sympathetic to those of Brand Y. We do not invariably seek the company of the same or like-minded people.

Commitment

Ehrenberg's analyses of consumers' brand purchasing behavior make it clear that, at least in fmcg markets, classical brand loyalty ("Us Tareyton smokers would rather fight than switch"—to quote an ancient, long-dead brand) is of trivial importance: the solus buyers of a brand are usually few and mostly light users of the category. (This has been known for 25 years from the Target Group Index in the United Kingdom, but in some markets, solus buyers may constitute more than 20% of category users, and carry more weight.) Loyalty is, in practice, habitual purchasing within a brand repertoire. Ehrenberg uses this evidence to deduce that brand loyalty is, at best, of marginal significance; it accounts, perhaps, for the marginal tendency of big brands to be bought more frequently, though this is mostly down to double jeopardy.

It is only in the past 3 or 4 years that major research companies have begun to introduce research products designed specifically to assess consumers' degrees of loyalty to the brands they buy, and to publish findings describing measures that purport both to assess loyalty and to predict trends in market share.[22] It seems to me that, although Ehrenberg has indulged in some public jousting with in particular Millward Brown's Brand Dynamics™ system,[23] he has neither taken much notice of these findings nor successfully undermined them.

Moving the Debate Forward

There is clearly a massive rift between the evidence that Ehrenberg has produced to show that advertising, although necessary, is usually unlikely to have any very significant effect on the fortunes of an established brand and the collective beliefs—and experience—of most advertising professionals. Is the whole edifice of advertising strategy and brand development built on sand?

Ehrenberg does not help this situation by further saying, in effect, that it does not matter much what an advertisement says, as long as it says it sufficiently "creatively" to achieve salience. This effectively removes almost all relevance from advertising strategic thinking, if taken literally.

The fact remains that there is a growing corpus of evidence, accumulating from around the world, that a lot of advertising works in the way that practitioners have always thought it does. The Institute of Practitioners in Advertising (IPA) in the United Kingdom established its Advertising Effectiveness awards scheme in 1981,[24] and now has a database of more than 1,000 cases; this scheme has been copied, so far mostly to a lower standard, in—at least—the United States (the Effies), Canada, and Australia. (Much of this material can now be accessed on-line through the World Advertising Research Center at http://www.warc.com.) It is, of course, possible to criticize this material as being the sparkling tip of an iceberg of mediocrity, but this ignores the fact that the majority of advertisers do not have the time, the inclination, or, in many cases, the data to support an entry for these awards. There are, certainly, many more successes than ever get published—although, equally, there is probably plenty of self-delusion, too.

It has to be recognized, also, that most of Ehrenberg's work has—inevitably, given its origins in brand purchasing patterns—been done on markets for repeat-purchase packaged goods. Although Ehrenberg and his colleagues say they have done a lot of work in other fields, little of this seems to have been published.

There is, it seems to me, no doubt that consumers can and do distinguish among brands, in most fields, in ways that are meaningful in relation to known purchase motivations. It is inconceivable that these distinctions do not have some effect on their purchasing propensities and behavior.

There is, equally, no doubt that consumers who take part in qualitative research—whether in focus groups or in-depth interviews—can paint detailed, clear, and distinctive pictures of brand characters and personalities that reflect the cumulative experience of both the brand-as-product and its communications. In a recent speech, Bruce Haines, CEO of British agency Leagas Delaney, described the complete contrast in image between Nike (creative, imaginative, flexible) and Adidas (professional, technical, controlled) based on research into commercials related to the 1998 soccer World Cup.[25] It is difficult to believe that this graphic differentiation between brands is not reflected in at least some purchasing decisions.

Interestingly, none of this discussion ever takes place in the context of direct-response advertising, where advertising research originated in the 1920s and 1930s. If this advertising is successful, it actually sells products—and it often does this over years, by being consistent in the way brand advertising is supposed to be. Of course, it achieves response rates of just 1%

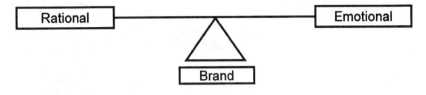

Figure 6.1. The Brand Seesaw

to 2%. But then, the whole thrust of recent media thinking—Ephron's "recency planning" [26]—is based on the recognition that, at any one time, only a few people are in the market for a given brand or category.

My view of all this is very clear. Brands are real in the minds of consumers. Strong brands exist because they have become deeply rooted in the minds of consumers and are part of the texture of people's lives. They become part of this texture because people are willing to respond to the brands and the ways in which they are presented, and advertising is often the most visible and dramatic aspect of this.

That said, in fmcg markets especially, consumer choices are often essentially trivial, so that consumers have, as Ehrenberg has shown, repertoires from which they are prepared to buy fairly erratically. How a brand gets on the repertoire and stays there is how advertising mainly works in such markets. It is the task of advertising to maintain, and ideally strengthen, the brand's place in the repertoire.

Ehrenberg argues that it is difficult to achieve this strengthening. It seems to me that he dismisses the findings of the "commitment" school of researchers altogether too cavalierly. The evidence appears to me quite strong that people can be, and are, moved along the scale of commitment to a brand, and that this has been demonstrated to relate to advertising inputs and is also able to predict brand share changes.

The relationship between brands and advertising is a complex one. A brand can be visualized as a form of seesaw, achieving a balance (which may vary widely for different types of brands) between rational and emotional elements or characteristics (Figure 6.1). From the marketer's point of view, this is constructed and articulated by the whole of the marketing mix, but, in particular, the communications elements of the mix, of which advertising is typically the largest part in dollar terms and also probably in impact over time (Figure 6.2). However, without the consumer, the brand barely exists. To

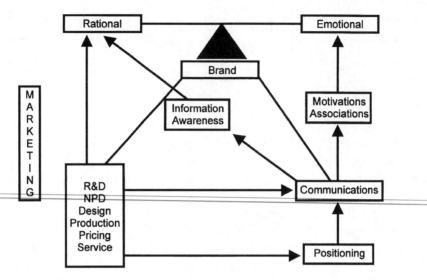

Figure 6.2. The Marketing Input

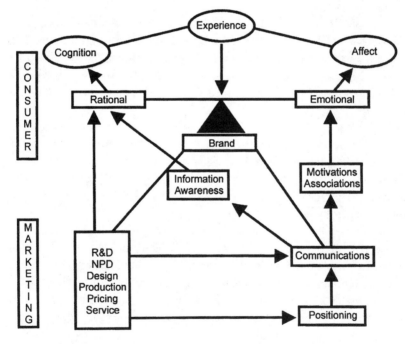

Figure 6.3. The Consumer's Input

complete the picture, we have to recognize the consumer's relationship with the brand, which, as we have seen, involves the three facets of cognition, affect, and experience. Each of these operates both as a recipient of the brand values and as a creative force upon them: The relationship is two-way (Figure 6.3). The tasks of the advertising planner are to understand these relationships and to learn how best to influence and—ideally—manipulate them for the benefit of his or her brand in its particular market.

Notes

1. Judie Lannon, "Mosaics of Meaning," *Journal of Brand Management,* vol. 2, no. 3, December 1994, 157.

2. Stephen King, *What Is a Brand?* (London: J. Walter Thompson, 1970), 37.

3. David A. Aaker, *Managing Brand Equity: Capitalizing on the Value of a Brand Name* (New York: Free Press, 1991).

4. Al Ries and Jack Trout, *Positioning: The Battle for Your Mind* (New York: McGraw-Hill, 1985).

5. Tim Ambler, "Advertising and Profit Growth," *Admap,* May 1998.

6. Herbert E. Krugman, "The Measurement of Advertising Involvement," *Public Opinion Quarterly,* vol. 30, 1966-1967, 583-596; see also Judie Lannon, "Asking the Right Questions: What Do People Do With Advertising?" *Admap,* March 1992 (and references therein).

7. Demetrios Vakratsas and Tim Ambler, *Advertising Effects: A Taxonomy and Review of Concepts, Methods, and Results From the Academic Literature,* Working Paper 96-120 (Cambridge, MA: Marketing Science Institute, 1996).

8. Ibid.

9. Erik Du Plessis, "The Advertised Mind: A New Paradigm of How the Mind Learns the Messages of Advertising," Telmar Awards Paper, presented April 15, 1998, New York.

10. Erik Du Plessis, "Frequency, Memorability, Ad-Liking: Where Is the Wisdom?" paper presented at the Communication Towards Open Societies Conference, School of Communications Research, Amsterdam, January 1998.

11. Russell J. Haley and A. Baldinger, "The ARF Copy Research Validity Project," *Journal of Advertising Research,* April/May 1991.

12. See M. Hall and D. Maclay, "Science and Art: How Does Research Practice Match Advertising Theory?" paper presented at the annual meeting of the Market Research Society, 1991. See also M. Hall, "Using Advertising Frameworks: Different Research Models for Different Campaigns," *Admap,* March 1992.

13. Gordon Brown, "How Indirect Response Advertising Works," paper presented at the Millward Brown International Seminar, September 1992.

14. R. Heath, "Brand Commitment as a Predictor of Advertising Effect," *Admap,* April 1997.

15. Andrew S. C. Ehrenberg, Gerald J. Goodhardt, and T. Patrick Barwise, "Double Jeopardy Revisited," *Journal of Marketing,* vol. 54, July 1990, 82-91.

16. For the complete set of references, see Andrew S. C. Ehrenberg and John Scriven, "Added Values or Propensities to Buy?" *Admap,* September 1997.

17. Ibid.

18. See Andrew S. C. Ehrenberg, J. R. Barnard, and John Scriven, "Differentiation or Salience?" *Journal of Advertising Research,* November/December 1997.

19. On the weak force argument, see John Philip Jones, "Advertising: Strong Force or Weak Force? Two Views an Ocean Apart," in J. C. Luik and M. J. Waterson (eds.), *Advertising and Markets: A Collection of Seminal Papers* (Henley-on-Thames, UK: NTC, 1996). See also John Philip Jones, "Is Advertising Still Salesmanship?" *Journal of Advertising Research,* May/June 1997; and John Philip Jones, *When Ads Work: New Proof That Advertising Triggers Sales* (New York: Simon & Schuster-Lexington, 1995).

20. Logical positivism, the philosophical doctrine of the Vienna school (1930s), acknowledges as true facts only those statements that are empirically verifiable. See, for example, Alfred J. Ayer, *Language, Truth and Logic* (Harmondsworth, UK: Pelican, 1954). B. F. Skinner, a leading behaviorist psychologist, is famous for his work with pigeons. As George Herbert Mead has stated, behaviorism "can only account for what people are doing, not what they are thinking or feeling"; quoted in Gordon Marshall (ed.), *The Concise Oxford Dictionary of Sociology* (Oxford: Oxford University Press, 1994).

21. Wendy Gordon, "Retailer Brands: The Value Equation for Success in the 90s," *Journal of the Market Research Society,* vol. 36, no. 3, July 1994.

22. Heath, "Brand Commitment."

23. See articles by various authors in the November/December 1997 issue of the *Journal of Advertising Research,* as well as the follow-up comments in the January/February 1998 issue. See also the May 1998 issue of *Admap* and the further comments in the June 1998 issue.

24. See the series *Advertising Works,* vols. 1-9 (London: Institute of Practitioners in Advertising, 1982-1998).

25. Bruce Haines, "Leverage via Creativity: Seven Sure Ways to Get More From Your Advertising Budget," paper presented at the Admap Conference, May 1998.

26. Erwin Ephron, "Recency Planning," *Admap,* February 1997.

7

Brand Equity

Do We Really Need It?

Paul Feldwick

What is the answer to the question being asked in cocktail lounges, all the time, all over America, "What is Brand Equity anyway, and how do you measure it?"

Thornton C. Lockwood
communications research manager, AT&T
"The Confessions of a Brand Equity Junkie"[1]

Methodological essentialism, i.e. the theory that it is the aim of science to reveal essences and to describe them by definitions, can be better understood when contrasted with its opposite, methodological nominalism. The methodological nominalist will never think that a question like "What is energy?" or "What is movement?" or "What is an atom?" is an important question for

NOTE: This chapter was first published as "Do We Really Need 'Brand Equity'?" *Journal of Brand Management,* vol. 4, no. 1, 1996, 9-28. © 1996 by Henry Stewart Publications. Reprinted by permission.

physics; but he will attach importance to a question like: "How can the energy of the sun be made more useful?" or "How does a planet move?" or "Under what conditions does an atom radiate light?" And to those philosophers who tell him that before having answered the "what is" question he cannot hope to give exact answers to any of the "how" questions, he will reply, if at all, by pointing out that he much prefers that modest degree of exactness which he can achieve by his methods to the pretentious muddle which they have achieved by theirs.

Karl Popper
The Open Society and Its Enemies[2]

From Brand Image to Brand Equity

Brands have been a major aspect of marketing reality now for more than a hundred years. The theory of branding came some time later. David Ogilvy was talking about the importance of brand image as early as 1951.[3] It was first fully articulated by Burleigh Gardner and Sidney Levy in their classic *Harvard Business Review* paper of 1955.[4] But despite such distinguished origins, the concept of "brand image" remained—until recently—peripheral to the mainstream of advertising theory and evaluation. Although it was endorsed from the 1960s onward by the British account planning movement,[5] it was also seen by many advertisers and researchers (especially in the United States) as a rather woolly theory—the sort of thing advertising agency people talked airily about when they failed to "get a hard product message across" or to "convert prospects" or to "make sales," as they were supposed to be doing. "Brand image" was associated with such things as the "soft sell"[6] and the "weak theory of advertising,"[7] which gave it, for many, the air of a whimsical luxury that a businesslike advertiser could hardly afford.

Then, in the 1980s, the hard-nosed businesspeople began to notice that brands appeared to be changing hands for huge sums of money. As takeover fever spread, the difference between balance sheet valuations and the prices paid by predators was substantially attributed to "the value of brands." Suddenly, the brand stopped being an obscure metaphysical concept of dubious relevance. It was something that was worth money.

This shift of perception was reflected in the way that the traditional term *brand image* (with its suggestion of a ghostly illusion) was increasingly displaced by its solid financial equivalent, *brand equity.* It is not clear who invented the expression, but few uses of it have been traced to before the mid-1980s.[8] It achieved respectability when it was taken up by the prestigious Marketing Science Institute, which held a major seminar on the subject in 1988 and has been going strong ever since.

In fact, the past few years have seen brand equity become one of the hottest topics in business. In the United States there is now an influential body, founded in 1991, called the Coalition for Brand Equity, which evangelizes for the importance of building brand relationships and brand loyalty. Interesting (and very different) books have been published on the subject.[9] It has spawned numerous conferences and seminars. It has attracted a lot of interest from academic researchers, although the greatest part of their work has been connected with brand equity as applied to brand extensions.[10] Meanwhile, commercial researchers have been busily designing and selling methods for measuring, tracking, and optimizing brand equity.

This can be seen as something of a paradigm shift in marketing thinking, and in my view a positive one. It seems right that the ideas formulated by Gardner and Levy and by King so long ago should at last be granted legitimacy as a serious part of business. In the conclusion to this chapter, I review the positive aspects of brand equity. But while I joined the cheering crowds lining the great brand equity parade, I was still bothered by two questions that did not seem to have clear enough answers:

- What exactly is meant by the term *brand equity*—and does it mean the same thing for everybody?
- How far can brand equity be measured in an objective way?

I have written this chapter in an attempt to answer these questions. The answers I have found suggest some further questions:

- Is brand equity a useful concept?
- Is brand equity, in fact, needed at all?

What Is Brand Equity, Anyway?

Karl Popper warned against a common mistake made by philosophers and scientists that he called "essentialism." [11] The mistake is supposing that you will find the truth by starting with a word and arguing about what it "really" means. Words, as Humpty Dumpty suggested, mean just what their users want them to mean. They can have various different meanings, and it is pointless to argue about which is right or wrong. When a common expression does have distinct meanings, however, it is well to be aware of the fact so as to avoid unnecessary confusion. This is true of the term *brand equity,* which seems to be used in three quite distinct senses (each of which has several further nuances of meaning):

1. The total value of a brand as a separable asset—when it is sold or included on a balance sheet
2. A measure of the strength of consumers' attachment to a brand
3. A description of the associations and beliefs the consumer has about a brand

Of these three concepts, the first could less ambiguously be called *brand valuation* (and often is). For the present argument, I refer to it as *brand value.*

The concept of measuring the consumer's level of attachment to a brand can be called *brand loyalty*—although this phrase is almost as ambiguous as *brand equity* itself. I prefer *brand strength* for this sense, and, although I am aware that this is also potentially confusing, that is what I will call it in this chapter.

The third could be called by the traditional name of *brand image,* but, for clarity, I will refer to it here as *brand description.* This reflects its fundamental difference from the other two senses of brand equity; it is unlike them because it would not be expected to be represented by a single number.

Brand value could also been seen as the odd one out in another way, as it refers to an actual or notional business transaction, whereas the other two focus on the consumer. In fact, brand strength and brand description are sometimes referred to as *consumer brand equity* to distinguish them from the asset valuation meaning.

Although it should already be clear that these three concepts are different, it is tempting to assume that they are closely related to each other. Brand strength could be a key determinant of the overall brand value; brand description might be expected to affect, or at least to explain, the brand strength. Underlying much of the talk about brand equity, and some of the more elaborate proposals for measuring it, such as Yankelovich methodology,[12] seems to be the assumption of a causal chain along the lines shown in Figure 7.1.

One theme to be pursued in this chapter is why both the links in this chain are weak or, at best, obscure. This being the case, there are clear dangers in using the same name for all three (or even any two) of these concepts—it gives

Figure 7.1. Brand Value: The Chain of Causality

the impression (deliberately or through carelessness) that they are all aspects of the same thing. Like the arrows in Figure 7.1, calling them all *brand equity* is an easy way to create the illusion that an operational relationship exists when, in reality, such a relationship cannot be demonstrated.

These three meanings of brand equity are distinct concepts that require separate discussion. If three different things are being talked about, there are three different questions about measurement. Brand description, in a sense, is not something that should be measured at all in the sense of a single scale, although of course brand attributes can be "measured" using multiple scales. I therefore deal with this fairly briefly. The lengthiest discussion below concerns brand strength, as this would seem to be what most of the brand equity debates have centered on. But it is also necessary to review the area of brand value, without going into any of the financial ramifications of this much-discussed area. These have been reviewed at greater length by others better qualified to do so.[13]

Sense 1: Brand Equity Equals Brand Value

The need to put a value on a brand arises for two main reasons: (a) to set a price when the brand is sold, and (b) to include it as an intangible asset on a balance sheet, a practice that is now possible in the United Kingdom but not everywhere. It has been suggested, following from this, that the balance sheet valuation of a brand should become one of the measures by which the management of the brand (and various inputs such as advertising) can be evaluated.

Consultants have devised formulas that are now widely used for creating brand valuations, foremost among these being Interbrand and management consultancies such as Arthur Andersen.[14] (See Haigh, Chapter 8, this volume.) However, there remain a number of difficulties that should be noted, particularly if these formulas are used as an indication of a brand's overall strength or health, or as a basis for evaluating performance.

First of all, there is the significant difference between an "objective" valuation created for balance sheet purposes and the actual price that a brand might fetch in a real sale. If brands are thought of like houses, it seems reasonable that an expert should be able to say within quite narrow limits what a particular one might fetch—its market value. However, estate agents and surveyors are able to do this for property (not always, but most of the time) because they have many points of comparison. They have seen similar houses sold and with a little experience can form a sound idea of a "market price." But brands are both more different and less frequently sold than houses, so the norms needed to estimate market price do not usually exist.

More important, a brand is likely to have a much higher value to one purchaser than to another. If a company already owns factories, manufacturing skills, means of distribution, or indeed other brands,[15] there may be synergies that make it worthwhile for that company to pay a great deal for a particular brand. To a company without the same assets, the same name could be worth relatively little. For acquisition purposes, the value of a brand to a particular purchaser is best estimated through scenario planning—what future cash flows could this company achieve if it owned and exploited that brand? Takeover price can be higher than current valuation because these incremental cash flows might be far greater than the brand could ever deliver to the existing owner.

Brands can be thought of in this sense as being like properties on a Monopoly game board. The face value of Coventry Street in the British version of Monopoly is £280 sterling, but if a player owns the other two streets in the set, and has plenty of cash to develop the set when complete, its value will be far more. Another player, even paying face value, would never be able to recoup his or her investment.

This is one reason there is no such thing as an absolute value for a brand. What it might actually realize, if sold, depends a great deal on who might be interested in buying it at the time and why. If two companies both want it, this might inflate the price considerably more as, in addition to the cash one could generate from the brand, the strategic advantage of keeping it out of the hands of a competitor is added. The battle between Nestlé and Jacob Suchard to own Rowntree (perhaps the most often cited example of "the value of brands") is a good illustration of this.

Another unresolved difficulty surrounding brand valuation is the issue of separability. John Stuart, when chairman of Quaker Oats, was famously quoted: "If this business were to be split up, I would be glad to take the brands, trademarks, and good will, and you could have all the bricks and mortar—and I would fare better than you." He may, in his particular case, have been right, but such a claim would not always apply. And a successful business has other assets besides trademarks and bricks and mortar. Many brand names, removed from the management, the skills, the culture, the support that they normally enjoy, would rapidly lose their customer bases. Again, this makes the point that a brand—essentially the right to a particular name or identity—has a value that fluctuates according to who uses it.

Balance sheet valuations can concern themselves only with the current user, and on this basis they try to estimate the future profit stream derived from the brand and, within this, how much can be attributed to the brand name itself. The main motives for having balance sheet valuations at all are financial, and these need not be discussed here. But it has also been argued that the act of valuing brands formally is a good discipline for a company; it can shift attention away from a concentration on the immediate profit-and-loss account to a consideration of the longer term.

This sounds as if it should be the case, but how far it really works depends on the formula used to create the brand's value. The preferred methods commonly in use start by considering the brand's current profitability. They then apply probabilities to the current situation growing or continuing, based on various measures of "brand strength," that in this sense may include consumer research and also other factors such as competitive position.[16] The in-depth analysis of all aspects of the brand that is involved may well be a valuable exercise. What is questionable is whether such approaches look at "brand value" in a pure sense or at the business unit as a whole. As sales and, particularly, profitability can be manipulated faster and more easily than can the underlying measures of brand strength (which are in any case necessarily subjective), the simplest way to increase a brand's valuation on this basis could be by continuing a short-term focus on profits. This is exactly what many advocates of brand equity are keen to get away from.

This raises another crucial issue to which I will return later—that of separating *brand strength* from *brand size*. Coca-Cola will appear a stronger brand than Pepsi, on most usual measures, because it is a bigger brand than Pepsi. One of the key issues in the whole field of brand equity measurement is how to find an indication of brand strength that is not simply a tautology for brand size. One extreme view is that the two are, in fact, the same.[17] Although I disagree with this, it is certainly true that large brands, particularly market leaders, derive a great deal of competitive strength from their relative size, and that many measures of brand strength are strongly affected by brand size.

There is, however, an even more fundamental issue about brand valuation. The most common (and most logical) way to estimate a brand's value is by discounting its future cash flows. This means forecasting the future. Now, forecasting is a necessary task, but it is different from objectively measuring something. To forecast, one must make all sorts of assumptions about the future, many of which will, in any event, turn out to be wrong. That is why forecasts tend to be volatile, and why buying and selling things (like stock) on the basis of forecasts has an element of gambling about it.

The American magazine *Financial World* does a valuation each year of the world's top brands. In 1992, it valued Marlboro at a very precise $51.6 billion. A year later, using the same procedures, the magazine valued Marlboro at only $33 billion. All that had happened in between was that Marlboro had cut its price. Many observers would probably agree now that had the brand not cut its price, it would have faced a disastrous long-term future; in fact, the brand was "stronger" when valued at $33 billion than it was when it was valued at $51.6 billion. It is unlikely that the brand had become any less attractive to its consumers as a result of the price cut. All this should suggest that whatever brand valuations show, they are neither objective measures of reality nor reflections of consumer brand strength.

In summary, then, a valuation for balance sheet purposes is not the same as a valuation made on behalf of a particular purchaser. Valuations are volatile, varying according to assumptions and context. They do not reflect current measures of a brand's strength with the consumer.

Sense 2: Brand Equity Equals Brand Strength— a Measure of Relative Consumer Demand for the Brand

David Aaker describes brand equity as having five components:

- Brand loyalty
- Awareness
- Perceived quality

- Other associations
- Other brand assets[18]

This is a pragmatic recognition of the different concepts that have been associated with brand strength and that can be measured. It can be criticized for lacking an underlying theory that relates these five ideas together,[19] but by the same token it is well to be prepared for the fact that no such underlying theory really exists—in which case the concept of brand equity can hardly be said to be a scientific one.

The many different methods that have been published can, for the most part, be described as using one or a combination of the following basic types of measures:

- Price/demand measures (including modeling approaches)
- Behavioral measures of loyalty (buying behavior)
- Awareness/salience measures
- Attitudinal measures of loyalty

Of these, the second is similar to Aaker's loyalty component, the third to his awareness component, and the last is related to—but not the same as—his concept of "perceived quality."

Aaker's term "brand associations" broadly describes the third principal sense of brand equity—that is, brand description. Aaker is quite right to include it as one of the dimensions on which a brand should be appraised; it has been dealt with separately because it seems essentially descriptive, rather than evaluative.

In my opinion, Aaker is also right not to include price premium as a core dimension of brand equity, though he discusses it briefly.[20] I would also agree that this is best seen as a measurable output of brand equity, rather than a part of brand equity itself (which raises another possible debate about what the term actually means). Because it has nevertheless formed one of the most popular approaches to measuring brand equity, it is dealt with first.

Price/Demand Measures
(Including Modeling Approaches)

One of the frequent benefits of a strong brand is its ability to command a higher price and/or its lower sensitivity to price increases compared with its

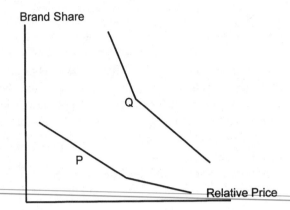

Figure 7.2. Two Demand Curves

competitors. It follows from this that two dimensions on which the strength of a brand can be measured are its price premium and its price elasticity. In other words, a brand is strong if people are prepared to pay more for it. Each of these dimensions can be measured in one of two ways: using market data or using experimental data.

Price 1: Using Market Data

Suppose it is considered that an improvement in price premium while sustaining share (or improving share while sustaining price) is an improvement in brand equity. This has the merit of simplicity and needs no special research beyond reliable data on relative price and share, such as can be had from a good retail audit. The simplest way to imagine this is by plotting brand share and relative price on two axes of a graph. For each brand, it is expected that a relationship between price and share will be seen, popularly referred to as the *demand curve*. "Changing the shape of the demand curve" and "moving the demand curve to the right" have long been recognized as possible desired outcomes of advertising.[21] This increase in demand could also be seen as an increase in the brand's equity.

In Figure 7.2, Brand Q has a higher share than Brand P when they both charge the same price premium over the market average, or can charge a higher price when they both have the same share. Also, Q loses less share than P when the price goes up; the slope of the line is steeper. These could be seen as two measures of Q's greater brand strength. If P and Q represent the same brand at different time periods, Q later than P, this could be taken as evidence of improved brand equity—caused, for instance, by advertising.

Price elasticity can also be estimated using econometric modeling; in the PG Tips case history, the Grand Prix winner in the 1990 Advertising Effectiveness Awards, sponsored by the British Institute of Practitioners in Advertising (IPA), there is an example of relative price elasticity quoted as evidence of brand strength/advertising effect.[22]

A refinement of the price premium approach is offered by Longman-Moran Analytics in the United States.[23] Here the definition of brand equity is as follows: Market Share × Relative Price × a "durability" factor. This last is an estimate of price elasticity based on market data. Crucial to this method (which makes it less easy than it sounds) is the importance of correctly defining the competitive set on which to base share and price differences, so that an apparently small brand may really need to be considered as a dominant niche player in a segment or small category.

A further development of this approach is also to take distribution into account. Distribution and price are thus regarded as two "contaminating" factors that disguise the "real" underlying demand for competing brands. Simon Broadbent has developed a measure of consumer brand equity that he defines as "the sales share we would get, if we were at average price and had average distribution—and average price and distribution elasticities applied. Equity is, in effect, the residual after price and distribution effects have been allowed for." [24] It is conceptually a short step from this to identifying equity with the underlying "base" or constant in an econometric model of sales or share. Broadbent has also been very active in exploring the idea that the constant in such equations can and does move over time, reflecting the underlying strength of a brand when all short-term factors—price, distribution, advertising, competitive activity, or whatever—have been allowed for.[25] This is referred to as the *floating base*. A similar concept can be found in the modeling approach to brand equity measurement offered by the Consumer Affinity Company in the United States.[26]

The idea of searching for brand equity (brand strength) by factoring out all influences on market performance other than the brand name itself can lead into some complex procedures, such as that used by Kamakura and Russell.[27] However, it is interesting that these American academic researchers validate their highly sophisticated approach by comparing results against a simple plotting of price premium versus brand share. In fact, this scatterplot approach remains one of the simplest and most practical ways to consider a brand's strength in the marketplace; for most purposes the use of multinomial logit models to estimate something similar may be using a complicated sledgehammer to crack a fairly simple nut.

Price 2: Experimental Approaches

Other approaches based on price take a different route. Instead of using market data, they use various forms of pricing research to estimate what share the brand would have at various different relative price levels. The equity measure is basically a calculation of the relative price at which each brand would have an equal share. (This is recognizable as the inversion of Broadbent's definition, given above.)

Joel Axelrod defines brand equity as "the incremental amount your customer will pay to obtain your brand rather than a physically comparable product without your brand name." [28] In order to measure this, customers are divided into different cells and shown different combinations of the test brand and competitors at different price levels; they express preferences using a constant sum technique.

Jim Crimmins of DDB Needham has a somewhat similar approach to measuring "the amount of value added by a brand name" (to his credit, he avoids the dreaded E word).[29] The interviewing approach sounds similar to that used by Axelrod. The output is an estimation of the price at which the test brand and each competitor are equally likely to be chosen. Notice that this measure of "brand value added" is not absolute, but varies according to which competitor is taken as the comparison. Crimmins reports that the value added by the number-one brand in a market averages at 40% compared with store brands, but averages only 10% compared with the number-two brand; in both cases there is a wide variation around this median figure.

Steve Roth describes the use of brand price trade-off analysis to estimate brand equity.[30] In this approach respondents choose their preferred brand at various different sets of price levels. By pooling all the respondents' individual decision processes, the computer program can simulate market outcomes at any set of prices. From a brand equity viewpoint, this micromodeling approach shows that a brand can have different "equity" for different respondents.

As one can see by examining behavioral or attitudinal loyalty measures, any serious investigation into quantifying consumers' degree of "attachment" to a brand is likely to discover this unsurprising truth: Some customers will be far more attached to the brand than will others. It follows from this that figures that average all customers to provide a total brand score may be misleading. Conversely, the process of decomposing a brand's user base into more-loyal or less-loyal users may be valuable in itself in planning marketing strategy. It may be that one of the main benefits of some brand equity research lies in this area, rather than in the quest for a single yardstick to use in measuring brand strength.

Trade-off or conjoint approaches make it appear quite easy to separate brand name effects from other factors, which may make people forget that in real life separability is not always so clear-cut. Can the Mercedes-Benz name really be separated, for example, from the reality of the Mercedes-Benz car?

Some General Observations on Price

The attraction of using price as an indication of brand strength is that it relates closely to one of the main business benefits of branding. It is helpful insofar as it takes the focus off volume and adds the dimension of commanding a fair price for a trusted product. However, there is more to brand strength than price premiums. There are strong brands that do not command a premium price, either because they are examples of "scale economy branding" or because there is no directly substitutable product in the market. Mars Bars would be an example of both. It is possible that relatively low price elasticity would still be an indication of brand strength, but if the policy of the manufacturer were to keep prices low—for example, to keep competitors out of the market—this would be a somewhat hypothetical measure.

Another danger is a possible lagged effect between price rises and share loss. It is a dangerous game to suppose that a brand can be made "stronger" by increasing its price premium, but this could be one logical outcome of a system that measures brand equity in this way. The story of Marlboro in the period leading up to "Marlboro Friday" illustrates the risks.[31]

This raises another question fundamental to defining what is meant by *brand equity.* Is it enough to consider a "snapshot" of the brand's relative position at one point in time? Or should people be interested in its future potential for growth, its future resilience against attack? Price premiums may be more a legacy of past strength (or present greed) than a guarantee of future performance. Many brands in the U.K. grocery market might be seen as illustrating this uncertainty.

Behavioral Measures of Brand Loyalty

Brand loyalty, as mentioned before, is another expression that can have varying meanings. It is sometimes used, for instance, to describe the consumer's attitudinal orientation toward the brand (to be covered later). Its narrower sense, however, is based on records of actual purchasing behavior as gathered in consumer panels.

One common method of using panel data to generate a measure of loyalty has involved the concept of *share of category requirements* (SCR), often abbreviated as *share of requirements* (SOR). The SOR for Nescafé is all Nescafé volume expressed as share of all instant coffee bought by respondents who bought Nescafé during the analysis period. This overall figure disguises wide variations among individual buyers, some of whom will have bought no other coffee in the period (SOR = 100%) and others of whom will have bought it only once out of n coffee purchases (SOR = $1/n \times 100\%$). On this basis the more loyal customer is the one for whom the brand represents a higher share of category requirements; for instance, someone who buys seven jars of Nescafé in 10 coffee purchasing occasions is more "loyal" than someone who buys only three.

A good deal of attention has been paid to this behavioral definition of loyalty as an indicator of brand equity, especially in the United States. The idea is that the buyer with a higher share of category requirements is, obviously, far more important to the business (overall weight of purchase being equal) and is also, implicitly, more emotionally attached to the brand and less willing to accept a substitute. (It does not, in fact, follow that this should always be the case, and I am not sure what evidence exists for this assumption.) Therefore, if a brand's buyers show, overall, a higher average SOR, this could be seen as a sign of brand strength. (More usually nowadays the criterion is a higher proportion of buyers with an SOR above a certain level, rather than the average. Crimmins suggests the proportion of buyers with an SOR over 60%; Christiani argues for considering the whole distribution.)[32]

Larry Light, a distinguished American advertising practitioner and chairman of the Coalition for Brand Equity, uses the following example to dem-

TABLE 7.1 U.S. Instant Coffee Market

Coffee	Annual Market Share (%)	Annual Share of Category Requirements (%)
Maxwell House	19	39
Sanka	16	36
Taster's Choice	14	32
High Point	13	31
All other brands	12	32
Folgers	11	29
Nescafé	8	28
Brim	4	21
Maxim	3	23

onstrate that brands with the same market share can differ in loyalty as measured by SOR.[33] He posits three imaginary brands: Brand A, which 100% of the user population buy 15% of the time; Brand B, which 15% buy 100% of the time; and Brand C, which half of the population buy 30% of the time. It will be seen that each of these brands has an identical 15% market share, but in terms of profitability, Brand B is claimed to be the most profitable (and the most secure?) and Brand A the least.

The problem with this (admittedly hypothetical) example is that brands like A, B, and C are not known to exist in normal markets. As I have already observed, every brand shows a distribution of different loyalty levels ranging from 100% loyalists to those who only bought the brand once. Andrew Ehrenberg and his colleagues have shown repeatedly that over any time period this distribution follows a standard pattern that can be predicted within fairly narrow limits from three parameters. Two of these are market-specific and can be estimated from the category rate of purchase and the number of brands in the market; the third is simply that brand's market share. Hence any brand's average share of category requirements can also be predicted, within narrow limits, from the same three parameters. Ehrenberg also shows that average share of requirements actually varies little among brands in a market, although it is normally higher for brands with a larger share, an instance of so-called double jeopardy.[34] Table 7.1, based on Ehrenberg and Scriven's data, illustrates a typical finding.

There is an apparent conflict between Ehrenberg's findings (which have never been seriously disputed, though often ignored) and much U.S. research based on SOR. The logic following from Ehrenberg's data is that brand strength measures based on share of category requirements are, once again, mere tautologies for brand share; share of category requirements will go up only if brand share goes up. In which case, SOR may discriminate between consumers, but not usefully between brands.

An alternative to using SOR as a way of defining loyalty is to look at patterns of purchasing over time and use these to estimate the probability of each panel member's buying the brand on the next purchase occasion. Alain Pioche of Nielsen describes such a system and illustrates how it can be more sensitive than SOR by using the following three purchasing sequences, where 1 represents a purchase of the brand and 0 represents purchase of another brand:[35]

$$1,1,1,1,1,0,0,0,0,0$$
$$1,0,1,0,1,0,1,0,1,0$$
$$0,0,0,0,0,1,1,1,1,1$$

The SOR here is identical for all three at 50%. On the basis that past buying is the best single predictor of future buying behavior, Pioche estimates the probability of each respondent's buying the brand next time as A = 0.21, B = 0.43, and C = 0.79. The results must be aggregated to create an overall measure for loyalty to a brand. This would then have the potential to vary continuously in time.

This idea has an intuitive appeal—it is like reading the form at a horse race. It may be thought, however, that at the aggregate level it will be unlikely to reveal anything new about the brand's health—if more people are buying the brand more often, this should be reflected in its overall brand share.

But what both SOR and this "stochastic" approach show is that any brand is bought by different groups of people, some very loyal (in behavioral terms), some not at all so. This mode of analysis is valuable in that it recognizes that some customers are far more important to the brand than others, and that if these can be identified and targeted there can be significant improvements in marketing efficiency. This is the reverse of traditional "conversion" models of marketing, where the target was essentially conceived of as a nonuser; it reflects a new and proper emphasis on the importance of the existing customer base.[36]

Once the attempt is made to decompose the customer base in this way, a number of interlocking segmentations become possible, and this can make the process a complex one. Three common divisions are as follows:

- Weight of category purchase can be employed where a wide distribution should be expected from heavy to very light users, that is, where (at least) the 80:20 rule generally applies—a minority of buyers account for a high proportion of total category consumption.

- Share of category requirements cuts across this, so that some of a brand's more loyal users will be heavy category users and some very light. Ehrenberg points out that customers whose share of category requirements is 100% are likely to include a lot of very light users, as the easiest way to be classified as 100% loyal is to have bought the category on only a single occasion in the analysis period.[37] This will also apply to others with a high SOR. Nevertheless, there will be some heavy category users who are 80%-100% loyal, and these will account for a disproportionate volume of the business.

- In the United States, where deep price discounting has become a major force in packaged goods markets, there have been attempts to find general consumer segmentations that hold true across categories—so that some individuals are more brand loyal, some buy across a wide repertoire, and some are particularly likely to buy on deal.[38] Discussion then arises as to whether an occasional buyer of a brand is a more or less attractive prospect if he or she is a loyal buyer of a competing brand or a "deal selective."

All this may seem to be straying far away from the topic of this particular inquiry, and so in a way it is. However, the relevance of this to an overall measurement of brand equity is that a buyer whose 50% SOR is based on preference would constitute a greater brand asset than a buyer whose same SOR was based on deal buying. This suggests that analysis of buying patterns alone can be misleading unless it also includes some information about price.

Measures of behavioral loyalty attempt to use consistency of behavior as a proxy for attitude, or what we might call commitment. Given the influence of other factors—such as inertia, availability, and price—it is not obvious that this is entirely sound. Another way of looking at brand equity is to get a fix attitudinally on the number of buyers who are strongly committed to a brand compared with the number who buy it simply because of price, because of habit or inertia, or because it is the only one there. I describe some of these below.

Attitudinal Measure of Brand Loyalty

This subsection is concerned with general evaluative measures (affective or "liking") more than with specific associations and beliefs about the brand (cognitive or "thinking"), which belong more properly under the third main definition of brand equity as brand description. The measures can take various forms that need not be described here in detail: scales ranging from "the only one I would ever consider" to "I would never consider"; constant sum preference scales; brand "for me" to "not for me." Any form of experimental price testing (such as those conducted by Axelrod or Crimmins, cited above) can be seen as a form of attitudinal research that takes claimed willingness to pay a price as its scale (hence it has been whimsically called "dollarmetric scaling"). General measures of "esteem" or "quality" are intended to be sufficiently vague to cover all types of products or services, so they can be included under general affective measures.

In a way, such attitudinal measures take the most direct approach to the underlying concept that needs to be measured—the relative preference, "want-ability," or attachment the consumer has for the brand, separated from "external" factors such as price and distribution. Brand strength defined in this way is essentially attitudinal, following Gordon Allport's classic definition of attitude as "a mental and neural state of readiness, organized through experience, exerting a directive or dynamic influence upon the individual's response to all objects and situations with which it is related."

If brand attitudes are handled crudely on an "8 out of 10 cats prefer" basis or, worse still, as a single averaged figure, care needs to be taken—again—that the numbers of a brand's devotees are not being confounded with the degree of their individual devotion to it. If this is done, then larger brands will tend to get the higher scores, and once again, nothing will be learned other than the fact that they are big.[39] In fact, the use of preference and other measures to stand for "brand equity" has led to renewed interest in trying to understand how they represent different parts of the customer base by disaggregating them into groups (as in the analysis of loyalty, with which some researchers have tried to combine it).

One method of attitudinal segmentation is the conceptually very simple one proposed by Cramphorn.[40] This method segments buyers of a brand into two groups, the discriminating and the undiscriminating, on the basis of a validated series of attitudinal statements. The percentage of discriminating buyers, plotted against brand share on the other axis, positions a brand as relatively stronger or weaker than others the same size.

A more complex attitudinal segmentation is Market Facts Inc.'s conversion model, which segments buyers and nonbuyers into four groups each: Users are *entrenched, average, shallow,* or *convertible,* and nonusers can be *available, ambivalent, weakly unavailable,* or *strongly unavailable.*[41] It is claimed that trends in movements among these groups anticipate and predict market share movements; in particular, as early as April 1991 the model predicted the decline in Marlboro share that led to the large price reductions of "Marlboro Friday."

If this is true, it means that the questions are a major advance from the traditional "intention to buy" question that was used for many years as a predictor of future behavior. In fact, as Bird and Ehrenberg found a number of years ago, claimed intention to buy reflects past behavior much more than future behavior.[42] So a brand with a higher intention to buy than its present brand share would imply that it is generally not, as might be expected, a brand that is about to grow, but a brand that is probably in decline. The number of respondents expecting to buy it is merely a reflection of past glories.

The proponents of the conversion model argue that behavioral loyalty alone can misrepresent consumers' level of emotional attachment to a brand, quoting evidence that many buyers with a high SOR have low emotional commitment. They also point out that in infrequent purchase choices, such as those concerning banks, cars, and credit cards, SOR is not a practically useful concept.[43]

Awareness/Salience Measures

Brand awareness is one of Aaker's five dimensions of brand equity. He defines it as "the ability to identify a brand as associated with a product category"—an important qualification. There is a difference between "mere" awareness of a name and associating that name with a particular product. Being the first name to come to mind when an individual thinks of coffee, hand drills, or mouthwash is one indication that a brand "owns" that particular category. Such associations can persist for a long time.

Brand awareness has a long pedigree as a desired outcome of marketing activity, deriving from the very earliest models of advertising effectiveness such as St. Elmo Lewis's AIDA (Attention–Interest–Desire–Action) in 1907. In most markets, recognition or a sense of familiarity with a brand name is considered a step toward improving acceptability and preference, other things being equal. Awareness can be measured as recognition (prompted by the brand name) or spontaneous (prompted by some definition of the product field), with a further refinement in collecting the first name mentioned.

One of the best-known general measures of brand equity, the Landor ImagePower Survey, consists of two parts: a simple measure of brand awareness and a more complex factor called "esteem" (a general quality rating).[44]

The findings of this survey indicate that these two measures are substantially independent of each other, showing that brands that are well-known or easily called to mind are not always highly thought of or likely to be preferred (although more so in the United States than in Europe).

Another major cross-category survey of relative brand strength, the Young & Rubicam (Y&R) Brand Asset Valuator, includes "familiarity" as one of four key dimensions of brand strength (the others are "esteem," "relevance," and "differentiation").[45] Even here Y&R is careful to point out that its definition of "familiarity" embraces more than mere name awareness.

In fact, it is generally true that high levels of awareness are created by a brand's size, ubiquity, and/or scale of promotional activity, but such awareness reveals relatively little about the brand's "strength" in the sense of the consumer's attachment to it or preference for it. Such measures tend to favor brands that are relatively or absolutely large, so that once more we are in danger of confounding size with strength.

Sense 3: Brand Equity Equals Description— Descriptive Associations/Attributes of the Brand

Some researchers talk about the collection of brand image data, positioning mapping, and the like as if this were "brand equity." David Aaker includes this as one of his dimensions of brand equity. It is widely assumed that the associations or attributes that a brand acquires are the main creators of the brand's strength, as when Alexander Biel argues that "brand image drives brand equity." [46]

A wide variety of techniques, qualitative and quantitative, exist for eliciting associations with and perceptions of a brand, by inviting respondents to link each brand with words or pictures or, in multidimensional scaling, to position them relative to each other. There is no need to describe them all here.

More relevant to the brand equity debate are attempts to relate the data gathered using these techniques, which are essentially descriptive, to dimensions of attitudinal or behavioral loyalty—that is, brand strength, as described above. It is through this linkage that what might be called brand image data have attached themselves to the brand equity concept, in procedures that are often known in the United States as "brand equity modeling."

Attempts to model general affective attitudes toward brands in this way can follow two main approaches, which can be called cross-sectional or time series. *Cross-sectional* analysis looks for correlations between the individuals in the sample—so that if the strongest preferrers show a strong tendency to rate the brand on attribute Y, the inference is that associating the brand with attribute Y creates preference. This procedure is not new—it goes back to the St. James model of the 1960s, and the objection made against it at the time, that it is impossible to distinguish cause and effect in such correlations, is still a matter for debate. *Time series* analysis requires a set of such data over time from a tracking study; if a sudden decline in one particular attribute happens at the same time as a decline in general favorability scores, that attribute is assumed to be an important "driver." Both approaches can be and often are combined with the loyalty segmentations described, so that the "drivers" for each brand's loyalists or rejectors (including competitive brands) can be computed.

All these procedures are controversial, but they are undeniably attractive for many reasons that go beyond the measurement aspect of brand equity. They offer guidance for advertising and marketing strategy, and an appearance, at least, of controlling complexity—"If we can improve this image dimension for these people, our brand equity—and profit—will go up this much." In their favor it must be said that they grapple with the complexity of a real user base, where different individuals vary. Not everyone will be convinced they deliver all they promise.

General Conclusions

What's Good About the "Brand Equity Movement"?

Before moving on to some more critical conclusions, I would suggest that the new focus on "brand equity" indicates a desirable paradigm shift in marketing thinking (this would be especially true in the United States). The key elements of this paradigm shift would be as follows:

- A focus on the value of *keeping* present customers, as opposed to converting new ones
- A recognition that marketing should be about selling at the *optimum price,* not just shifting volumes
- A focus on protecting and developing a *long-term profit stream,* not just getting the next sale

- An understanding that a brand survives and prospers only if it keeps its *contract* with the customer
- A revival of interest in the concepts of *differentiation* and *positioning*

But the idea that all this is somehow explained by the motions and dimensions of a mysterious substance called *brand equity* is much harder to defend.

Dispelling the Brand Equity Myths

Brand value is not the same as brand strength.

I have argued throughout this chapter that financial valuation of a brand as a separable asset is fundamentally different from the concept of measuring a brand's "strength" relative to the consumer. Calling the two things by the same name is confusing, even misleading. Although the two concepts both have some kind of validity as ideas, the connection between them is a very tenuous one. Valuation is essentially a forecast, and therefore can be volatile and dependent on variable assumptions. A measure of brand strength, on the other hand, ought to reflect some kind of objective reality, and should therefore be reasonably stable and replicable. One represents the future, the other represents the present. And present brand strength is only one factor—not necessarily an important one—in constructing a future forecast. (Barwise points out that none of the short-term measures of brand loyalty has yet been shown to have any long-term predictive power.)[47]

It should follow from this that the idea of using brand valuation as a yardstick for judging and rewarding management is a dangerous one. Why pay a brand manager a bonus for something his successors may or may not succeed in doing in future years?

There is no single number that represents brand strength.

It should at least be clear that whatever the different measures of "brand strength" represent, they do not all measure the same thing. For instance:

- A brand's ability to command a price premium is different from its SOR. (The brand leader may have 40% more "equity" than the store brand measured as price premium but the same SOR among its buyers, or less.)
- "Loyalty" as shown by probability models is different from attitudinal measures;[48] also, as mentioned, it is different from SOR.

- Different price measures give quite different results. (Crimmins is explicit in pointing out that his measure of brand value is not the same as the price premium in the market.)[49]

- Ceurvost points out that the conversion model's measure of "commitment" is not related to SOR.[50]

And so on.

To talk about a brand's "strength" or "health" is after all to use a metaphor. Such metaphors are employed all the time (e.g., the sun "rises"), but they should not be confused with science. Advertisers are so used to the metaphor of "brand as person" that they may need to remind themselves that it is not literally true.

What is meant by the statement "A brand is strong" is really something like "The main performance indicators look positive." And there may be many different performance indicators, and the ones that matter may vary from brand to brand and from time to time. No sensible person would expect to represent the health of an individual, or of a nation's economy, by a single figure (and the results of such a mistake, if made, could be disastrous). So it is with brands.

It is difficult to separate
"brand strength" from "brand size."

Another theme in this chapter is that many of the performance indicators discussed tend to be largely a function of a brand's sales in the market. Some key performance indicators are, indeed, sales based (as in the price/share charts). Attitudinal and awareness measures relate largely to brand size, and even SOR has been shown to be predictable from it.

However, this does not entirely justify Ehrenberg's apparent view (if this is the correct interpretation) that brand strength and brand size are exactly the same, so that the first term is completely redundant.[51] It is easy to imagine situations where research shows a degree of consumer demand for a brand not reflected in sales, or where sales are inflated by factors other than consumer demand. These would be very valuable situations for a brand manager to know about, the one representing an opportunity and the other a threat. It is the object of "brand monitors" and other attitudinal research to provide information like this. But providers and users of such data need to be aware of the pitfalls involved.

What Is It That Needs to Be Measured?

What I have really discussed in this chapter is not the elusive brand equity, but a variety of different performance measures and forecasting techniques. Instead of the nominalist mistake (invent a thing called brand equity and find ways to measure it), a decision should be made about what needs to be measured (and, if necessary, names should be found for each of these things). The main things a brand manager or brand owner might want to measure, then, will be as follows:

- *Current performance:* How well is the brand doing now, relative to competitors or to previous years? Indicators would include share/price combinations and modeling techniques that attempt to separate underlying consumer demand from external factors such as distribution (a simple version of this, of course, being rate of sale).

- *Diagnosis of current trends and "early warning systems":* This is where the various consumer measures of attitudes, awareness, and buying behavior come into their own—as long as it is remembered that these data usually to a large extent reflect sales performance. They are also extremely valuable in decomposing aggregate sales patterns into different consumer groups. More perceptual measures, such as surveys of a brand's relative positioning or differentiation, are relevant here too.

- *The brand's chances of future, long-term profitability:* The real goal for brand owners is to achieve what Larry Light has called enduring, profitable growth. This brings us to the heart of what the various attempts to measure brand equity are trying to do. Current performance indicators can show short-term increases in sales (e.g., by promoting) or in profit (e.g., by increasing price) or even, occasionally, both (by promoting while reducing quality or investment), but at the same time be reducing the chances of the brand's succeeding in the future. It would be a good thing if there were a performance indicator that rewarded brand management for protecting the long-term health of the brand, rather than merely maximizing its share or profit in the current year. However, it is not clear that such an indicator has yet been found, or even whether it is possible for one to exist.

  Certainly many of the simple measures put forward as representing brand equity, such as relative demand, do not by themselves fit the bill, as I have already argued. Conceptually, the problem is the same as with brand valuation for financial purposes—what people are looking for is an estimate of how the brand will perform some years into the future. Although this may be something that management should form a judgment about, there is no objective way of capitalizing current investments in a brand's future. What people can be alert to are improvements in current performance that are merely a result of manipulating price or investment, and a judgment can be made—it can hardly be put more strongly than this—on whether these changes in policy are likely to maintain the brand's competitive position into the future. This returns us, in fact, to considering current performance and diagnosing the reasons for current performance.

- *Overall performance:* For buying, selling, or valuing a brand, or as an aid to future strategic planning, an overall valuation can be attempted. There are various ways of tackling this tricky job, but they tend to be essentially forecasts of future performance (translated into net present value). Such forecasts involve competitive and strategic judgments and other considerations, such as legal ownership, as well as current performance measures.

Another question often asked (but hardly discussed in this chapter) concerns *branded extendability:* How can a brand's reputation be used in other product fields? Although quite a lot of academic work has been done in this area, it is questionable whether any really useful principles have been discovered, and rather doubtful whether there will ever be. Consumer research might be of some use in making this kind of decision. From a valuation point of view, to include hypothetical performance of a brand in a different category is about as speculative as one can get. It is, surely, part of the great brand equity myth that "a strong brand" can stroll with ease and impunity into neighboring territories and clean up. Experience rather tends to show the contrary.

Final Conclusions

Brands need to be managed with a view to their long-term market position, respecting their contract and relationship with the consumer. There are many different kinds of performance indicators that will monitor these factors. A value can also be put on brands as assets when necessary, and they can be bought and sold. But all this can be done without assuming the existence of anything called *brand equity.* In fact, the whole area might be easier to understand if people stopped using those words altogether.

Notes

1. Thornton C. Lockwood, "The Confessions of a Brand Equity Junkie," in Advertising Research Foundation (ed.), *Exploring Brand Equity* (New York: Advertising Research Foundation, 1995).

2. Karl R. Popper, *The Open Society and Its Enemies,* vol. 1 (London: Routledge & Kegan Paul, 1945), 32.

3. Quoted in Alexander L. Biel, "Converting Image Into Equity," in David A. Aaker and Alexander L. Biel (eds.), *Brand Equity and Advertising* (Hillsdale, NJ: Lawrence Erlbaum, 1993), 67.

4. Burleigh B. Gardner and Sidney J. Levy, "The Product and the Brand," *Harvard Business Review,* March/April 1955, 33-39.

5. See Stephen King, *What Is a Brand?* (London: J. Walter Thompson, 1970); see also Don Cowley (ed.), *Understanding Brands* (London: Kogan Page/Account Planning Group, 1989).

6. Rosser Reeves, *Reality in Advertising* (New York: Alfred A. Knopf, 1961), 77-86.

7. John Philip Jones, "Over-Promise and Under-Delivery," paper presented at the ESOMAR seminar, What Do We Know About How Advertising Works and How Promotions Work? Amsterdam, April 1991, 13-27.

8. Tim Ambler and Chris Styles, *Brand Equity: Towards Measures That Matter,* Pan'agra Working Paper 9902 (London: London Business School, 1995).

9. See, for example, David A. Aaker, *Managing Brand Equity: Capitalizing on the Value of a Brand Name* (New York: Free Press, 1991); and J.-N. Kapferer, *Strategic Brand Management: New Approaches to Creating and Evaluating Brand Equity* (London: Kogan Page, 1992).

10. Patrick Barwise, "Brand Equity, Snark or Boojum," *International Journal of Research in Marketing,* vol. 10, no. 1, March 1993, 93-104.

11. Popper, *The Open Society.*

12. See James A. Taylor, "Brand Equity; Its Meaning, Measurement and Management," paper presented at the ESOMAR seminar, The Challenge of Branding Today and in the Future, Brussels, October 1992, 55-75.

13. Patrick Barwise, Christopher Higson, Andrew Likierman, and Paul Marsh, *Accounting for Brands* (London: London Business School/Institute of Chartered Accountants, 1989). See also Kapferer, *Strategic Brand Management.*

14. John Murphy, "Assessing the Value of Brands," *Long Range Planning,* vol. 23, no. 3, 1990, 23-29; Howard Barrett and Nick P. Bertolotti, "Brand Evaluation," paper presented at the ESOMAR seminar, The Challenge of Branding Today and in the Future, Brussels, October 1992, 1-12.

15. Patrick Barwise and Thomas Robertson, "Brand Portfolios," *European Management Journal,* vol. 10, no. 3, September 1992, 277-285.

16. Murphy, "Assessing the Value of Brands."

17. Andrew S. C. Ehrenberg, "If You're So Strong, Why Aren't You Bigger? Making the Case Against Brand Equity," *Admap,* October 1993, 13-14. See also the comments by Ambler and Feldwick, as well as Ehrenberg's reply, in the December 1993 issue of *Admap.*

18. Aaker, *Managing Brand Equity.*

19. Gil McWilliam, "A Tale of Two Gurus," *International Journal of Research in Marketing,* vol. 10, no. 1, March 1993, 105-111.

20. Aaker, *Managing Brand Equity,* 23.

21. John Philip Jones, *What's in a Name? Advertising and the Concept of Brands* (New York: Simon & Schuster-Lexington, 1986), 95-96.

22. Paul Feldwick (ed.), *Advertising Works 6* (Henley-on-Thames, UK: NTC, 1991), 13.

23. William T. Moran, "Brand Equity: The Durability of Brand Value," paper presented at the ARF Brand Equity Workshop, New York, February 1994.

24. Simon Broadbent, "Using Data Better: A New Approach to Sales Analyses," *Admap,* January 1992, 48-54.

25. Simon Broadbent, "Advertising Effects: More Than Short Term," *Journal of the Market Research Society,* vol. 35, no. 1, January 1993, 379.

26. Sandra K. Eubank, "Understanding Brand Equity: A Volumetric Model," paper presented at ARF Brand Equity Research Day, New York, October 1993.

27. W. A. Kamakura and G. J. Russell, "Measuring Brand Value With Scanner Data," *International Journal of Research in Marketing,* vol. 10, no. 1, March 1993, 9-22.

28. Joel N. Axelrod, "The Use of Experimental Design in Monitoring Brand Equity," paper presented at the ESOMAR seminar, The Challenge of Branding Today and in the Future, Brussels, October 1992, 13-26.

29. James C. Crimmins, "Better Measurement and Management of Brand Value," *Journal of Advertising Research,* vol. 32, no. 4, July/August 1992, 11-19.

30. Steve Roth, "Pricing, Profits and Equity," paper presented at the Third ARF Advertising and Promotions Workshop, New York, February 1991.

31. Paul Feldwick and Françoise Bonnal, "Reports of the Death of Brands Have Been Greatly Exaggerated," *Marketing and Research Today,* vol. 23, no. 2, May 1995, 86-95.

32. Crimmins, "Better Measurement and Management"; Arthur Christiani, "Measuring and Monitoring Brand Loyalty and Its Role in Managing Brand Equity," paper presented at ARF Brand Equity Research Day, New York, October 1993.

33. See Larry Light, *The Fourth Wave: Brand Loyalty* (New York: American Association of Advertising Agencies, 1996), 28.

34. Andrew S. C. Ehrenberg, *Repeat-Buying: Facts, Theory and Applications,* 2nd ed. (New York: Oxford University Press, 1988). See also Andrew S. C. Ehrenberg, Gerald J. Goodhardt, and T. Patrick Barwise, "Double Jeopardy Revisited," *Journal of Marketing,* vol. 54, July 1990, 82-91; Andrew S. C. Ehrenberg and John Scriven, *JOAB Report 1: Added Values or Propensities to Buy* (London: South Bank Business School, 1995).

35. Alain Pioche, "A Definition of Brand Equity Relying on Attitudes and Validated by Behavior," paper presented at the ESOMAR seminar, The Challenge of Branding Today and in the Future, Brussels, October 1992, 27-40.

36. Garth Hallberg, *All Consumers Are Not Created Equal: The Differential Marketing Strategy for Brand Loyalty and Profits* (New York: John Wiley, 1995), chaps. 3, 4.

37. Ehrenberg, *Repeat-Buying,* 174.

38. Carol Foley, Josh McQueen, and John Deighton, "Decomposing a Brand's Consumer Franchise Into Buyer Types," in David A. Aaker and Alexander L. Biel (eds.), *Brand Equity and Advertising* (Hillsdale, NJ: Lawrence Erlbaum, 1993), 235-246.

39. Patrick Barwise and Andrew S. C. Ehrenberg, "Consumer Beliefs and Brand Usage," *Journal of the Market Research Society,* vol. 27, no. 2, April 1985, 81-93.

40. Michael F. Cramphorn, "Are There Bounds on Brand Equity?" paper presented at the ESOMAR seminar, The Challenge of Branding Today and in the Future, Brussels, October 1992, 41-54.

41. Robert W. Ceurvost, "A Brand Equity Measure Based on Consumer Commitments to Brands," paper presented at the ARF Brand Equity Workshop, New York, February 1994.

42. Michael Bird and Andrew S. C. Ehrenberg, "Intentions to Buy and Claimed Brand Usage," *Operational Research Quarterly,* vol. 17, 1966-1967, 18, 27-46, 65-66. See also Neil Barnard, "What Can You Do With Tracking Studies and What Are Their Limitations?" *Admap,* April 1990, 23.

43. Ceurvost, "A Brand Equity Measure."

44. Stewart Owen, "The Landor ImagePower Survey: A Global Assessment of Brand Strength," in David A. Aaker and Alexander L. Biel (eds.), *Brand Equity and Advertising* (Hillsdale, NJ: Lawrence Erlbaum, 1993), 11-30.

45. Young & Rubicam Ltd., *Brand Asset Valuator Prospectus* (New York: Young & Rubicam, 1994).

46. Alexander L. Biel, "How Brand Image Drives Brand Equity," paper presented at the ARF Workshop, New York, February 1992.

47. Barwise, "Brand Equity."

48. Pioche, "A Definition of Brand Equity," 37-39.

49. Crimmins, "Better Measurement and Management," 18.

50. Ceurvost, "A Brand Equity Measure."

51. Ehrenberg, "If You're So Strong."

Putting a Price
on Brand Equity

David Haigh

Analyses of brands are normally based on their value to consumers and to manufacturers, with "value" interpreted in quasi-philosophical terms rather than measured in dollars and cents. Many such analyses—including a number in this book—are robustly empirical, but the data relate to nonfinancial measures, such as consumers' awareness of and attitudes toward brands and complex details of their purchasing behavior.

For more than a decade, manufacturers and advertising agencies have attempted to make financial estimates of the worth of brands' equity, but these efforts have not been entirely successful for two reasons: (a) their methodology and (b) the conservatism of the American accountancy profession in demanding a virtually ironclad valuation of brand equity before it is allowed to appear on manufacturers' balance sheets. British accountants have been more innovative in this regard, and it is not surprising that much of the work

AUTHOR'S NOTE: David Haigh is Managing Director, Brand Finance.

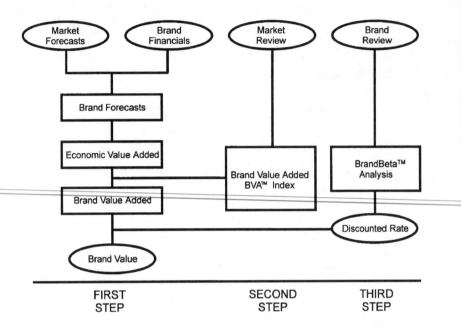

Figure 8.1. Brand Valuation Framework: Three Steps
SOURCE: Brand Finance Limited.

of estimating the worth of brands has taken place in Britain. British accountants have in fact responded to strong pressures from their clients to put values
on their brands.

Brand valuation theory and practice have come under increasing scrutiny
over the past 10 years as the need to identify, disclose, and build brand value
has grown. The increased spotlight on brand valuation has led to growing
demands for transparency and clarity in methods used. There is no longer
room for "black box" techniques that cannot be reconciled back to the
management of the business.

In response to this demand, a highly transparent approach to brand valuation has been developed that is grounded in investment, business, and
marketing theory. It provides brand valuation solutions on a modular basis,
fitting the approach to the particular client need. This is the work of my
company—a British consulting organization called Brand Finance Limited.
Our approach is summarized in Figure 8.1, which shows the three steps in an
economic use valuation.

Brand Valuation Methodology

The "economic use" approach is the most popular method for conducting brand valuations. Such valuations consider the economic value of a brand to the current owner in its current use. In other words, they consider the return that the owner actually achieves as the result of owning the brand—the brand's net contribution to the business, both now and in the future.

This can be measured using an estimate of the increase in gross profit attributable to selling a branded rather than an unbranded product or service. However, brand valuations are more commonly based on net, "fully absorbed" profits through identification of the excess net earnings attributable to ownership of the brand. Such valuations draw on internal information, supplemented by external market research. They do not normally consider the value of the brand in use by a different owner or any "hope value" based on new uses of the brand.

What we really want to know is the value of future earnings stemming from the brand's pact with its consumers. It is therefore increasingly common for economic use valuations to be based on the discounted value of future brand earnings. This approach depends on the accuracy of future sales and earnings projections.

Theoretically, the economic use approach should use pure cash flows from future brand sales. However, it is more straightforward to use an adjusted profit-and-loss account figure as an approximation of the pure cash flow. This has the benefit of simplicity.

The approach uses the future earnings stream attributable to a brand after making a fair charge for the tangible assets employed (both maintenance and financing costs). The result is earnings attributable to the intangible assets as a whole. A charge is also normally made for tax at a notional rate. The resulting "excess" earnings are discounted back to a net present value representing the current value of the branded business.

One part of the total branded business value is the brand alone, which is valued through an estimation of the proportion of total business earnings that can be attributed specifically to that brand.

Typically, brand valuations are based on 5- to 10-year earnings forecasts prepared on an annual basis. In addition, an "annuity" is calculated on the final year's earnings on the assumption that the brand continues beyond the forecast period, effectively in perpetuity. As brand rights can be owned in perpetuity and many brands have been around for more than 50 years, this is not an unreasonable assumption.

Just as analysts now value shares on the basis of sustainable cash flows from the business, putting a value on that cash stream, the economic use brand valuation process is essentially a cash-flow valuation. In fact, this type of cash-flow approach has been endorsed by the British Accounting Standards Board in Financial Reporting Standard 10 (FRS 10), which I describe later in this chapter.

Using the discounted cash-flow approach, the brand valuer discounts estimated future brand earnings, at an appropriate discount rate, to arrive at a net present value—the value of the brand. Such a brand valuation typically comprises four elements:

1. *Total market modeling,* to identify market demand and the position of an individual brand in the context of all other market competitors. Usually the model is segmented to reflect the relevant competitive framework within which the brand operates. Such models allow for "dynamic" assumptions to be tested, making brand valuation a portfolio management tool as well as a financial reporting technique.

2. *Specific branded business forecasting,* to identify total branded business earnings.

3. *Business drivers research,* to determine what proportion of total branded business earnings may be attributed specifically to the brand—Brand Value Added BVA™.

4. *Brand risk review,* to assess the security of the brand franchise both with customers and with end consumers and therefore the security of future brand earnings. This is known as BrandBeta™ analysis.

A prerequisite of this process is that a legal audit has been completed confirming ownership of all intellectual property components of the brand being valued, to establish that the brand is a true piece of legal "property." In many cases brand owners believe they have good title to all elements of the brand but on inquiry turn out to be poorly protected against infringement.

The Steps in a Brand Valuation

In the first step depicted in Figure 8.1, a wide range of information is gathered about the brand, its performance, and its history from a number of different sources. Data are collected through a mixture of desk research, questionnaires, and face-to-face interviews. The information is then analyzed to assess the brand in various terms, beginning with the financial data.

Calculating Economic Value Added

Once a brand's background and its earnings have been established, it is possible to produce a 5- to 10-year cash-flow forecast that can be assessed for reasonableness.

Clear definition of a brand's earnings for valuation purposes is important. The earnings used must be the fully absorbed earnings of the brand after the allocation of central overhead costs.

Elimination of Private Label or Nonbranded Activity

The earnings used in the discounted cash-flow calculation must relate only to the brand being valued and not to other, unbranded goods or services that may be produced in parallel with the brand but are not sold under the brand name.

Remuneration of Capital Employed

To avoid overvaluation of the brand it is necessary to make a fair charge for the value of the tangible assets employed in the business, such as the distribution system, the manufacturing plant, and the stock. Until a fair return has been made on the fixed assets and working capital tied up in the business, it cannot be said that the brand is adding value to the business. The resulting stream of earnings, after the finance charge is made, represents the economic value added to the business by the intangible assets.

Taxation

Brand valuations are typically prepared using post-tax earnings. The result of this analysis is a thorough assessment of the historic and prospective economic value added attributable to all the intangible assets employed in the branded business. The next step is to establish what proportion of the total economic value added relates to the brand as opposed to other intangible assets.

TABLE 8.1   BrandBeta™ Analysis

Composite rate analysis
  Risk-free borrowing rate
  Equity risk premium
  Weighting for market risk
BrandBeta™ based on
  Stability, scale, and growth of the brand

SOURCE: Brand Finance Limited.

Calculating Brand Value Added

This is the second step in Figure 8.1. Different businesses rely in varying degrees on branding to stimulate demand and support price. By identifying what it is that drives demand in the specific market, it is possible to estimate the contribution made to the business by the brand. This is typically achieved using a form of trade-off analysis known as the Brand Value Added BVA™ analysis. This is a research-based way of systematically estimating earnings attributable to the brand. It produces reliable conclusions, particularly where it is supported by large-sample trade-off or conjoint analysis. By applying the BVA™ index to economic value added, one can estimate the brand value added.

Assessing Brand Risk

This is the third step in Figure 8.1. A brand value reflects not only the potential of a brand to generate income, but also the likelihood that the brand will do so. It is therefore necessary to determine an appropriate discount rate that takes into account economic, market, and brand risks. This is accomplished through BrandBeta™ analysis.

First, the risk-free borrowing rate is obtained for the geographic market in which the valuation is being completed. Next, an appropriate equity risk premium is obtained (see Table 8.1). Such risk premiums are available for most worldwide stock markets and reflect the expected returns for equity investors in those markets. The composite discount rate determined by this process is then adjusted for the specific risks associated with the market within which the brand operates. Finally, the average market risk rate is either increased or decreased by reference to the specific risk profile of the individual brand to be valued.

TABLE 8.2 BrandBeta^{TM} Scoring Template

Attribute	Score
Time in the market	0-10
Distribution	0-10
Market share	0-10
Market position	0-10
Sales growth rate	0-10
Price premium	0-10
Elasticity of price	0-10
Marketing spend/support	0-10
Advertising awareness/effect	0-10
Brand awareness/loyalty	0-10
Total	0-100

SOURCE: Brand Finance Limited.

TABLE 8.3 Brand Ratings

BrandBeta^{TM} Score	Rating
91-100	AAA
81-90	AA
71-80	A
61-70	BBB
51-60	BB
41-50	B
31-40	CCC
21-30	CC
11-20	C
0-10	D

SOURCE: Brand Finance Limited.

The BrandBeta^{TM} Scoring Template

BrandBeta^{TM} scoring achieves this by considering a number of objectively verifiable key indicators of historic and current brand performance (see Table 8.2). All brands in the market are scored relative to one another to arrive at the relevant BrandBeta^{TM} for the brand being valued.

When all brands in a given market have been scored against the 10 objectively verifiable criteria, brand ratings—effectively, credit ratings for brands—are determined (see Table 8.3). These drive the discount rate used in the valuation.

An average brand, achieving a BrandBeta^{TM} score of 50 and rated as B, will attract the average composite discount rate for that sector. A brand scoring

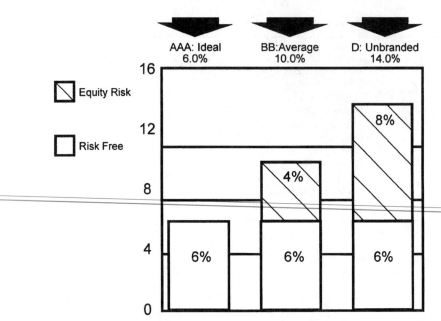

Figure 8.2. Applying BrandBeta™ Analysis (Based on U.K. Risk-Free Borrowing Rate and Equity Risk Premium)
SOURCE: Brand Finance Limited.

100 and rated as AAA is theoretically risk-free and is discounted at a risk-free rate. In practice, few if any brands are likely to attract such a rating. A brand scoring 0 and rated as D attracts the highest discount rate, with a doubling of the equity risk premium.

So the BrandBeta™ score is used to determine the discount rate to be used in the brand valuation. It is applied to the average equity risk premium for the sector in question to arrive at the equity risk premium appropriate to the particular brand in that particular market (see Figure 8.2).

Brand Valuation

Armed with forecast BVA™ for the brand, and with a robustly and transparently determined discount rate, one can calculate brand value by applying the appropriate discount rate to the expected future brand cash flows.

As the following simplified example shows, we begin with operating earnings calculated in the conventional way. Capital employed in the opera-

TABLE 8.4 Example of a Discounted Cash-Flow Brand Valuation (based on forecast BVA™)

	Year 0	Year 1	Year 2	Year 3	Year 4	Year 5
Net sales	500	520	550	580	620	650
Operating earnings	75	78	82.5	87	93	97.5
Tangible capital employed	250	260	275	290	310	325
Charge for capital @ 5%	12.5	13	13.8	14.5	15.5	16.3
Economic value added	62.5	65	68.8	72.5	77.5	81.3
Brand value added @ 25%	15.6	16.3	17.2	18.1	19.4	20.3
Tax rate (%)	33	33	33	33	33	33
Tax	5.2	5.4	5.7	6	6.4	6.7
Posttax BVA™	10.5	10.9	11.5	12.1	13	13.6
Discount rate (%)	15					
Discount factor	1	1.15	1.32	1.52	1.75	2.01
Discounted cash flow	10.5	9.5	8.7	8	7.4	6.8
Value to year 5	40.4					
Annuity	45.1					
Growth 0%						
Brand value	85.1					

SOURCE: Brand Finance Limited.

tion of the brand is determined, and a full financing charge is made against operating earning for the finance required to support the brand. The charge for capital is normally at a risk-free borrowing rate on the principle that the capital is included at its realizable market value and therefore no risk is involved in ownership of the capital.

Having made the financing charge, we are left with economic value added in the branded business. It is this surplus, after all factors of production have been rewarded, including tangible capital employed, that can be realistically attributed to the intangible assets at work in the business—including the brand. The total value of the economic value added from the business is used to calculate a branded business value, part of which is the brand value. Both values are calculated through the application of the appropriate discount rate to the expected future cash flows (see Table 8.4).

Segmentation and Aggregation of Brand Values

Brands have value only in the contexts of specific marketplaces. In one market a brand may add a great deal of value, and in another it may add very little.

For example, in established airline and music recording industries, the Virgin brand adds a great deal, whereas in the cola or vodka markets it appears to add very little. Similarly, in Scotland the Irn Bru brand adds a great deal, but in Italy or Greece it adds little if anything. Consequently, brand valuations are normally segmented by discrete market and then aggregated back to a total value. In some markets the brand may even be destroying shareholder value, and this should be aggregated into the total valuation as part of the overall segmentation.

Such segmentation brings brand valuation down to the level at which markets and businesses actually operate. It allows a better understanding of where brand value is really being added, and from a management point of view allows for modeling of how overall brand value might be increased at the aggregate level. It is this that takes brand valuation from the realm of global financial reporting into the area of better business management. For example, Brand Finance Limited has recently created "dynamic" brand segmentation models for clients in sectors as diverse as banking, insurance, petrochemicals, food, and alcoholic drinks.

The imminent entry of brands like Virgin and Sainsbury's into certain financial services markets means that traditional banking and insurance brands have been forced to consider in great detail what value they actually add to those markets. They have been forced to reengineer themselves and their marketing efforts. Brand valuation techniques are the ideal vehicle for reviewing performance in this new world.

It is possible to imagine at some point in the future that we may be able to track brand value at the individual customer level. There are already plenty of data and powerful information technology systems to manipulate them. In the life insurance market, embedded value calculations already start at the individual customer level. But for the moment, tracking of awareness, marketing, and financial data occurs mainly at the product segment level.

In my experience, segmented brand valuation models provide a consistent way of valuing and managing branded goods and service companies. Their use is growing rapidly, and the results seem increasingly likely to flow straight through into external reporting.

New Financial Reporting Requirements

The International Accounting Standards Committee's "Framework for the Preparation and Presentation of Financial Statements" states that "the objective of financial statements is to provide information about the financial position, performance and changes in financial position of the enterprise that is useful to a wide range of users in making economic decisions." Investors, employees, lenders, suppliers, customers, governments, and their agencies and the public all need to understand the particular enterprise's asset base and risk profile. Financial statements should also "show the results of the stewardship of management, or the accountability of management for the resources entrusted to it."

Finally, after many years of deliberation, the U.K. Accounting Standards Board has passed Financial Reporting Standard 10, which should go a long way toward achieving the objectives set out in the conceptual framework for accounting. At present, FRS 10 applies only to acquired brands, but it requires a much more consistent approach to reporting brand values and will probably lead to much greater disclosure of underlying data and trends. It will most likely lead to the separate disclosure of more information about the total brand portfolio and the integration of internal and external reporting information for brands. It is a major step in a continuing journey toward ideal brand value reporting.

Summary of FRS 10

FRS 10, "Goodwill and Intangible Assets," sets out the new rules on accounting for both goodwill and intangible assets, including licenses, franchises, publishing titles, and brands. The new standard removes an important inconsistency found in U.K., international, and U.S. practices by making it a requirement in the United Kingdom to place goodwill and acquired intangibles on the balance sheet.

FRS 10 requires a significant change for most U.K. companies in their treatment of goodwill and intangibles, including brands. The previous accounting standard on goodwill, Statement Standard Account Practice 22 (SSAP 22), permitted a choice of accounting treatment. Its preferred treatment, adopted in the vast majority of acquisitions, was for purchased goodwill to be eliminated immediately against reserves. More than 95% of U.K. companies adopted this approach, which has been criticized on two counts:

- It gave the impression that the acquirer's net worth had been depleted or even eliminated.
- It caused financial statements to overstate the rates of return achieved on acquired investments.

The problem of equity depletion, and even negative equity, particularly among large companies making huge brand purchases, encouraged such companies to reduce amounts attributed to purchased goodwill and separately value brands as nondepreciable fixed assets in the balance sheet. SSAP 22 allowed this treatment although only a small percentage of the largest, most acquisitive companies actually chose that route—companies like Grand Met, Guinness, and Cadbury's.

Under FRS 10, individually identifiable intangible assets—including brands—will have to be capitalized as assets on the balance sheet, as will residual purchased goodwill. Those intangible assets that are believed to have limited lives will be amortized to the profit-and-loss account over their expected useful lives. Amortization will not, however, be required for those assets that can be demonstrated to have indefinite lives. Such assets will need to be written down only if and when their values drop below those recorded on the balance sheet.

Impairment Reviews

The general presumption of FRS 10 is that the lives of goodwill and intangible assets will be no more than 20 years. A longer or indefinite life may be assigned only if the durability of the asset can be demonstrated and if it is possible to remeasure its value each year to identify any reduction. These measurements—so-called impairment reviews—must be performed annually when lives of more than 20 years are chosen. For lives of fewer than 20 years, impairment reviews are required only in the year after acquisition and in other years if there is some indication that the value of the goodwill or intangible asset might have fallen below its recorded value. The detailed rules for such reviews are set out in a separate but parallel statement, FRS 11.

The emphasis on impairment reviews is a key feature of FRS 10. The British Accounting Standard Board believes that a formal requirement to monitor the value of acquired goodwill and acquired intangible assets using standardized methods, and to report any losses in the financial statements, will enhance the quality of information provided to users of financial statements. The Accounting Standards Board recommends the discounted cash-flow valuation approach based on "income-generating units"—likely to be brands in many cases. This requirement effectively endorses best-practice brand valuation methods. The procedures for performing impairment reviews are set out in FRS 11.

Christmas Comes Early for Brand Owners

FRS 10 is effective for financial years ending on or after December 23, 1998. U.K. companies will be permitted, but not required, to restate goodwill that was eliminated against reserves before that date. All new brand purchases will need to be capitalized.

The inclusion of acquired brands in balance sheets should come as a welcome surprise for management and shareholders alike as they finally become aware of the valuable assets that conservative U.K. accountants have conspired to hide from view for so long.

Side by side with the new U.K. accounting standard, the International Accounting Standards Committee (IASC) has produced International Account Standard (IAS) 58, which is effective from July 1999. It recommends that all acquired brands be capitalized. This is a persuasive standard rather than a requirement for members of the IASC. However, it is likely to be widely adopted everywhere except the United States. The American Financial Accounting Standards Board (FASB) has so far rejected the FRS 10 and IAS 58 approach.

Despite the FASB's reservations, I believe 1999 is the start of a new millennium for brands, starting one year early. It will be the start of a new era of dynamic brand value management and the reporting of brand value information to stakeholders.

9

Parity

Consumer Perceptions
That All Brands Are Alike

John Philip Jones

During the early 1990s, the large advertising agency group Batten, Barton, Durstine and Osborn Worldwide (BBDO) carried out groundbreaking research into how consumers perceive brands, and in particular the degree to which brands are seen as similar to one another. The research, which was a standardized quantitative investigation, was carried out by 28 agencies in the BBDO network, and a total of 4,200 consumers worldwide were interviewed. The countries covered were Canada and the United States, seven countries in Latin America, nine countries in Europe, two countries in Africa, one country in the Middle East, and seven countries in the Pacific Rim. The investigation covered 13 different product categories: 9 repeat-purchase packaged goods, 2 durables, and 2 services.[1]

Overall, the consumers surveyed felt brands to be very much alike. Nearly two-thirds of the worldwide sample considered the brands in the categories covered to have "no relevant or discernible differences." In blind and named product tests independent of the BBDO research, competitive brands are often seen by consumers as differing significantly from one another in functional terms. However, the BBDO research asked about the similarity/dissimilarity between brands as an abstract proposition. The consumers' responses demonstrate as much as anything a degree of disillusionment.

The average perceptions of parity in all categories are listed below, with the countries shown in rank order:

- 80%-99%
  Japan
  Korea

- 60%-79%
  Malaysia
  France
  Australia
  Mexico
  Italy
  Canada
  Germany
  United States
  Nigeria
  Kuwait
  Argentina
  Austria
  Hong Kong
  Singapore
  Great Britain
  Spain

- 40%-59%
  Belgium
  El Salvador
  South Africa
  Denmark
  Chile

    Costa Rica
    Netherlands
    Philippines
    Puerto Rico

- Below 40%
    Colombia

There were also wide variations in parity perceptions by product category, as shown in the following list (categories are shown in rank order):

- 70% or more
    Credit cards
    Paper towels
    Dry soups
    Snack chips

- 60%-69%
    Bar soap
    Cola
    Personal computers

- 50%-59%
    Airlines
    Television sets
    Beer
    Ground coffee
    Shampoo
    Cigarettes

The rankings of the various product categories are slightly surprising in that there is low perception of parity (i.e., belief in differences) for categories as rich in added values as beer, ground coffee, shampoo, and cigarettes.

BBDO clusters countries and categories according to degrees of parity perceptions. Strong clustering is an important factor when the agency comes to develop global advertising strategies. However, BBDO's clusters are not cut-and-dried, and there are exceptions within them. The fact is that perceptions of parity in different product categories differ widely between apparently similar countries.

The reasons suggested by BBDO for the remarkable findings of this research are threefold:

1. In a world in which competitive response to product innovation has become very rapid, categories (or at least subcategories) tend toward actual brand parity in functional terms.

2. The proliferation of brands and varieties (a response in many countries to a flattening of category growth) has led to consumer disillusionment, a feeling that "all of the available brands cannot possibly possess unique and relevant features."

3. There has been much "parity advertising" (i.e., similarity in product claims and advertising styles between competing brands), which has led to an erosion of added values, so that brands increasingly lack nonfunctional distinctiveness, in line with their perceived lack of functional distinctiveness.

BBDO uses the lessons from this research operationally. The research sends up warning signals for the future of brands that BBDO believes advertisers should heed.

Note

1. BBDO Worldwide, *Focus: A World of Brand Parity* (New York: BBDO Worldwide Inc., n.d.). Karen Olshan, BBDO's director of research services, helped in the preparation of this chapter.

10

Brand Management

John Philip Jones

B rand management is a system by which most manufacturers of packaged goods, as well as many advertisers in other fields, control their advertising on a day-to-day basis. One of the most interesting managerial developments of the mid-1990s was the introduction of brand management in all three of the major American automobile companies. This is a move of the system into a totally nontraditional field. Ford has even established it in Europe, with the objective of encouraging more international harmony in the corporation's advertising campaigns.[1]

The brand management system has two important features. First, a brand manager is a general manager rather than a specialist; his or her functions embrace all aspects of a brand, but with specific emphasis on advertising and sales promotions. The second feature of the system is that the job is "staff" and not "line." It demands that the brand manager generate ideas and shepherd these through the often plentiful management layers of the advertiser's organization. Most important, the brand manager coordinates all activity in marketing the brand—production, packaging, and sales, as well as advertising and promotions.

Because the function is a "staff" one, and brand managers are not empowered to make major policy or financial decisions about brands, brand managers are mostly young executives carefully selected for their energy and promise. Brand management is considered excellent training for general "line" management.

Entrepreneurship—the ability to control brands and operate them aggressively—is central to the system. Brand managers are expected to be opportunistic—the opposite of the bureaucratic style of management that might be expected in large manufacturing organizations. If, as is common, a company markets a portfolio of brands in any category, these brands have to be clearly separated from one another in strategic terms to prevent cannibalization. The brand managers in charge of individual brands are allowed to compete with one another, and the company relies on the strategic divisions between its brands to prevent loss of business through the competition's becoming too destructive. However, controlled competition is an important aspect of the brand management system—a point underscored by the fact that competing brand managers normally use different advertising agencies.

Brand managers were first introduced by Procter & Gamble (P&G) in 1931:

> The brand manager leads the brand group [in] developing the annual marketing plan; developing and executing the advertising copy strategy; planning and selecting media; planning sales promotions; co-ordinating package design; and analyzing and forecasting business results.[2]

In this system, each brand is expected to stand on its own feet. P&G in fact first appointed brand managers for the sole purpose of enabling its leading bar soaps, Ivory and Camay, to be independent from and indirectly competitive with one another. Both brands prospered, and brand management was extended within P&G and soon widely copied elsewhere.

There is little doubt that brand management was one of the engines—perhaps the most important one—driving the growth of brands during the half century between 1930 and 1980. During this period, the system was adopted by the majority of packaged goods advertisers worldwide.

The brand manager is the main point of contact between the client and the agency account executive, and he or she is therefore of key importance in all client-agency cooperation. Agencies reinforce this relationship through a system of "covering" the brand manager's superiors via links with people higher than the account executive in the agency hierarchy. This involves some duplication of work, but agencies consider that this procedure helps detect any problems that develop between brand manager and agency before these become too serious.

The advantages of brand management outweigh the disadvantages of the system. There have, however, always been two problems with it:

1. Because brand managers are "staff" and not "line," they do not have the authority to accept and implement agency recommendations, but can only pass these up the hierarchy. Brand managers can, however, make negative decisions and reject agency recommendations with which they disagree. This ability of the brand manager to say no but not yes causes a great deal of frustration within agencies.

2. Agency recommendations that are endorsed by the brand manager have to be approved by a number of layers—in some cases as many as six separate ones—within the client's organization. Brand managers are generally required to provide objective support for their proposals, and this causes them to use market research as a standard procedure to evaluate all advertising recommendations. Much of this research may be methodologically flawed, and can lead to the rejection of potentially effective campaigns if they research badly.

Brands have encountered manifest problems during the 1980s and 1990s: a stagnation in category growth and a high degree of fragmentation within categories, a difficulty exacerbated by the growth in promotions and a relative stagnation of media advertising for much of the period. Such problems have caused many manufacturers to reevaluate their brand management systems, Procter & Gamble again taking the lead. The main move has been toward category management, a system that attempts to control all the company's brands in a category as a more or less cohesive whole.

This in some ways represents a return to the system that predated brand management. By aiming to avoid the potentially wasteful competition between brand managers, category management imposes a judgmental (and bureaucratic) system for establishing priorities between brands—brands that had formerly fought it out independent of one another (often with great success). It is therefore by no means certain that the new system will act as powerfully as brand management to nurture and develop individual brands. It will encourage arbitrary decisions to be made in favor of some brands and not others. Some analysts believe that the strength of a manufacturer's position in a category depends essentially on the self-reliant independence of each separate brand in its portfolio, with the forces of the market boosting some brands and trimming others. This is precisely what the brand management system was set up to achieve.

Notes

1. Suzanne Bidlake, "Ford Shuffle in Europe," *Advertising Age,* July 20, 1998, 31.

2. Oscar Shisgall, *Eyes on Tomorrow: The Evolution of Procter & Gamble* (Chicago: J. G. Ferguson, 1981), 163. See also the Editors of Advertising Age, *Procter & Gamble. The House That Ivory Built* (Lincolnwood, IL: NTC Business Books, 1989); and Alecia Swasy, *Soap Opera: The Inside Story of Procter & Gamble* (New York: Random House/Times, 1993).

Part II

New and Growing Brands

A Marketing Template
for New Brands

John Philip Jones

In Chapter 13 of this volume, Jan S. Slater describes the odds against success in new brand ventures. However, there are ways—described in this chapter—in which manufacturers can reduce these odds. If clients and their agencies make effective use of all eight parts of what I call the *marketing template for new brands,* they will greatly improve their chances of success. But if there are weaknesses in any of these elements, failure is almost certain.

Launching a new brand is an expensive endeavor. Not only does it cost a great deal in terms of product research and development, it calls for management commitment (which has a serious opportunity cost), and—most of all—there must be an investment in distribution, promotions, and advertising to provide the essential cost of entry into the market. It is rare for a new brand to make money during its first 3 years at least. One of the major challenges of new brand activity is to build volume and reduce investments according to a well-calculated payout plan, so that losses are gradually diminished and the brand moves eventually into targeted profit.

The eight parts of the template include four endogenous factors—factors that describe characteristics of the brand itself:

- Functional performance
- Positioning
- Name
- Price

Two parts are concerned with the retail trade:

- Distribution
- Trade promotions

And two parts are rooted in the relationship between the brand and its eventual consumers:

- Consumer promotions
- Consumer advertising

All of these elements are interrelated. In particular, price and trade and consumer promotions are essentially different ways of looking at the same thing.

Factors Characterizing the Brand Itself

Functional Performance

In Chapter 2 of this volume, I make the point that a brand comes naked into the world. Without superior competitive functional performance in at least some respect, it has little chance of succeeding; it will not persuade a person who buys it on a trial basis, or who receives a free sample, to buy it again. One of the roles of the package design, introductory promotions, and initial advertising is to communicate this functional performance clearly and forcefully.

The packaging (an extremely important advertising medium) and the advertising itself should also begin to build those added values that are vital to protect the brand's often rather fragile franchise once competitors have moved toward functional parity with it. In other words, the new brand needs the edge of added values to maintain its position when, as often happens, it loses within months the advantage of its initial functional lead. But added values take time to build. At the time of launch, if the brand is to be bought more than once, buying decisions are essentially based on its functional properties.

A. C. Nielsen has generalized from the experience of many hundreds of American examples that functional superiority is the most important factor in the success of new brands, and functional weakness is the most important cause of failure.[1] British Nielsen data add a time dimension to suggest that functional weakness as a cause of failure is becoming even more important with the passage of time.[2]

An analysis by Davidson of 100 new grocery brands in the United Kingdom provides data that closely confirm and supplement the Nielsen findings.[3] Of these brands, 50 succeeded and 50 failed, a rate of success rather better than the general average. Of the successes, 37 offered better performance than the competition, and 22 of these offered significantly better performance. Of the failures, 40 offered functional performance that was the same as or worse than that of the competition.

Competitive functional performance is not something that is important to new brands and unimportant to mature brands; the added values that brands acquire over the years cannot provide a permanent bulwark against functionally superior newcomers. The large British food manufacturer Brooke Bond Oxo (part of Unilever) has published evidence that the repeat buying of its brands correlates closely with product performance as evaluated by the blind product tests the firm carries out repeatedly (itself an unusual procedure). The conclusion of the analysts who published this case is that, given that repeat purchase is essentially determined by consumer satisfaction with the functional performance of a brand, advertising does not have much role in this process and "may find its greatest potential at the periphery of the user group."[4]

Aggregated Nielsen information supports the data from Brooke Bond Oxo on the importance of competitive functional performance to existing brands. During the 15-year period after the end of World War II, leading brands in a third of 34 different product categories in the United States lost their leadership. In two-thirds of these cases, the cause of the loss was competitive technological advances. In the 6 years from 1965 to 1971, well over half of the brands losing market leadership in major product fields in the United Kingdom lost it for this same reason. "It is a cardinal fact that a consumer franchise will not protect a brand against a well-advertised technical breakthrough by competition." [5]

There is a further point to be made about the functional properties of a brand. They help to describe the competition, and thus become a tool to specify the best target group for advertising: the users of defined competitive brands. What makes this such a relatively efficient planning device is the looseness of alternative (demographic and psychographic) descriptions and their general inability to discriminate between competitive brands.

Paradoxically, users of a brand are best defined by that very fact of usage. This is not as circular a definition as it appears, because once a brand joins the homemaker's repertoire, inertia and habit begin to play a role; usage becomes entrenched. Repeat purchase comes about at least in part because it saves the homemaker trouble, although of course a new brand with functional superiority will always pose a threat to the brands already in the repertoire. This is why it is so important for a manufacturer of a new brand to target it specifically at existing competitive brands with the intention of elbowing them out, so that the inertia will gradually work for the new item instead of for the others (unless it is creating a new market or building one from a low existing level, both of which are now the exception and not the rule in economically developed countries).

The first question the manufacturer of a new brand should ask is, From which brands do we want to take business? Once this question has been answered, the firm can direct research and development efforts to the specific functional characteristics for which it must provide superior performance with the new brand.

Positioning

The best policy for a manufacturer introducing a new brand alongside others is to introduce it into a different subdivision of the market, on the assumption that a market is already segmented or can be segmented by advertising and promotion into recognizably different although not necessarily completely self-contained parts. This can often be done, and the segmentation of a market that is easiest to exploit is one based on functional differences. This in turn leads to psychographic and demographic segmenta-

TABLE 11.1 Category X: Market Shares, 1975, Equivalent Case Basis

Market Share	(%)
Manufacturer A	42
Manufacturer B	20
Manufacturer C	14
Manufacturer D	9
Other manufacturers	14
Total	100

TABLE 11.2 Category X: Market Shares and Segments, 1975, Equivalent Case Basis

	Total Market Share (by volume) (%)	Number of Brands	Average Share per Brand (%)	Segments in Which Manufacturer Operated
Manufacturer A	42	4	10.5	red, blue, green
Manufacturer B	20	2	10.0	red, green
Manufacturer C	14	4	3.5	red, green
Manufacturer D	9	2	4.5	blue, green, yellow

tion (e.g., people with active lifestyles will use deodorant bar soaps and mothers of young children will buy presweetened breakfast cereals), but the principal motivating argument for buying these products or brand groups is the functional one (e.g., the deodorant feature of the soap and the presweetening in the cereal).

Here are the details of a historical real-life example of a manufacturer's use of segmentation to create the opportunity for an important new brand. The market in question (Category X) is for an important personal product bought with the greatest regularity. The market is large, static, and mature. Like most such categories, it is an oligopoly, although the leading manufacturer has a larger share than is normally the case in such markets. In 1975, the four main manufacturers (all nationally known names) had the shares shown in Table 11.1.

Brands in the market can be classified into four functional segments; I use the code words *red, blue, green,* and *yellow* to describe these. Typically enough, these segments are not absolutely self-contained. For instance, green and yellow overlap with one another, with yellow having grown out of green in the 1970s; yellow is the newest, its development initially having taken place in Europe (see Table 11.2).

TABLE 11.3   Category X: Market Shares, 1975 and 1980, Equivalent Case Basis

| | Market Share (%) | |
	1975	Mid-1980
Manufacturer A	42	46
Manufacturer B	20	17
Manufacturer C	14	14
Manufacturer D	9	8

Manufacturer A was in much the strongest position in 1975, with the largest market share in total, the largest average share per brand, and the best coverage of the market segments (although this was not quite complete). By way of contrast, Manufacturer C had four brands, each with a small market share, with three of these in fact clustered uncomfortably into one single segment. Manufacturer A was in such a powerful position that in any other circumstance, it or any other firm with a 42% market share would have been happy to preserve the status quo. But Manufacturer A's awareness of an opportunity in the yellow sector supported the company's natural aggressiveness—such is the nature of competition between oligopolists. And A's expansion-based strategy was indeed successful, as can be seen from the market shares 5 years later, displayed in Table 11.3.

Manufacturer A had added 4 percentage points of market share, taken directly out of competitors B and D. The firm had in fact done this by introducing a new brand aimed at the yellow segment, and had managed to gain 7% in the process for the new brand, cannibalizing its own existing brands by 3%, but, more important, taking 1% from manufacturer D and 3% from manufacturer B.

This is a neat, opportunistic, and successful piece of positioning. But to put it into perspective, we should go back to the point that the new and attractive market segment, yellow, had originated in Europe. Of our four oligopolists, three are multinationals (the exception being B, which lost most to A's new brand). The success stemmed unquestionably from A's awareness of European trends and the company's ability to move quickly into the U.S. market with a well-conceived brand, capitalizing on them.

But do not assume that Manufacturer A's analysis of market trends and subsequent new brand entry were a simple sequential process that any firm could have followed. It so happens that the growing importance of the fourth market segment had been known from European experience for more than 10 years, and for all that time Manufacturer C had been trying to break into this segment. Manufacturer C, it will be remembered, had a total of four brands, with three crowded into one market segment. C was acutely aware of the need to broaden its base by moving into new parts of the market. And yet the brands directed at the yellow segment that C had introduced into test since 1968 had invariably failed, despite C's track record of successful innovation in Europe and its considerable resources, and despite great energy on the part of the manufacturer itself and its advertising agencies.

Name

It might strike the reader that the choice of a name for a brand is a less substantial matter than the concerns discussed so far: making sure that the brand is functionally effective and is properly positioned in the market. Many people believe, however, that the added values of a brand are in some way embodied in its name, and that these values can be transferred to another product through the use of the brand name as a common property. This is the rationale for the strategy of using an umbrella name for a number of different products (a strategy described as *line extension*).

The first and most obvious point is that the danger of cannibalization is likely to be greater where the products with the umbrella name are in competition with one another (e.g., powder Tide and liquid Tide) than when they are not (Ivory bar soap and Ivory shampoo).

In one case published by A. C. Nielsen, a manufacturer introduced a new brand on top of an existing successful entry. In the fifth year, the new brand was about a third the size of the first, which had by then been cannibalized to a significant degree, so that the overall share of the two brands together was one-fifth larger than the company's former share with one. This is not a disastrous achievement, but a second case of a similar type shows much better performance. Here, by the fifth year the manufacturer of the new brand had virtually doubled sales. The original brand had remained at its previous level, but the second brand had put on additional sales almost as large as these again. How can we account for this much better performance?

It will be no surprise that much of the difference stems from functional performance. In the less successful of the two cases, the existing brand was not improved, thus leaving it vulnerable to cannibalization, and the new brand was slightly disappointing in performance, thus inhibiting its growth. In the more successful case, the existing brand was improved so that it was protected,

TABLE 11.4   New Names Versus Umbrella Names

Market	Number of Examples	Median Market Share at End of Second Year (%)	
		New Brands With New Names	New Brands With Umbrella Names
Household (U.S.)	28	6.7	3.3
Food (U.S.)	36	6.5	1.9
Food (U.K.)	26	14.0	7.6
Health/toiletries (U.S.)	51	2.7	2.6
Health/toiletries (U.K.)	26	8.8	8.2

and the new brand performed up to expectations. Moreover, in the less successful case, the existing brand was milked in the way normally expected of manufacturers who believe in life-cycle theory—support was reduced in the expectation that decline was inevitable (thus inexorably accelerating decline). In the more successful case, support was maintained for the existing brand. This is not, however, the whole story, because before getting to these causes, a more obvious one suggested itself. Very simply, in the first case the names of the old and new brands were similar to one another, which tended to attract an undue proportion of the second brand's customers from the first brand rather than from the field as a whole.[6]

But what about the more obvious advantage of umbrella naming—that people who use one product under an established brand name can presumably be persuaded easily to sample a second perhaps different category of product using that same name? We are talking here about extending a franchise across product categories.

Nielsen can provide important aggregated information on this subject: The database is 167 new brands in a variety of packaged goods categories and shows their market share levels at the end of their first 2 years. New brands using existing or umbrella brand names are compared with new brands using completely independent brand names. At first glance, there are big differences (see Table 11.4).

On the basis of the data shown in Table 11.4, a good case can be made for using new brand names rather than existing ones, emphatically so in the household and food categories. However, this is not the end of the story. There is also strong evidence that manufacturers follow an umbrella naming policy largely because they think that they can save promotional money by doing so, presumably by relying on the added values of the other products carrying the umbrella brand name. This is a very dangerous conclusion.

When the Nielsen figures just cited are weighted to take into account the different levels of advertising investment behind each new brand, the performance of new brands with umbrella names is brought almost exactly into line with that of new brands with new names. In other words, the generally lower level of performance of new brands with umbrella names is a result of the generally lower level of advertising investment put behind them.

> Many marketing executives who have seen these results seem to feel that it is largely a matter of marketing psychology: realizing that marketing a new brand under a new name is tough, manufacturers gear up their marketing efforts proportionately. On the other hand, because it is commonly (and erroneously) believed that an established brand name is already presold, less money and effort is directed at the brand and a smaller market share results.[7]

The data in these examples lead to a clear but negative conclusion. The economic advantages of umbrella naming are not at all obvious in the short and medium term. Umbrella names are in general no worse and no better than completely new names. As a general rule, the level of success of a new brand is much more dependent on support levels than on the name per se. It is possible that umbrella names provide greater staying power, by enabling a greater addition to added values, which is essentially a long-term process; the examples of Ivory, Palmolive, Cadbury's, Kellogg's, and Kraft support this contention. But the payoff is likely to be protracted and not really discernible in the analysis of a 2-year sales effect, which we have just seen. In the longer term, umbrella naming is really a part of a manufacturer's corporate policy, in particular its stance vis-à-vis retail customers.

Price

In perhaps two-thirds of all cases, a new brand enters an existing market at a premium price. The manufacturer, if it feels the need, justifies this to itself and (it hopes) to the consumer on the basis of the innovation and functional superiority of the new brand over the competition. In reality, the premium price is necessary to fund the high cost of achieving sampling by expenditures above and below the line. These expenditures must be at a high or "investment" level to compensate for the established position of existing brands with their stock of added values, which have been acquired over the years. And whereas a new brand only rarely makes a profit during its first 3 years, deficit budgeting puts an automatic upward pressure on the consumer price. Of course, the negative effect of the premium price is often concealed by the use of temporary price reductions and other promotional methods to encourage sampling.

There is also a good deal of evidence that, although new and different brands will normally command a significant price premium, this premium tends to narrow during the first few years of a brand's life. William T. Moran, formerly a senior Unilever executive, has published analyses illustrating this trend in the prices of new brands of deodorants, mouthwashes, cough syrups, and sandwich bags.[8] Simple observation of the retail scene can add confirmation.

There are also facts to support the contention that premium prices are reasonably well accepted as a justification for functional improvement, although consumers are hearteningly skeptical about manufacturers' attempts to charge premium prices for no obvious functional advantages at all. Davidson, whose investigation was cited earlier, examined 50 successful new brands and 50 failures. Of the 50 successes, more than half were sold at a premium price, and in virtually every case the higher price was accompanied by a better performance than was provided by competitive brands. Of the 50 failures, 35 were sold at a premium price, but 25 of them were accompanied by a similar or a worse performance than that of competitive brands.[9]

These analyses and their lessons are useful as far as they go, but this is not far enough to provide operational advice for a manufacturer that wishes to launch a new brand. Stephen King, whose treatment is based partly on academic studies and partly on practical experience in the United Kingdom, suggests a useful investigative and pragmatic approach to the question of initial pricing, working on the assumption that the best price for the manufacturer to charge must be based roughly on what consumers will accept. The technique recommended is research into consumer attitudes based on direct and indirect questions, which will provide guidance concerning the feasibility of "skimming" or "penetration" pricing (aimed, respectively, at skimming the cream from the market by pricing high and opening up the market by pricing much lower).[10]

It is also true that econometric techniques are helpful in pricing, although they are essentially a fine-tuning device for the period after a brand is launched. The most useful such device is a calculation of price elasticity: the percentage increase in sales that will follow a 1% price reduction on its own. The trouble with this type of analysis is that it is constructed from historical data, which take some time to build for any brand. But a useful procedure in a brand's early planning stage is to make guesstimates of the price elasticities of competitive brands in the market; any internal consistency could provide guidelines.

As the reader can infer from this discussion, judgment plays an important role in the establishment of an individual price. Once a brand is launched and progressing, the sensible manufacturer will take steps to estimate price elasticity as soon as a range of data becomes available. (Sales data from different regions and in different types of stores provide a surprisingly large amount of information quickly.) The range of elasticities for brands is quite wide—from virtually zero to beyond –2.0.[11]

Factors Concerned With the Retail Trade

Distribution

One key factor influencing the immediate success (or failure) of a new brand is the ability of the manufacturer's sales force to get it into distribution. A superficial glance at the Nielsen data suggests that manufacturers in general have little trouble in achieving quick distribution. This is a result of the efficiency and concentration of the American retail trade, with its relatively small number of buying points nationally and regionally. This significant scale economy is also evidence of the muscle exercised by the sales force of the average large manufacturer.

Peckham investigated 64 new brands and estimated that on average these achieved the satisfactory weighted distribution level of 57% to 72%, depending on type of store, within 8 months of launch.[12] What his analysis does not show, however, is the different growth patterns for successful and unsuccessful brands. King, using British Nielsen data, draws this distinction and shows differences in degree between the two countries, in particular in the absolute distribution levels in the United Kingdom, which are lower. For example, successful brands reached a weighted distribution of well under 60% within the first 8-month period, and unsuccessful brands achieved much less than this. The differences between Britain and the United States are difficult to explain but are probably the result of differences between the two countries in manufacturers' and retailers' attitudes toward new brand activity.

King shows that both successful and unsuccessful brands make noticeable distributional headway during their first 4 months, although even in this short period the successful brands do rather better. But it is at this point that their paths seriously diverge. The distribution of successful brands continues to climb, to the 60% weighted level and beyond. The unsuccessful ones remain static and eventually begin to fall. Is this a reflection of differences in the effort of the sales force? Or is it a result of the initial acceptance of the product by the consumer, a matter influenced primarily by the brand's functional performance? The latter is almost certainly the more important cause: "Distribution is a result of success. If the brand goes well in the early stages, the public demands it, retail branches hear from head office, the word gets around and more retailers want to stock it." [13]

But functional performance is not important to the consumer alone. Retailers themselves and, even more important, manufacturers' sales personnel are conscious of functional superiority and its contribution to a brand's success. Functional superiority will provide conviction to the sales force and draw commitment from the retailer. When Nielsen executives actually sat in as observers on new brand presentations to chain and independent supermarket buyers, they found that a very important—perhaps the most important—reason for acceptance of a new brand was evidence of salability. This is a direct reflection of functional excellence. [14]

Distribution factors should also influence the initial decision about the case size for a new brand, because too small a size brings the immediate danger of shops running out of stock before the end of the manufacturer's sales cycle. Changing the case size is obviously more difficult and troublesome once a brand is under way than at the beginning. It is at the earliest stage that the manufacturer should do its homework (which means making a careful estimate of likely rates of sale in different outlets), introduce the optimum size from the outset, and explain to the retail trade exactly why this particular size was chosen. [15]

Trade Promotions

Trade promotions are regrettably very important for the sales success of a new brand. I say "regrettably" because of the great expense of all promotional activity.

Trade promotions, consumer promotions, and advertising are funded out of the manufacturer's advertising and promotional (A&P) budget. Large manufacturers distribute this budget on average in the ratios of 50:26:24, respectively, among the three activities.[16] Taking a brand's A&P budget and percentaging this on the aggregate A&P budgets of all brands in the category provides an estimate of the brand's A&P share of voice. A. C. Nielsen recommends that this share for a new brand should be a good deal greater than the new brand's anticipated market share: between 1.1 and 2.5 times as large, depending on the specific brand and its category.[17] A rule of thumb is an A&P share of voice twice the anticipated market share.

Although it is much more difficult to estimate competitive brands' expenditures on trade and consumer promotions than their expenditure on advertising, because both types of promotions are income reductions and not real expenditures, it is possible for a manufacturer to calculate in approximate terms the huge sums of money required. It is most important to control and if possible minimize these. As explained, trade promotions can be expected to account for half the new brand's A&P budget, which can in turn be expected to be proportionately much above the category average.

A manufacturer's trade promotion budget is made up of large numbers of items because promotions are tailored to individual retail groups. However, all trade promotions are variations on the theme of price cutting: rebates on the price charged by the manufacturer to the retailer. Beyond discounts per brand and overriding rebates, specific individual types of discount include the following:

- Slotting allowances (i.e., special allowances for carrying new brands; these discounts grew rapidly during the 1980s as a result of the increase in brand fragmentation—the introduction of myriad brand varieties that took place during that decade)
- Display allowances
- Cooperative advertising allowances (i.e., contributions to the cost of the retailer's advertising featuring the manufacturer's brands)
- In-store product demonstrations
- Consumer coupons on the retailer's shelf

Retail groups are extremely tough about the size of the trade promotions they will demand to handle a new brand. Negotiations with individual stores will determine the manufacturer's exact promotional expenditure, but, as indicated, these promotions should be employed as sparingly as the retailers will accept. A 10% saving below planned cost will yield a very large dollar sum in most circumstances, as well as impose a valuable discipline for the future.

Besides being a basic operating cost, do trade promotions offer specific benefits to new brands? To a very limited degree they do. Nielsen's experience suggests that the different individual benefits can be graded as follows:[18]

- *Excellent effect:* Stimulates interest of the sales force.
- *Good effect:* Increases inventories at retail level; works synergistically with advertising.
- *Very limited or very temporary effect:* Increases purchases by present users; attracts new users; obtains broader distribution; cushions introduction of consumer price increases.
- *Virtually no effect:* Countercompetitive inroads; ensures adequate shelf space; obtains more in-store displays.

The above is not an impressive list. We are, however, left with the key argument that the retail trade demands rebates and the manufacturer must pay this price as a cost of doing business.

A helpful way of looking at promotions is by using the analogy of the pipeline—the imaginary tube connecting the manufacturer with the end user. Insofar as trade promotions have any effect in the marketplace, they exercise a push effect on the merchandise, driving it down the pipeline toward the consumer. They operate in an essentially different way from consumer promotions and advertising, which pull the goods through, with the consumer doing the pulling. To a limited degree, some of the financial benefits of trade promotions are passed on to the public in the form of retail rebates (e.g., double-value coupons). When this happens, trade promotions can be seen to have some pulling effect on consumer demand, but this is not a factor of enormous importance.

Factors Relating the Brand and the End Consumer

Consumer Promotions

As mentioned above, the average large manufacturer spends 26% of its total A&P budget on consumer promotions. Like trade promotions, consumer promotions are expensive compared with their benefits to the brand, because of the large amount of lost revenue. However, manufacturers of new brands are compelled to spend considerable resources on consumer promotions, not only because of the importance of product sampling—an expensive activity—but because the retail trade requires consumer promotions as a means of injecting adrenaline into sales. The enthusiasm of retailers is such that consumer promotions actually work to some extent to push the merchandise through the distributional pipeline as well as carrying out their main pulling function.

The nine main types of consumer promotion are as follows:

- Samples delivered to the home (the best but most expensive way of demonstrating the functional excellence of the new brand)
- Premium redemption plans using tokens in the package
- Self-liquidating offers
- Premiums and sweepstakes
- Premiums in the package
- Refund offers
- Coupons—with or without sampling, and freestanding or in the package
- Banded packs and extra goods
- Cents-off-label packs

In terms of their ability to build a consumer franchise, the various types of promotions are listed here in their approximate order of effectiveness. However, the ability to build a franchise is not at all the same as having an immediate effect on sales. Direct financial incentives—the last four items on the list above—are the most effective in terms of raw sales, but their cost is high in terms of profit forgone. Consumer promotions stimulate sales on a once-and-for-all basis, with no repeat business. Indeed, they even discourage repeat purchasing by "mortgaging" future sales—that is, they stimulate consumers to stock up at the promotional price, and thus avoid subsequent purchases at the full price.

A. C. Nielsen's research into the effectiveness of different types of consumer promotion has revealed the circumstances under which consumer promotions are most effective for building a franchise, which should be the prime objective for a manufacturer launching a new brand.[19] Consumer promotions are most effective

1. where there is a major functional improvement,
2. where the brand is on the rise in terms of competitive share,
3. when used in conjunction with a sales drive to increase retail distribution,
4. when used only occasionally, and
5. when run alongside instead of as a replacement for brand advertising.

Nielsen also lists the least effective ways of using promotions for franchise building. Such promotions are not very effective

1. when used on established brands with no product change,
2. when used on established brands with a declining market share,
3. when used as replacements for intelligent media support,
4. when used in categories where consumer promotions are already a way of life, and
5. when used in categories where intense marketplace activity constantly stimulates response from competitive brands.

This list applies as much to existing brands as to new ones.

Consumer Advertising

Most of the chapters in this book have things to say about the role of consumer advertising in building and defending brands. I shall avoid too much duplication in what I say here by being brief. I shall make only two points.

Advertising Arguments

A new brand must of course announce its functional innovations in the launch advertising; the word *new* is overused, but it still carries great weight. However, a brand's launch campaign should also say something about the psychological added values the manufacturer is trying to build. There is an urgent reason the campaign should do this.

The new brand's sine qua non—a demonstrable functional superiority in at least some respects compared with the competition—gives it a good chance of establishing an initial consumer franchise. But what happens when competitive brands improve their performance to match the newcomer—a process that normally takes place within months? These older brands already have batteries of added values that have been built over the years, but a similar battery is of course not available to the newcomer.

During the period from the initial introduction to the time when competitive response makes itself felt, the new brand must build its own added values in order to keep up with the competition. This means that the advertising must quickly and progressively focus on these values and give less prominence to the straightforward announcement of the product news. In other words, the advertising must embark on a creative direction that it could very well continue to follow for years rather than months in the future.

Initial Advertising Budget

As I have indicated above, a new brand must devote uneconomically large resources to trade and consumer promotions and consumer advertising. Determining promotional budgets is an ad hoc procedure, largely governed by the detailed negotiations the manufacturer carries out with its retail customers. With consumer advertising, on the other hand, the decisions are less pragmatic. There are objective principles to follow.

The advertising budgets for new (and also for established) brands should be determined by the advertising noise level in the market, adjusted for the advertiser's experience of the productivity of previous investment levels for similar brands.

The best way to factor into the calculation the competitive noise in the marketplace is to compute the advertising budget in terms of share of voice (SOV), measured in percentage points. This is simply the brand's anticipated share of total advertising expenditure in the product category. (This category must be carefully defined.) There is general experience to help establish the appropriate SOV level.

The regression displayed in Figure 11.1, which is called the *advertising-intensiveness curve* (AIC), is derived from 666 brands in 23 different countries. It relates share of voice to share of market (SOM) for each brand (clustered in groups determined by their size). The horizontal line halfway up the diagram represents parity, where SOV = SOM. Above the line, SOV is larger than SOM; below it, SOV is smaller than SOM.[20]

As is clear from the AIC, small brands overspend as a general rule, and large brands underspend. For a new brand, the anticipated share of market will certainly be small, and the necessary investment in share of voice must always be relatively high. A targeted SOM of below 4% calls for an SOV of about

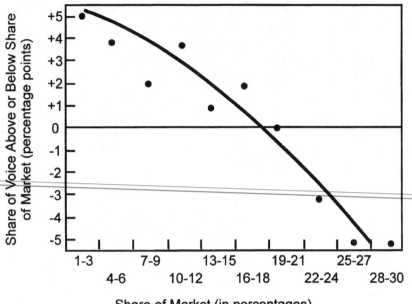

Figure 11.1. The Advertising-Intensiveness Curve

8% (4 percentage points above 4% SOM). This two-to-one relationship jibes with the rule of thumb for A&P expenditure described earlier in this chapter.

A Final Note on the Importance of a Brand's Functional Performance

I have emphasized the importance of functional excellence a number of times in this chapter. This is a point that I am not shy to reiterate, because large numbers of marketers, advertising agency practitioners, and academics tend to underplay the point and seem sometimes even to be unaware of its importance.

I am reminded of an anecdote from the 1980s about the now virtually defunct beer brand Miller High Life. Five different specialists commented on a new advertising campaign for this brand: the head of a major advertising agency, a securities analyst, a Miller distributor, a marketing professor, and a bartender. The first four people were concerned exclusively with the marketing and advertising reasons for Miller's problems and how these had influenced the new campaign. Only the bartender referred to the functional performance of the beer: "I think High Life is very bland. It has no significance at all. No character. It is a little watery." [21]

Notes

1. James O. Peckham, Sr., *The Wheel of Marketing,* 2nd ed. (privately published, 1981; available through A. C. Nielsen, New York).

2. *Nielsen Researcher,* vol. 14, no. 1, January/February 1973, 10-11.

3. J. Hugh Davidson, "Why Most New Consumer Brands Fail," *Harvard Business Review,* March/April 1976, 117-122.

4. Peter Carter and Roz Hatt, "How Far Does Advertising Protect the Brand Franchise?" *Admap,* May 1983, 280. I recommend that interested readers examine this important article in its entirety.

5. Peckham, *The Wheel of Marketing,* 73.

6. Ibid., 86.

7. Ibid., 91.

8. William T. Moran, "Why New Products Fail," *Journal of Advertising Research,* April 1973, 5-13.

9. Davidson, "Why Most New Consumer Brands Fail."

10. Stephen King, *Developing New Brands* (New York: John Wiley, 1973), 161-167.

11. Gerard J. Tellis, "The Price Elasticity of Selective Demand: A Meta-Analysis of Econometric Models of Sales," *Journal of Marketing Research,* November 1988, 331-341.

12. Peckham, *The Wheel of Marketing,* 16.

13. Stephen King, *Advertising as a Barrier to Market Entry* (London: Advertising Association, 1980), 14.

14. Peckham, *The Wheel of Marketing,* 23.

15. *Nielsen Researcher,* vol. 13, no. 5, September/October 1972, 7-9.

16. Cox Direct, *Navigate the Promotional Universe: Cox Direct 19th Annual Survey of Promotional Practices* (Largo, FL: Cox Direct, 1997).

17. Peckham, *The Wheel of Marketing,* 13.

18. Ibid., 51.

19. Ibid., 67.

20. John Philip Jones, *How Much Is Enough? Getting the Most From Your Advertising Dollar* (New York: Simon & Schuster-Lexington, 1992), chap. 5.

21. Quoted in *New York Times,* March 3, 1985. See also James Rudolph, letter to the editor, *New York Times,* April 7, 1985.

12

The Initial Growth Cycle of a New Brand

John Philip Jones

The first problem a manufacturer faces with a new brand is how to achieve consumer trial. Various techniques are used to bring this about—in the main, consumer promotions of different sorts are employed, although advertising also has a part to play. As a result of the initial activity, a consumer base is built: People who have tried the brand once. The critically important stage now is first repurchase. It should be emphasized that the brand must offer functional superiority in at least some respect in order to achieve repurchase; the consumer will be aware of how well the brand performs after having used the first package. But, naturally, not all trial purchasers will repeat.

In functional performance a new brand cannot be all things to all people, and any brand will have functional weaknesses as well as functional strengths. It follows that the brand will not be bought again by those people who were more disappointed by the weaknesses than satisfied by the strengths. It is also likely that some people are going to be wedded to their existing brands, which may have added values that are particularly strong and personally relevant to these consumers, so that the new brand will need to offer considerable functional superiority to compensate.

The largest increases in the sales of a new brand will be those accompanying the growth in its distribution; when the brand has achieved a high level of distribution, growth must then come from increasing sales in the average store, which is a reflection of consumers' buying the brand repeatedly. It is, incidentally, surprising how low a level of sales is achieved by even a major brand. In a fairly large supermarket, three-quarters of all brands/varieties sell a maximum of 12 packages per week.

As a brand becomes accepted by consumers, distribution grows at a continuous and often rapid rate. Advertising has an important role to play in encouraging distribution. It helps to keep the brand before retailers as well as before consumers.

It is not uncommon for a new brand to achieve a 70% weighted distribution level after about 8 months (i.e., distribution in stores accounting for 70% of the sales of all brands in the relevant class of trade—food, drugs, and so on). But the growth is often slower than this. In observing the growth of distribution, we can normally discern a relationship between distribution and sales that can help us predict the eventual sales level when the brand has reached its long-term stability. This is a modeling procedure, and the mathematics are not complicated.[1]

The first thing to do is to look at a new brand's sales and weighted distribution in test market and compute the ratio between them. This shows sales volume per percentage point of weighted distribution. A case of a real new brand, published by A. C. Nielsen, shows that it achieved in its first 2-month period sales of 61,000 units and weighted distribution of 41%—a ratio of 61,000:41, or 1,490 units per percentage point of weighted distribution. This is more simply expressed as 1.49 thousand units per distribution point.

As the brand grows, sales and distribution both grow, and we can calculate this ratio of sales to distribution for each period. If the brand is becoming successful, we will immediately see that this ratio steadily increases. In other words, sales are going ahead faster than the number of shops stocking the brand, because the sales per shop are increasing due to the growing popularity of the brand, which results in repeat purchase. The actual progression of the ratio over the course of the first year in our example was as follows: 1.49, 1.51, 1.76, 2.13, 2.27, 2.50. As the ratios are calculated for further periods,

TABLE 12.1   Second Year, Unit Sales (in thousands) per Percentage Point of
Weighted Distribution

Period	Unit Sales	% Increase Over Previous Year
1	2.65	78
2	2.26	50
3	2.48	41
4	2.88	35
5	3.02	33
6	3.28	31

the rate of increase is seen to be slowing up. Table 12.1 shows the figures for the second year, with a calculation of the increase over the same period in the previous year, showing how this progressive increase is being reduced.

We now have a series of figures from which three specific predictions can be made:

1. The future ratios of sales to distribution can be predicted on the basis of the declining rate of growth, projecting forward the trend in increases over the year before (the figures in the right-hand column of Table 12.1).

2. Distribution growth can be forecast, or at least targeted, separately. It is substantially under the manufacturer's own control, in that it is directly influenced by promotional and sales force activity.

3. By taking the unit sales from the projected ratio (point 1 above) and applying it to the targeted distribution (point 2), we can make a forecast of sales. This tool is of day-to-day value to the brand manager.

Another pronounced pattern about which generalizations can normally be made is the primary growth cycle for a brand. We are talking here about a medium-term period (of an average length of 2 years or so) and a sales pattern that shows a peak of initial sales followed by noticeable decline. This decline can be explained partly by the loss of some initial users—those who are not sufficiently convinced of the new brand's functional superiority to repurchase it. It is also partly the result of a slowing in the growth of new trial users following the normal reduction in promotional and advertising expenditures from an initial peak to a more normal ongoing level. And it is also commonly the result of competitive retaliation. The reader will note that this primary growth cycle (something finite, predictable, and to some extent within the control of the manufacturer) is a totally different concept from the long-term supposedly uncontrollable life cycle (see Jones, Chapter 16, this volume).

The concept of the primary growth cycle is relatively straightforward, and it is a useful tool to help us plan the restaging that is normally necessary to maintain a brand's long-term strength, thus prolonging its mature life. The data quoted below are based on a Nielsen examination of a large number of newly introduced brands in scores of different product categories.

Nielsen's observation of these brands suggests that the normal pattern is for a brand to grow to its sales peak and then decline to a relatively stable level of 80% of that peak. The primary growth cycle is defined as the period between the brand's introduction and when it drops to this 80% level. The first thing to examine is the length of the cycle. The average figure calculated from an examination of 86 cases is 28 months, with a spread from less than a year to more than 4 years. The average brand takes slightly longer to peak (15 months) than to decline to the 80% level (13 months).

Four points can be made about this cycle as it affects different types of brands:

1. There is a direct relationship between a brand's share of market and the length of the cycle. The brands with the longest cycles are those with the highest achieved market shares.

2. Brands in the health and beauty fields have longer primary cycles (an average of 34 months) than do brands in the household and food fields (averages of 23 and 24 months, respectively).

3. Brands with long primary cycles tend to have high levels of advertising support and innovation but low levels of new brand activity in their categories.

4. Brands with short primary cycles tend to be in large, crowded markets with a high degree of new brand activity but a low degree of innovation and relatively low advertising support.

These characteristics point to the likelihood of the cycle becoming shorter over time, as markets become more densely crowded with brands and as it becomes increasingly difficult for new brands to gain large market shares. Additional Nielsen analyses demonstrate that this has indeed been happening, with cycles falling to as little as 18 months in many cases.

An interesting sidelight is that in a less developed market like the United Kingdom, the share of market of a new brand is on average two to three times greater than in the United States. This suggests that overall economic development (as in the United States) may be leading to progressively lower average market shares and shorter primary cycles.

Because of the characteristics of the primary growth cycle, the operational lesson from this analysis is the importance of regular restaging, and that plans for the first restage must be developed in the period following the initial launch of a brand. Increasingly long lead times will be required to develop and implement product innovations and packaging and advertising changes that restages always call for, whereas the initial growth cycle itself may be growing shorter.

A rather different illumination of the primary growth cycle is provided by a classic investigation of British test market experience by John Davis. Davis examined 44 test markets, both successes and failures. Although he does not make direct comparisons with Nielsen's analyses (which are mainly American), his observed primary growth cycle

1. is of much shorter duration (as little as 8 months in most cases),

2. shows a very pronounced drop from peak to relative stability (on average about 40%), and

3. is associated with generally lower levels of distribution than in the United States.

The differences from the mainly American experience of Nielsen are not too easy to explain. Some of these differences must stem from the fact that Davis's examples include a large number of test market failures, which probably cause both the extent and speed of the drop to be exaggerated. The American Nielsen data appear to exclude early failures, although some of the analyses do not make this absolutely clear. It is also probably true that the differences between the American and British findings are a reflection of the differences between the two countries, with the likelihood of a greater general volatility in Britain, as is evidenced by the larger initial market shares there.

The thing that makes Davis's study so interesting is a supplementary investigation into the levels of the drop from peak to stability. Davis's conclusion has not been tested in the United States, but there is no intrinsic reason to believe that it would not operate here. What he suggests is a consistency in the extent of the drop from peak to stability for individual brands, as they are moved from test to national distribution. In other words, no matter if the initial peak is different between the test and the national launch, the ongoing level can be predicted.

Here we have the makings of another simple model in which it should be possible (on the assumption that American and British experiences are similar) to forecast the extent of the drop to the ongoing national sales level. This can be done quite simply by working from the national peak sales level and applying the same percentage drop as that which actually occurred in the test market.

Note

1. See John Philip Jones, *What's in a Name? Advertising and the Concept of Brands* (New York: Simon & Schuster-Lexington, 1986), chap. 4 (including detailed bibliography).

13

New Brands

Success Rate and Criteria for Success

Jan S. Slater

Companies are successful not because they manufacture products, but because they produce brands. Procter & Gamble (P&G) is profitable not because it makes soap and laundry detergent; it is successful because consumers want Ivory, Tide, Cheer, Cascade, and Dawn. Coca-Cola does not manufacture and bottle a mere soft drink; people like the quenching, refreshing taste of Coke. And McDonald's hasn't become the leading family fast-food palace just because it flips burgers; children ask for Happy Meals and their parents crave Big Macs and Quarter Pounders. These companies, and countless others, have invested enormous amounts of time and money in the skillful development of brands that make promises to the consumer beyond their labels.

This distinction is vital: There is a difference between a product and a brand—a difference that might be the underlying force deciding whether a

147

new product succeeds or fails in the marketplace. Of the 25,261 products introduced in a recent year, it is variously estimated that 50% to 80% of them have failed or will fail.[1] No one can agree on the exact proportion, because each company measures success in a different way. For example, success might mean returned profit, share of market, or simply survival.

Regardless of the rate, there is little doubt that at least half of the 25,261 will not survive. Why? What makes some products succeed while others quickly die? What makes Lever 2000, Healthy Choice, Snackwell's, Aleve, and other new brands succeed? There is no real formula, no hard-and-fast rules for the success of new brands. But perhaps by understanding the fundamentals of branding and the difference between a product introduction and a brand introduction, we might gain some insight.

History of Brands

Branding is not a new practice. Tradesmen have long put their names on bricks, shoes, and metalwork as signatures to identify themselves as the makers of goods. In the 18th century, whiskey distillers burned their names into the barrels used for shipping. But branding as we know it, and the use of individual brand names, began in the 19th century. The Industrial Revolution led to the development of advertising and marketing techniques, which led to the significance of brand names.

The Industrial Revolution expanded not only the population of the United States, but the country's transportation systems and production opportunities. The growth in population influenced a vast growth in output by stimulating a demand for new products. Furthermore, the railroads made it possible to transport products throughout the country, eliminating the face-to-face contact most manufacturers had with their customers up to that time. As the variety and quantity of products grew along with their distribution, manufacturers needed to ensure their products were easily identified by the customers, and they also needed to protect their products from duplication by competitors. Thus manufacturers would name their products and employ trademarks or brands. This not only provided legal protection for the manufacturers, it served as a means of identification for consumers and a guarantee of homogeneity and quality.[2] Several factors influenced the early brand names and to a certain extent are relevant today: The name should have memorability, ease of pronunciation, and originality, and should be directly or indirectly descriptive of the product.[3]

Yet another factor also influenced the emergence of brands, an economic factor. As a new brand was introduced, the manufacturer would enjoy a monopoly for a short time, which boosted profits. Competition then would infiltrate the segment, and if the competitor could achieve competitive economies of scale, it could survive and profit as well. Thus the emergence of oligopoly—a situation in which a few manufacturers affect but do not control the marketplace. Brands therefore succeeded in differentiating the products in an oligopolistic marketplace. Branding was a device that allowed manufacturers to control their markets by preventing substitution of competitive products.[4]

During the late 1800s and early 1900s, several brands that are still familiar today were born: Coca-Cola, Ivory soap, Camay, Campbell's soup, Hershey chocolate bars, Budweiser, American Express Traveler's Cheques, Quaker Oats, and Kodak. What made these products "brands"?

Definition of Brands

All brands are products; not all products are brands.[5] A product is something that is made in a factory; a brand is something that is bought by a consumer. A product can be copied by a competitor; a brand is unique. A product can quickly become outdated; a successful brand is timeless.[6] What makes a product a brand? It is a combination of tangible and intangible benefits that must appeal to the consumer. First, and foremost, a brand must meet the needs, wants, and desires of the consumer. No amount of research and development, advertising, low pricing, or massive distribution will sell a product no one wants. Two elements establish that desire in consumers: functionality and added values.

Functionality refers to a demonstrable difference in how the brand performs in comparison to its competitors. It might be a better taste, a whiter wash, a moister cake, a faster cooking method, or decaffeination of a soft drink. This functional point of difference between brands must be one that is easily recognizable to the consumer and one that is desirable. Functionality is usually demonstrated with blind product tests. A blind product test is conducted without disclosing the product names, so that the focus is exclusively on the functional properties of the product.[7] Functionality becomes the tangible difference between brands, a tangible difference that is not only inherent to the product but obvious to the consumer.

Added values formulate the intangible or discriminating benefits that prompt the consumer to buy one brand over another.[8] Added values are over and above the functional benefits of the product, but added values should never be considered a substitute for functionality. The nonfunctional benefits are beyond reliability, taste, nutrition, smell, or safety. Added values are the reason successful brands are preferred in named product tests by a higher margin than in blind product tests.[9] Added values are established through the following elements:[10]

1. *The consumer's experience of the brand:* A brand is a pact between the manufacturer and the consumer. It is a guarantee of quality, of value and product satisfaction.[11] Brands become part of family loyalty; many consumers buy the same brands their mothers bought. Familiarity with the brand reduces the consumer's risk of dissatisfaction or disappointment. The brand develops a personality based on the consumer's experience and on the reliability of the brand.

2. *The type of people who use the brand:* Many consumers relate to others who also use the brand. This association, often depicted in the advertising, is an added value. Furthermore, as people become more affluent, added values and brand personalities are likely to become more important to them. They get more and more of their rewards in life from the nonfunctional.[12] User association is a common value in designer fashion, weight-loss programs, automobiles, and luxury items, as well as beer and soft drinks.

3. *The belief that the brand is effective:* Obviously, the consumer must believe the product will work before he or she will buy it. But there is evidence that consumers believe branded products work better than unbranded products. This is especially true of over-the-counter drugs. This belief also plays an important role in cosmetic brands, where the users feel more beautiful by using the product.[13]

4. *The appearance of the brand:* Here the packaging is key. This is how the product is presented. The package must be attractive and recognizable, and must appeal to the consumer. The appearance of the brand is not only important on the retailer's shelves, it is also a key element in advertising, especially for packaged goods.

Added values are built over time. They are developed through consumers' satisfaction with the brand and reinforced through the advertising of the brand. That is the power of Coca-Cola, Kodak, McDonald's, and thousands of others.

The power of brands and the expense of establishing and maintaining them are indicative of the value of brands. Kraft was purchased for nearly $13 billion, and the collection of brands under the RJR Nabisco umbrella sold for more than $25 billion.[14] So, how does a new brand gain that value?

New Brand Criteria

An extreme proliferation of products exists in the market today. Supermarkets and discount stores are bursting at the seams, and there is little evidence that consumers want 25,000 or more choices while doing their weekly grocery shopping. In addition, not all new products are new. Many are simply extensions of existing brands with a new flavor, color, or other variation, such as caffeine-free Coke, Canada Dry Raspberry Ginger Ale, Coffee-Mate flavored creamers, Tide with Bleach, and Honey Nut Cheerios. There are new brands as well, such as Miller's Red Dog Beer, Hershey's Chocolate Drink, Nestlé's Lion King candy bar, Hershey's NutRageous bar, Nabisco's Snackwell's, General Mills' Bugs Bunny and X-Men Fruit Snacks, and Procter & Gamble's Aleve pain reliever (now owned by Bayer). Of the 20,000-plus products introduced in a recent year, 75% were food products.[15] And what will be the secret ingredients that will afford some of these brands success? There is no magical answer, no scientific formula to follow for successful brand introduction. But some companies, such as Philip Morris, Nestlé, Procter & Gamble, Campbell's, and Hershey have been able to succeed. Based on the previous discussion of brand fundamentals, a few criteria checks suggest themselves.

1. *A new brand must provide functional superiority over its competitors and be evaluated in blind product tests.*[16] In many cases, a new brand has no point of difference—it is simply a replication of an existing brand. The consumer is already satisfied with the existing brand and the new brand offers no differentiation or incentive to switch.[17] In addition, the point of difference must be recognizable by the consumer. This may sound simple, but often products are developed with technical differences that can be measured in a laboratory, but are not evident to the consumer. For example, when Procter & Gamble introduced the Duncan Hines Moist & Easy cake mix, it was technically more moist than the competition, Betty Crocker's Snackin' Cake. However, when consumers tasted it in blind test, the moistness did not make

up for the deficiencies in the product's taste. Although P&G launched the brand, it was withdrawn from the United States 7 years later.[18] A. C. Nielsen has long recommended that no new brand be launched without a minimum preference in blind product testing of 60:40 over the direct competitor.[19]

A Nielsen study examined 53 successful new brands introduced over a 2-year period and found that the most important reason for success was functional performance.[20] A study of 100 new brands in the United Kingdom confirmed that 74% of the successes offered the consumer better performance at the same or higher price.[21]

Another point about functionality is that it helps to describe the competition and assists in determining the target group for advertising: the users of defined competitive brands. A new brand with functional superiority should always target users of the competitor.[22]

2. *A new brand must have added values.* As discussed earlier, brands depend on added values. Therefore, added values become central to making a new brand successful. The brand must have a coherent totality, the totality of the consumer's wants and needs, both functional and nonfunctional. The functional and nonfunctional features are interrelated. Added values are not simply tacked onto the brand after the functional features are determined. Together, they are integral to the personality and the appeal of the brand.[23] Therefore, the functional features of the new brand are not the only features to be tested in preliminary research.

Furthermore, many believe that added values of the brand are embodied in its name.[24] It is most common for a new brand to be introduced under an established name (e.g., Dial Hand Sanitizer, Ultra Downy, and Honey Nut Cheerios). The belief is that the established name will carry the new brand because of the already established added values the name implies. This may be true, and there are data to suggest that this practice can be successful. However, the new brand must live up to the consumer's expectations of the established name in order to succeed, and—an important point—using an established name should not suggest that the financial investment in the new brand can be reduced.[25]

3. *A new brand requires effective positioning.* This pertains to the brand's position within the product segment the brand is entering. Manufacturers often introduce new brands to keep pace with competitors. What they must determine is whether the new brands will hurt or cannibalize their own

existing brands in the segment. For example, many of the same people buy Kellogg's Corn Flakes and Nabisco Shredded Wheat. If Kellogg's were to introduce a new brand to attract Shredded Wheat users, Kellogg's no doubt would cannibalize its Corn Flakes by taking users from its own brand as well. A less destructive strategy is to introduce a new brand into a subdivision of the category on the assumption that segmentation already exists or can be created by advertising and promotion. The important element, however, is that this segmentation must be based on functional differences of the brand.[26]

4. *A new brand requires an effective pricing strategy.* Obviously, there are many pricing strategies a manufacturer can use. But most often a new brand will be introduced at a premium price. There is no problem with this if indeed the brand has functional superiority over its competitors. The 1976 Davidson study found that of the 50 successful brand introductions, more than half were introduced at a premium price, and in every case the price was reflected by superior performance. Of the 50 failures, 35 were sold at a premium price, but 25 were either similar or worse in performance than the competition.[27]

The investment in a new brand introduction is enormous, and rarely does a new brand make a profit in the first 3 years. So the decision to charge a premium price often reflects the manufacturer's necessary investment in the brand, not the brand's functionality. This type of pricing will provide an estimate of whether and when introductory costs will be recovered, but provides no indication as to whether consumers will buy the brand at the premium price. The most effective and efficient way to determine initial brand pricing is to determine what consumers will accept. It is just as important to test pricing strategies among consumers as it is to conduct blind preference tests.[28]

5. *A new brand must gain distribution.* This is a key factor influencing the success or failure of a new brand. In today's marketplace, the retail trade is concentrated, and large manufacturers have significant advantages because of their powerful and experienced sales forces. During the first 4 months of introduction, both successful and unsuccessful brands make some headway in the distribution chain. After this, it is the successful brands that continue to grow and the unsuccessful brands that remain static and eventually decline. What makes the difference? Is it a result of differences in sales forces or is it a result of consumer acceptance of the product based on the brand's functionality?

As I have noted throughout this chapter, functional performance is the basis of the success of a new brand. The consumer is interested enough to try the brand in the early months and, if satisfied, will support the brand. As more consumers demand the brand, the more retailers want to stock it. However, functional performance is not exclusively a matter of consumer satisfaction. Retailers and the sales force are conscious of functionality, and if the brand succeeds, everyone wins. Functional superiority is a great boost to the sales force, providing them with a salable brand for their customers, the retailers. And superior brand functionality garners commitment from the retailers to stock the brand because of that salability.[29]

Conclusions

No doubt manufacturers will continue to view new brand introductions as opportunities to grow their business. And the pace of new brand activity is heated, not least because manufacturers in oligopolistic markets are afraid of being preempted by their competitors. New brands are risky; there is more chance of failure than success. New brand introduction invariably takes resources from existing brands, thus existing brands may suffer at the same time new brand ventures are very likely not to succeed.[30]

To reduce their risks, manufacturers must lay the groundwork to ensure long-term growth from their brands. This suggests not starting with a ledger sheet and a formula, but with the consumer. Without understanding the consumer, a company cannot establish the need to be met, a demonstrable functional superiority. This has been the dominant theme of this chapter and the dominant reason for success in new brand introductions.

Finally, it is important to learn from new brand failures and successes. There is no absolute consensus on the failure rate for new brands, but most estimates put it at more than 50%. Nor do we know what makes a new brand successful, because manufacturers and their agencies have not made the data available for study. The risks involved justify post hoc research into successes and failures by independent and qualified personnel.[31] This would be the best way to uncover the patterns that influence the failure or success of new brands and thus reduce some of the risks that manufacturers face in this process.

Notes

1. Nancy Ten Kate, "New and Improved," *American Demographics,* March 1998, 32.

2. John Philip Jones, *What's in a Name? Advertising and the Concept of Brands* (New York: Simon & Schuster-Lexington, 1986).

3. Adrian Room, "Developing New Brands," in John M. Murphy (ed.), *Branding: A Key Marketing Tool* (New York: McGraw-Hill, 1987).

4. Jones, *What's in a Name?*

5. Ibid.

6. Stephen King, *Developing New Brands* (New York: John Wiley, 1973).

7. Jones, *What's in a Name?*

8. Ibid.

9. Ibid.

10. Ibid.

11. John M. Murphy, *Brand Strategy* (Englewood Cliffs, NJ: Prentice Hall, 1990).

12. King, *Developing New Brands.*

13. Jones, *What's in a Name?*

14. David A. Aaker, *Managing Brand Equity: Capitalizing on the Value of a Brand Name* (New York: Free Press, 1991).

15. "Product Categories," *New Product News,* November 10, 1994, 11.

16. John Philip Jones, *How Much Is Enough? Getting the Most From Your Advertising Dollar* (New York: Simon & Schuster-Lexington, 1992).

17. Murphy, *Brand Strategy.*

18. Tom Blackett and Graham Denton, "Developing New Brands," in John M. Murphy (ed.), *Branding: A Key Marketing Tool* (New York: McGraw-Hill, 1987).

19. Jones, *How Much Is Enough?*

20. Jones, *What's in a Name?*

21. J. Hugh Davidson, "Why Most New Consumer Brands Fail," *Harvard Business Review,* March/April 1976, 117-122; Laurie Freeman, "Aleve Promises Relief," *Advertising Age,* February 27, 1995, 22.

22. Jones, *What's in a Name?*

23. King, *Developing New Brands.*

24. Jones, *What's in a Name?*

25. Ibid.

26. Ibid.

27. Davidson, "Why Most New Consumer Brands Fail."

28. Jones, *What's in a Name?*

29. Ibid.

30. Ibid.

31. Jones, *How Much Is Enough?*

14

Exploring Brand Magic

Alexander L. Biel

The most valuable financial assets that a firm owns are arguably its brands. This chapter explores a key driver of financial value that I call *brand magic*. Functional excellence is fast becoming a necessary but not sufficient attribute of strong brands. I suggest here that brand strength depends far more upon the development of a unique, vivid, and meaningful identity for a brand.

Financial Value of Brands

A study by the consulting firm of Swander Pace has shown that although the sales growth rates of firms producing branded and unbranded products were virtually identical between 1990 and 1995, the return on sales for the branded products firms was twice as high.[1] Moreover, branded products marketers enjoyed a significantly higher return on total assets and shareholder return. Operating profits increased 50% faster for branded products marketers during this 5-year period (see Table 14.1).

TABLE 14.1   Does Branding Pay? Firms Manufacturing Food Products,
                 1990-1995

	Branded (%)	Unbranded (%)
Sales growth rate	5.2	4.9
Return on sales	9.2	4.4
Operating profit growth rate	4.8	3.2
Return on total assets	12.0	8.7
Shareholder return	11.1	9.2

Another way to find out about the financial significance of brands is to examine brand value as a proportion of the firm's replacement value. Economists Simon and Sullivan, funded by the Marketing Science Institute, have developed a way of separating brand value from the other assets of a firm.[2] They start by computing the value of the firm on the basis of its capitalized share value minus its debt. After deducting the replacement value of tangible assets, they developed a way of separating brand value from other intangibles (see Figure 14.1). Using this unique approach, they calculated the value of the brand portfolios of a number of prominent marketers. At the time of their analysis, Seagram's brands, for example, were valued at about 75% of the firm's replacement value, Quaker's were valued at 60%, and Campbell's were valued at around 35%. In effect, investors are saying that brands have a value above and beyond the capability of making or providing the underlying product or service. (See also Haigh, Chapter 8, this volume.)

Defining Brand Equity

Although definitions of brand equity abound, many of them fall into the trap of being rather more appropriate to brand image. I would suggest that a meaningful definition of brand equity must relate financial value to consumer behavior. In my view, brand equity consists of two linked elements: one expressed in financial terms and the other described in terms of consumer response.

Brand equity is the additional discounted future cash flow achieved by associating a brand with an underlying product or service (see Figure 14.2).

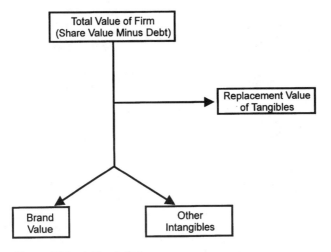

Figure 14.1. A Firm's Value

That additional future cash flow is, at the end of the day, predicated on a buyer response to the branded offering that exceeds the response that would be achieved by that same offering without brand identity.

Indeed, it was Philip Morris's exploitation of just such a response that led the firm to demand double-digit price increases for more than a decade during the late 1980s and early 1990s. The company's price retreat in 1993, on what is now remembered as "Marlboro Friday," was based on the realization that although the brand was, and remains today, one of the world's strongest, it was nonetheless possible to raise the price beyond the point sustainable by the brand's perceived value. The Marlboro experience naturally raises a question: Where will brand value go tomorrow?

The evidence suggests that brands will become more—rather than less—important, for one very good reason: Brands are important to consumers. Indeed, if brands were not important to consumers, few marketers would find them of interest. Consider the observation of Donald Keough, former chairman of Coca-Cola, after the unsuccessful introduction of New Coke:

> The most important source of Coca-Cola's continuing success is not the bottlers, the Coca-Cola system, the corporation itself, its executive committees, employees, boards of directors, company presidents, or chief executives.
> It derives from the consumer.[3]

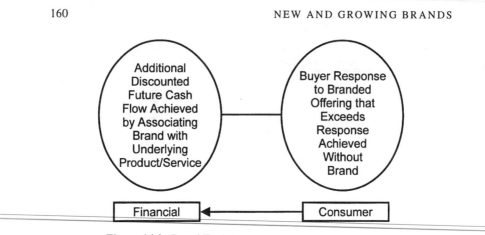

Figure 14.2. Brand Equity

Mr. Keough should know; one of the great near-missteps of marketing took place during his watch, in 1985, when Coca-Cola introduced New Coke. Coke's mistake was an honest one; in taste tests with no brand identification, consumers preferred New Coke. But people don't buy *blind* products. Half a million letters and phone calls later, Coke bowed to consumer demand. Under the circumstances, a very rapid response for a gigantic organization previously convinced that it controlled the brand. Coke Classic was back just 60 days after New Coke was introduced.

And of course the Coke story since then has been an amazing success, with an average annual 7% increase in sales and 26% increase in share value. The cover of a recent Coca-Cola annual report showed the silhouette of the firm's famous bottle with the words "Quick. Name a soft drink." The name of the company was absent. As the *New York Times* put it, it was "a brilliant way of reminding investors of the brand equity enjoyed by Coke." Coca-Cola is merely a high-profile, extreme example of the relationship people have with many of the brands in what anthropologist John Sherry has referred to as their "personal brandscapes." [4]

Over the past two decades, the brand equity concept has moved brands all over the world from marketing departments to boardrooms. But in our fascination with the economic value of brands as demonstrated by their ability to escalate a firm's value to stratospheric heights, we sometimes lose track of just *how* strong brands cast their spells. Brands do not spring to life in boardrooms. And, arguably, they are not really produced in marketing departments, although the latter may facilitate—or impede—their development. Strong brands are created in the minds of consumers.

Consumers use the information that marketers present to help them develop their perceptions of brands. But consumers—or customers, or prospects, if you like—also use other information, which they process to develop their own idea of a brand.

Jeremy Bullmore, former chairman of J. Walter Thompson in London, put it well when he said, "We [consumers] build images as birds build nests; from the scraps and straws we chance upon." Another advertising luminary, David Ogilvy, was one of the first to use the term *brand image*. "A brand's image," said Ogilvy in a speech to the American Marketing Association in 1955, "is the picture people carry around in their heads of a brand. It is the intangible sum of a product's attributes, its name, packaging and price, its history and reputation and the way it's advertised." Two decades later, brand image went mainstream, at least among advertising people. The notion that brands per se had equity was introduced to explain the rationale behind the frantic merger and acquisition activity of the 1980s.

Brand equity, of course, is a *result* of the brand-building process. Brand image, on the other hand, is broadly accepted as a key driver of equity.

Consumers Value Brands

Brands are important to consumers because they make choice easier.[5] Brands serve as shorthand for a bundle of both functional and emotional attributes. In effect, brands are problem solvers.

On a personal level, brands reduce performance risk. On a social level, the brands an individual chooses, and the brands he or she rejects, are self-expressive. Driving a Jeep Grand Cherokee defines me differently than would my driving a Buick Riviera. Owning a Mac distinguishes me from those who own other PCs.

The strongest brands are those that have developed distinct, meaningful images that set them apart in the minds of consumers. These discriminators can be functional, emotional, or a combination of both. In the past, functional differences often distinguished strong brands. However, in today's world of exploding technology, functional, physical differences between competing brands have diminished, and the time advantage that a functional innovator used to enjoy has largely disappeared.

- When the cold medicine Contac was introduced, it was the first cold remedy with sustained-release medication. This advantage was sustained for well over a decade and was used as the brand's central selling argument. Today, there are at least half a dozen competitors offering this feature.

- American Airlines introduced the first frequent-flier program in the early 1980s, to be followed literally within days by United with a virtually identical program.

- When Macintosh introduced the Graphical User Interface in 1984, it was a unique, relevant functional difference. But that distinction diminished when Microsoft brought out Windows.

- In the United States, Unilever's Chesebrough-Pond's unit recently launched its very successful Mentadent toothpaste, which contains baking soda and peroxide, two ingredients long associated with good dental hygiene that had never before been commercially combined. A competitor, Church & Dwight, has since introduced PeroxiCare with the same ingredients, less than 2 years after Mentadent's launch.

Beyond this, functional distinctions have become progressively more marginal. Product tests indicate that when consumers are blind to the brands tested, they cannot distinguish between leading brands in very many product categories. When the brand is introduced, however, perceived differences emerge. I am certainly not suggesting that functional excellence is irrelevant, but it has become a "table stake" rather than a compelling differentiator.

The "Softer" Side of Branding?

Ironically, the so-called softer side of branding—the identity of the brand—is increasingly being recognized as in reality the harder, cutting edge of brand differentiation. Brand identity is reflected in the image and personality of the brand and in the quality of the relationship between the brand and the consumer. More often than not, a brand's identity is deeply rooted in the marketer's corporate culture. Elizabeth Nelson, the distinguished American-born British researcher and founder of Taylor Nelson, has noted, "It is almost as if a brand is like a glass door through which the consumer can perceive the true values of [the corporation]." [6]

I refer to these unique values as *brand magic*. Functional benefits invite imitation, but brand magic, sharply etched, although difficult to build, is easier to own. Examples of this phenomenon are not hard to find:

- Many insurance companies promise to indemnify their policyholders when things go wrong, but only with Allstate is the buyer promised the protection of the "good hands."
- With every pair of Nike shoes, the purchaser also gains a share in a passion for excellence, encouragement to "do your own thing," and bragging rights to a brand with "an attitude." The cutting edge of competitiveness is inextricable from the brand.
- In the United Kingdom, Andrex toilet tissue, through the use of the Andrex puppy, clearly promised a special kind of softness, as well as a personality that exuded warmth and playfulness that no other brand could easily borrow.

Although virtually all marketers can wax eloquent on the functional properties of their brands, very few are able to articulate their brands' magic with confidence. To build strong brands and keep them strong, it is important for marketers to understand the ways in which consumers gain brand insights and form brand relationships. With such understanding, marketers can guide the actions through which consumers interpret the characters of brands.

Understanding Brand Magic

Many brands, of course, go slogging through life with very little magic. Undistinguished, though not necessarily unprofitable, they are typically the third- or fourth-ranked brands in a category. Although in some cases their magic really is absent, in many others it is simply undernourished. The strongest brands discover, nurture, and enhance their magic, developing it as a critical brand asset.

In this context, we need a framework for analyzing a brand's magic—those properties that both set the strongest brands apart from their competitors and create compelling desire. If we start with consumers, it follows that we need to know how they think about brands (see Figure 14.3). Not surprisingly, consumers want to know what a brand does on a very basic, functional level. What skills or expertise does the brand offer? Skills are those familiar functional and emotional attributes that relate to brand performance. For a bank, examples might include reliability, convenience, and helpfulness; for a

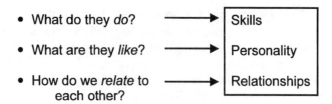

Figure 14.3. How People Think About Brands

detergent, cleaning power and gentleness. The value of such skills is undeniable.

However, when competing brands offer similar, hard-to-distinguish sets of skills, consumers require additional information to make decisions. They need to know more about a brand than simply what it does; they also want to know what it is like and how it might relate to them. Even a cursory examination of strong brands—such as Nike, Mercedes-Benz, Marlboro, Coca-Cola, Microsoft, Jack Daniels, and Harley-Davidson—leads to the inescapable conclusion that these brands have very well developed personalities that set them apart from their competitors.

The idea that personality plays a role in commerce is hardly new, of course. Before the growth of retailing and the emergence of brands, the traditional mode of commerce was strictly personal: a one-on-one transaction between a buyer and a seller, who more often than not were neighbors. Although quality was clearly important, so was the personality of the seller. Indeed, people have always preferred, other things being equal, to buy from people they know, or at least from people they feel they know.

As commerce flourished, the direct retail transaction between a buyer and a producer clearly became inefficient. Under these conditions, it is hardly surprising that the personality of the brand has developed as a substitute for that of the seller. This very natural transition explains why consumers take the trouble to impute personality to brands even when those brands have not consciously focused on developing and managing their personas. Today, the personality of the brand serves as a vital surrogate for personal intimacy in commerce.

But intimacy is an *interactive* phenomenon. It includes the notion of relationship. This is the construct that Blackston first developed in 1992.[7] His research suggests that to understand the interactive nature of the brand relationship, marketers must not only discover what consumers think of a

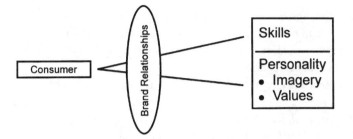

Figure 14.4. Lens Model of Brand Perception

brand, they must also question consumers about what they believe the *brand* thinks of *them*. Fournier later expanded this concept by developing a scale that measures the quality of brand relationships, the BRQ scale.[8] She has reported that the quality of brand relationships can be described on the dimensions of intimacy, commitment, partner quality, attachment, interdependence, and love. Fournier suggests that these relationships are formed on the basis of brand actions that can build or dilute the quality of the relationship, and thus affect brand equity.

One way of putting these constructs together employs a lens model in which skills and personality are mediated by brand relationships (see Figure 14.4). Traditionally, marketers have concentrated on managing their brand skills and have largely neglected brand personality and brand relationships. Today, most—though certainly not all—marketers accept that there is such a thing as brand personality. Indeed, anyone who has spent much time behind the one-way mirrors of focus group rooms has quickly realized that consumers and customers alike easily and naturally attribute personality traits to the brands that populate their personal brandscapes.

Although a small proportion of marketers have attempted to measure the personalities of their brands, virtually all of those measurements have utilized casual cobble-togethers of a few items that looked as if they ought to measure something related to human personality. Not surprisingly, the results have been largely unenlightening.

Recently, however, there have been some important new developments in brand personality research. Rather than trying to fit brands into the framework of human personality, one investigator, Jennifer Aaker, has developed a dedicated measure of brand personality.[9] It is related to, but is by no means identical to, human personality. Aaker has found five overarching factors that explain brand personality: sincerity, excitement, competence, sophistication, and ruggedness. Her scale discriminates between brands both within and across product categories.

Aaker recently reported that a replication of her U.S. work in Japan had revealed some potentially important differences in brand personality dimensions across cultures. Four of the five overarching factors that Aaker discovered in the United States also appeared in Japan; however, the dimension of ruggedness simply does not exist in the Japanese brandscape. Moreover, a factor labeled *peacefulness* was uncovered in Japan, but not in the United States.

Cultural differences in the organization of brand personality have important implications for international brand building as well as brand personality measurement. The conventional method of simply translating a personality battery in a questionnaire developed in, say, New York and using it around the world may miss important personality dimensions in different cultures.

Brand personality, brand skills, and brand relationships, taken together, constitute brand magic. As I have noted, these are areas that many managers have difficulty thinking about. They are not the stuff that is talked about much in business schools. But in fact, understanding the personification of brands by consumers and the relationships consumers have with brands is a critical step on the road toward grasping a brand's magic.

Brand magic is very real. It is the source of added value. It is why Coke scores much higher on identified product tests compared with its performance blind. Elaboration of a brand's magic, in turn, is vital to the development of a strong brand identity.

Personality Cues

How do consumers around the world learn about a brand's personality? Media advertising, of course, still plays a dominant role in developing the personalities of some brands. But today there are many other sources from which consumers and customers derive their perceptions of brand personality. Figure 14.5, which illustrates some of these sources, is messy, but so is life. In the 1960s and 1970s, when packaged goods dominated the world of marketing, for those lucky brands where media advertising was a far more controlling source of influence, advertisers at least had it within their power to shape

Figure 14.5. Sources of Inference of Brand Personality

consistent, coherent personalities for their brands. Today, media advertising's share of the mix is much smaller. The sources of brand information are multiple, complex, and likely to become more so. Often the sources of information are not consistent, so the consumer must resolve ambiguity.

As but one example, consider United Airlines. For years, travelers were exhorted to fly the "Friendly Skies of United." Today we are also told by United's advertising that the firm empathizes with its customers and is responsive to them: United, say the ads, is "rising." But when a traveler calls for a reservation and is told, "Your call is very important to us, please stay on the line," as he is thrust into the limbo of what seems like interminable hold, he may sense a certain discontinuity. As he searches the Internet for the United Web site and instead happens across the "Untied" Web site, a haven for customers' complaints, he sees yet another side of United.

Later, when he boards one of United's airplanes, the flight attendant recites all the "rules" with which passengers must comply, in a manner that suggests the airline expects them to try to smoke in the lavatory or turn on their computers at the wrong time. Rationally, the traveler understands that the attendant is merely conforming to regulations. Emotionally, however, he continues building the mosaic of United's brand personality as well as his relationship with the brand. Although the customer may have no doubt that

United's skills are competitive, it is not unlikely that he may start to question the company's frankness and sincerity.

When I contact IBM by phone, even though it is not possible to see the person at the other end of the line, I am likely to imagine that he is businesslike, that he is wearing a suit and tie. I unconsciously search his telephone manner for clues. Is the voice that of a knowledgeable person? Are there undertones of precision? Does he call me "Mr. Biel?"

But if I call Apple or Dell, my expectations are very different; I imagine the person is surely not wearing a tie—he may not even own one! I may not like it if he calls me "Alex," or even "Al," but I am not surprised.

Increased sensitivity to the clues to brand personality and brand relationships is a critical first step for marketers who want to develop more coherent brand identities. One way to do this is to start with a brand input assessment (BIA).

The Brand Input Assessment

The brand input assessment is simply an inventory and analysis of the objects, policies, and interactions that the brand has with its consumers. Although the specifics of the BIA process differ by product category, it typically consists of a review of the advertising that the brand and its direct competitors are running currently as well as the advertising that they ran in the recent past. It involves an examination of the brand's packaging and promotions (and comparison with those of the competition) as well as a review of the brand's media coverage. A thorough BIA also reviews policies and behavior at the consumer-brand interface. Depending on the nature of the business, this might include sales call protocols, company help lines, reservation systems, service contacts, and telemarketing programs. In effect, a BIA is an analysis of the elements that lead to the image and personality of the brand and the relationships the brand has with its consumers.

Clearly, advertising is one important source of image and personality. Michelin's long-running campaign featuring babies, with the theme "Because so much is riding on your tires," is one example of this. But, as I have suggested, advertising is almost never the sole source. Consumers interpret the actions, language, location, and dress of a brand and thereby interpret the brand's intentions.

- A brand like Celestial Seasonings, which gives purchasers a toll-free phone number and invites them to call with questions or comments, may seem more open and approachable than one that does not.

- The tongue-in-cheek manner of advertising for Apple's Macintosh evokes the impression that the brand is warm and friendly, and not stuck-up. The computer's breezily written manual enhances this perception. When the buyer of an Apple product opens its plain-Jane, recycled packaging, this signals that Apple is a brand that cares about the environment.

- L. L. Bean's folksy manner, its rural Maine location, its offer to resole the boots it sells, and its straightforward, no-caveats guarantee all tell consumers that it is a brand with which they can have a long-term, mutually satisfactory relationship.

But many brands do not speak with a consistent voice. For example, contributors to the Humane Society, arguably a "brand" in the nonprofit sector, occasionally include the names of their dogs as donors. The aims of the Humane Society are laudable, but when a preapproved credit card arrives in the pet's name, indicating that the organization sold the donor's name to other institutions in the for-profit sector, that donor may well feel less kindly toward the charity.

Many executives admire the *Wall Street Journal.* They appreciate its news coverage, and the publisher makes it easy for subscribers to suspend service when they are out of town. But when the *Journal* engages a telemarketer to call subscribers at dinnertime—generally the time with the highest probability of finding subscribers at home—to solicit subscription renewals, they chip away at the goodwill the publication has nurtured. Instead, subscribers see a pushy, intrusive side of the *Journal.*

Indeed, it is arguable that most outbound telemarketing—and, for that matter, direct mail—is more destructive than marketers realize. The accounting procedures that demonstrate financial success at single-digit response rates may well be misleading in that they do not reflect the reactions of the more than 9 in 10 who, having been interrupted, must go to the trouble of ridding themselves of the unwanted caller or piece of mail.

Conducting a brand input assessment is an interesting exercise and almost invariably leads to some useful insights. Although it sounds extremely pedestrian, and some managers initially question the BIA's utility, I have found that this very elementary activity almost never occurs as a standard, periodic review activity of any firm. Yet for most brands, these input acts are uncoordinated events that simply "grew," based on immediate needs. Often, different organizational units of the company execute them. Seeing them as elements of a branding task casts them in a whole new light. However, as the name implies, the brand input assessment is "input," rather than consumer reaction. And consumer response to the brand's input is key to the process of understanding brand magic.

Promising New Approaches to Understanding

There have been important developments in research methodology to support the investigation of brand magic. In addition to the work of Aaker, Blackston, and Fournier already mentioned, other investigators have been probing this area. Olsen and Allen have suggested the use of narrative stories elicited from consumers as a powerful way of gaining insights about brand personality.[10] For example, they might ask a respondent to imagine the brand as a person and to play the role of a private investigator who follows the brand around for a day. They have found that this sort of personification task poses no great difficulty for respondents, and that a good deal of consensus emerges across respondents. Both of these findings suggest that personification tasks are meaningful to consumers rather than mere artifacts imposed by researchers.

Zaltman's Metaphor Elicitation Technique is another new and exciting approach to understanding brand magic.[11] Arguing that most human communication is nonverbal, Zaltman starts with pictures. He arms consumers with scissors and cameras and asks them to bring back pictures of the brand experience. Based on these *consumer-generated* intermediate stimuli, he then conducts an intensive interview that includes Kelly grid and laddering tasks, in which he elicits the consumer's own interpretation of *her* pictures.

There have been important breakthroughs in research in the quantitative measurement of brand image as well. Researchers have been describing these images for more than 30 years, but although the descriptions were either comforting or disturbing, they did not lead to any action. Today it is possible, through research techniques based on micromodels, actually to design a brand's image to give it optimum marketplace positioning.

An example of this kind of model is Locator[SM], developed by Morgan of Research International.[12] Ordinary Likert scales are used to enable consumers to describe the major brands competing in a market on the basis of their personalities and skills. A constant sum preference task contributes the dependent measure. Locator models the responses of each consumer on an individual basis. It is therefore possible to predict the impact of changes in perception upon brand choice. If the brand were to be positioned, for example, as more frugal, would this increase or decrease brand preference?

This exercise does not tell the marketer *how* to make a brand more frugal—that is properly a creative task. But the micromodel addresses what would happen to preference if the brand were to be successful in moving in a specific direction.

Still another promising approach combining the element of qualitative insight with the rigor of quantification is the work that Sterenberg has been doing using nonverbal stimuli to explore brands.[13] Sterenberg has developed a set of pictures whose meanings have been intensively explored and validated cross-culturally. The pictures form the basis of a photo sort that is then used to explore brand values.

Taken together, the tools described above offer marketers important new resources for the discovery and development of brand magic.

Characteristics of Strong Brands

Recently, I had the opportunity to examine the characteristics that distinguish strong brands from their weaker sisters.[14] The data set consisted of 137 brands across 49 product categories. This sort of analysis highlights the importance of a brand's magic in setting it apart.

Two sets of attributes distinguished the strong from the weak. Some characteristics were "output" or response items. They reflected consumer reaction to strong versus weak brands and included such characteristics as relative perceived quality. Another set consisted of what we might call "input" items. These are characteristics such as length of time in business (see Figure 14.6). Among the output items, stronger brands were more likely to be seen as unique. They enjoyed higher perceived quality relative to their competitors. And they were more likely to evoke vivid, rich imagery among consumers.

Input factors that differentiated strong brands included a sense of history: Stronger brands had a higher likelihood of having withstood the test of time. Strong brands also were more likely to exhibit a singularity of focus, a factor I have labeled *category leadership*.

Advertising spending played a dominant role in some brands' marketing mix. A dimension I have labeled *refreshment within consistency* was found in the advertising themes of stronger brands. These brands were likely to run the

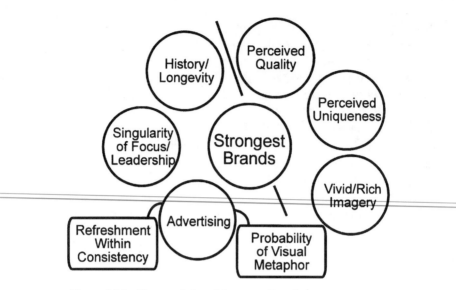

Figure 14.6. Characteristics of Strongest Brands

same campaigns for extended periods of time, changing the executions frequently, but not the campaign themes.

Visual Metaphors

A higher probability of the presence of visual metaphors was also found for stronger brands. Metaphor, of course, is the use of one object to describe another. Visual metaphors take this principle into the world of the nonverbal. Examples of visual metaphors include Planters' Mr. Peanut, the dancing California Raisins, the umbrella of Travelers Insurance, Merrill Lynch's bull, and Kellogg's Tony the Tiger.

Visual metaphors are clearly not new, but their power in brand building has not always been recognized. Visual metaphors are powerful for a number of reasons, several of which I describe below.

Different Rules

Probably the most important feature of visual metaphors is that they communicate using a very different set of rules from that employed in verbal communication. Whereas verbal exaggeration quickly reaches the point of rejection on the grounds of disbelief, this does not happen with the visual metaphor. Whimsy and hyperbole are acceptable in metaphor, but can be counterproductive in verbal communication.

When Exxon, through the ingenuity of television, shows a moving car turning into a tiger, and then becoming a car again, no one literally believes that the car has become a powerful beast. But the association is clear, unmistakable, and laden with meaning.

In the world of the visual, the use of exaggeration and distortion merely represents playing by a set of rules that is both understood and accepted by the viewer. Around the world, the Marlboro cowboy is masculinity and independence. Outside North America, he is Americana as well.

Cognitive Processing

Visual metaphors evoke mental processing on the part of consumers, who must interpret the metaphors to extract their meaning. There is mounting evidence that this active processing enhances attitude formation and retards the decay of attitudes so formed.

Low Susceptibility to Wear-Out

The "good hands" have been part of the Allstate magic for more than 30 years, but they have been used in many different ways. At times the hands have been photographs of real hands that have dissolved into artwork hands; at other times, they have been a drawing. Sometimes they have contained animated people. At other times, they have held houses and cars. Like the "good hands," visual metaphors can be refreshed and used in different ways without substantially changing their meaning.

Ability to Convey Complex Messages

Wells Fargo Bank in California effectively uses a stagecoach to symbolize the idea that the bank will always come through for you. It also conveys the idea that Wells Fargo has been around a long time—an important association for an institution to which people entrust their money. The identification with the West also projects an image of friendliness and straight talk. And finally, the people who settled the West are viewed as heroes, as people who shrugged off adversity.

The stagecoach works brilliantly on television, and Wells Fargo also does an excellent job of using it consistently across all forms of communication. Indeed, because the company has built the visual metaphor so consistently over a long period, it also works well on radio. The sound effects of the horses' hooves as they pull the coach and the exaggerated Western accents of the riders conjure up visual images in the minds of listeners.

Ownability

Because they can be designed to be unique, visual metaphors provide distinctiveness to brands that words cannot equal. To the extent that the distinctiveness imparts meaning, it contributes a powerful message that is not subject to the skepticism encountered by verbal argument.

Possible Negatives

Is there a downside to the visual metaphor? Of course. One risk is that consumers will not interpret a metaphor in the manner that was intended. The processing requirements may be too demanding. Another risk is that a metaphor may be misinterpreted and thus may result in an undesirable message. Yet another potential problem is that a metaphor may become limiting as the nature of the business evolves and changes over time. However, these are risks that can be identified and managed. The branding advantages of a well-developed visual metaphor are clearly worth considering.

The greater risk, ironically, is closer to home—it is the marketer who does not recognize the value of his or her property. Possibly the best example of this is the abandonment of the Andrex puppy in the United Kingdom by Kimberly-Clark on that company's acquisition of Bowater-Scott, the owner of the metaphor. The puppy's ability to convey softness, strength, and product quantity was one of England's most striking and best-documented marketing success stories.

Andrex is not alone. Hathaway shirts recently abandoned its man-with-an-eyepatch metaphor on the dubious grounds that it is no longer contemporary. And the flying red horse of Mobil, although still present in the firm's signage, is clearly eschewed by the marketer in favor of the stylized *O* in the word *Mobil.*

Summary

In this chapter I have argued that brands will increase in importance to consumers, and therefore to marketers. That is good news for manufacturers committed to brand building. The bad news, for manufacturers, is that retailers recognize this, and the best of them are learning how to build strong brands of their own.

I have also suggested that what many view as the softer side of branding has a very hard edge indeed. The emotional, personal, relational aspects of branding are more likely to provide lasting economic advantage than are the functionally based aspects. Marketers who take the trouble to understand and manage the identities of their brands will increase their probability of winning in ever more competitive markets.

Notes

1. Swander Pace & Company, *State of the Food Industry Report* (San Francisco: Swander Pace & Company, 1997).

2. Carol Simon and Mary Sullivan, *A Financial Approach to Estimating Firm-Level Brand Equity and Measuring the Impact of Marketing Events,* Working Paper 92-116 (Cambridge, MA: Marketing Science Institute, 1992).

3. Donald Keough, "The Importance of Brand Power," in Paul Stobart (ed.), *Brand Power* (New York: Macmillan, 1994), 78.

4. John Sherry, paper presented at the 14th Annual Meeting of the Association for Consumer Research, as cited in Alexander L. Biel, "Converting Image Into Equity," in David A. Aaker and Alexander L. Biel (eds.), *Brand Equity and Advertising* (Hillsdale, NJ: Lawrence Erlbaum, 1993).

5. Biel, "Converting Image Into Equity."

6. Elizabeth Nelson, chair, Taylor Nelson, personal communication, May 1992.

7. Max Blackston, "Beyond Brand Personality: Building Brand Relationships," in David A. Aaker and Alexander L. Biel (eds.), *Brand Equity and Advertising* (Hillsdale, NJ: Lawrence Erlbaum, 1993).

8. Susan Fournier, "A Consumer-Brand Relationship Perspective on Brand Equity," paper presented at the Marketing Science Institute Conference on Brand Equity and the Marketing Mix, Tucson, AZ, March 2-3, 1995.

9. Jennifer Aaker, "Dimensions of Brand Personality," *Journal of Marketing Research,* August 1997.

10. Jerry Olsen and Doug Allen, "Building Bonds Between the Brand and the Customer by Creating and Managing Brand Personality," paper presented at the Marketing Science Institute Conference on Brand Equity and the Marketing Mix, Tucson, AZ, March 2-3, 1995.

11. Gerald Zaltman and Robin Higie, *Seeing the Voice of the Customer: The Zaltman Metaphor Elicitation Technique,* Working Paper 93-114 (Cambridge, MA: Marketing Science Institute, 1993).

12. Biel, "Converting Image Into Equity."

13. Greet Sterenberg, "BrandSight: A Non-Verbal Method to Measure Brand Personality," paper presented at the RIQ Seminar on Qualitative Research, Singapore, November 1997.

14. Alexander L. Biel, "Discovering Brand Magic: The Hardness of the Softer Side of Branding," *International Journal of Advertising,* vol. 16, no. 3, 1997. See also Alexander L. Biel and Judie Lannon, "Steel Bullet in a Velvet Glove? The Use of Metaphor in Advertising," *Admap,* April 1993.

How Advertising Builds Brand Equity

Andy Farr

This chapter addresses two key questions that are taxing the minds of advertisers and marketers all around the globe. First, how can we evaluate a brand's equity with the consumer? And second, how can we determine which advertising campaigns are likely to generate brand equity in the long term? The framework for answering these questions is based on Millward Brown's experience over more than 15 years of linking tracking data to sales modeling, and the initial results from a research project looking at the consumer research measures that are common across successful brands.

Why do we need to measure consumer equity? With sophisticated scanner data, we should expect to be able to identify an immediate short-term sales response to most fast-moving consumer goods (fmcg) advertising. The problem is that this is likely to show that much advertising is not justifiable on the basis of its short-term payback. However, my own experience, as well as an analysis of the Institute of Practitioners in Advertising (IPA) advertising

177

effectiveness award winners and Nielsen's pilot analysis of 45 major U.K. brands over the past 3 years, indicates that advertising does have a role in long-term brand building.

There is, however, a proviso. Not all advertising and not all innovations will be successful—some strategies will be more powerful than others, and some executions will be more effective at delivering those strategies. What marketers need is proof that today's advertising investment is going to be worthwhile in the longer term.

This means we must look for changes in the brand's underlying long-term core sales and other measures of sales equity. But because by its nature a long-term effect occurs only over a 1- to 5-year period, we need to know which short-term measures are precursors to long-term brand building. The consumer researcher's role is to identify the measures that are leading indicators of advertising's effects on the brand as well as the strategies and executions that are moving the brand in the right direction—but at an early stage.

Research Measures of Consumer Brand Equity and the Link With Advertising

Survey research measures only one part of a brand's equity, but it is an important part. The ideas, associations, and images that people have of a brand determine the demand side of the brand equity equation. They define the brand's worth to the consumer—what makes a user willing to pay the price asked and a nonuser willing to consider the brand for purchase. If the brand's standing is strong enough in consumers' minds to warrant their paying the price asked for it, then the brand will have realized its consumer equity and turned it into sales equity. This consumer brand equity can be summarized through the five elements shown in Figure 15.1.

Brand Presence

The brands in a marketplace can be arranged on a continuum from no awareness to passive name recognition, to brands consumers have some knowledge of, or familiarity with, to brands they know well through actual experience or marketing activity, and finally to those brands that are felt to be dynamic or growing in popularity. Using standard research measures of

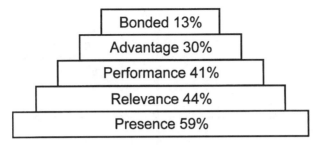

Figure 15.1. Building the Pyramid

prompted awareness, salience, familiarity, and brand dynamism, it is possible to place the brands on a grid showing the level of awareness and the extent to which this is active or passive (see Figure 15.2). Brands in the top right quadrant of this grid are those with active brand presence.

The concept and importance of brand presence become clearer when we look at examples of this dynamic.

Brand Launches

Advertising has a key role in putting a new brand on the map, and success in creating awareness is one of the first steps toward a successful launch. Figure 15.3 shows the level of prompted awareness for 51 fmcg product launches. All the data shown are taken from 6 months after launch. Across the bottom of the figure are the levels of television ratings (TVRs) during the first 6 months. There is a wide variation in awareness, but a generally positive trend. After 400 ratings, we would typically expect about 40% brand awareness; after 600 TVRs, about 50%; and after 1,000 ratings, 60% or more.

For a new product, brand presence can be seen as the gateway to the brand for consumers—they are unlikely to buy a brand they know nothing about— except in the lowest of risk categories. An analysis of launch awareness against trial within the product field shows a strong correlation. Awareness does not guarantee trial, but it is an important factor.

Established Brands

Creating a "buzz" or sense of excitement about a brand is one of the ways of generating an increase in the underlying sales trend. The example of the

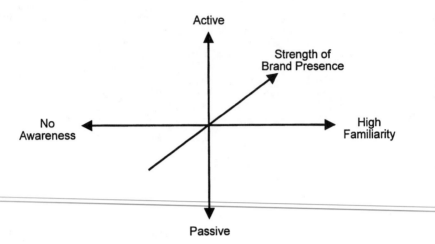

Figure 15.2. Brand Perception Grid

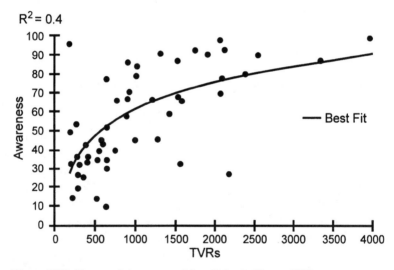

Figure 15.3. Prompted Awareness After 6 Months Versus TVRs

successful British snack Pepperami, detailed below, demonstrates this point
excellently. However, it is only one of a number of highly effective campaigns
that have succeeded in raising a brand's presence to new levels, including the
famous work for Wonderbra and the orange soda Tango. Pepperami, prior to

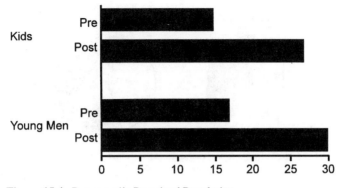

Figure 15.4. Pepperami's Perceived Popularity

its award-winning advertising campaign in 1992, already had prompted awareness of 90%, but sales had plateaued after rising in the late 1980s. The introduction of the high-impact "bit of an animal" campaign had the effect of raising advertising awareness from 11% to 67%, placing the brand above major confectionery brands such as Mars, with one of the smallest budgets in the snacks sector. And it doubled the brand's perceived popularity among children and young adults, as shown in Figure 15.4. The brand moved from having a passive presence to a highly active presence in the snacks market-place. The resulting impact on sales was a 35% average increase.

For established brands, increased brand presence is a genuine leading indicator of sales growth—sustained increases in brand salience or a sense that the brand is growing in popularity often precede changes in the brand's core sales.

Proving That Advertising Is Driving Brand Presence

The new launch data presented in Figure 15.3 show a generally positive response of awareness to increased weight. But some launches, despite invest-ing heavily in above-the-line media, fail to put their products on the map. This can be due to a number of factors, the most important being lack of distribu-tion. However, the effectiveness of the execution in cutting through and leaving a branded advertising message is also a key factor. Figure 15.5 shows that the amount of variance explained just by the TVR weight increases by a third (from 41% to 55%) when the TVRs are factored by the Awareness Index to create a measure of "effective weight." (The Awareness Index is Millward

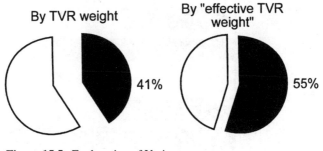

Figure 15.5. Explanation of Variance

Brown's advertising efficiency index calculated by relating the rise in advertising awareness to increased media weight.)

In the case of established brands, it is also no surprise that dramatic changes in brand presence have resulted from advertising that generates awareness indices in the top few percent of all ads tracked. One of the earliest indicators that a campaign has the potential to generate an increase in consumer equity is an increase in the level of advertising awareness among the target group.

Thus brand presence can be created by all styles of advertising, from the simplest announcement of a new product and its primary functional benefit to the most highly creative approach. However, the branded visibility of the advertising is a key component in its success.

Brand Relevance

If the brand's presence is the gatekeeper for the consumer, then the relevance of the brand's promise to the consumer's needs and aspirations will determine the potential size of the market available to the brand. For example, in the toothpaste market we can see in Table 15.1 that a niche brand like Sensodyne can have a very clear positioning. It is seen as the most effective brand for sensitive teeth by three-quarters of the market, but because the relevance of this to most consumers is limited, its market share is only 4% by volume.

Proof That Advertising Is Creating Relevance

Nigel Hollis has shown that the degree to which advertising is immediately motivating is driven by a combination of news content, relevance, enjoyment,

TABLE 15.1 Positioning of Two Toothpaste Brands

	Sensodyne (%)	Colgate (%)
Best for sensitive teeth	75	11
Relevant to mine or my family's needs	14	51
Market share (volume)	4	30

and branding.[1] Relevance on its own accounted for nearly half the variance Hollis found in persuasion scores. This was particularly true of "lapsed users" and "non-trialists."

Most new innovations will be immediately motivating for some people; however, advertising has the power to enhance this. For example, in the United Kingdom, was there a need for round tea bags before Tetley launched and then advertised them? Would Toilet Duck cleanser have been so successful without the simple creative device of the woman turning upside down? Or would Radion have generated sales at launch without advertising to make smell removal an issue? In each of these cases, it is highly doubtful.

The role of relevance is even more clear-cut for established brands. Advertising can be used to leverage existing advantages by making them relevant to a new need or group of consumers. The most famous example of this is SmithKline Beecham's Lucozade, which was switched from a drink for convalescents to a fashionable sports drink.

In such cases the evaluation/proof of the advertising's effectiveness is not just the measure of increases in trial and repeat, but also a demonstration that the opportunity has been maximized. Did the advertising deliver the message effectively to the target group? Was it clear? And was it as credible and relevant as it should have been?

Product Performance

Actual product performance is a highly subjective measure, but ultimately if the product fails to deliver, or fails to keep up with the competition, then in the long term its sales will decline. As Paul Feldwick and Françoise Bonnal note, "If you look at brands that are really in trouble today, you will often find products that have lost their competitive advantage through devaluation or just failure to innovate, and yet still expect to command an ever-widening price gap against parity competitors."[2] In other words, advertising can have a profound effect on the perceptions of product performance, but it cannot make a weak product strong. However, it can give a product at parity performance a perceived edge. Having a clear understanding of what the product is actually delivering is an important strand in understanding the brand's consumer equity and its ability to warrant a premium.

Product and Brand Advantages

A brand's advantage can be a direct extension of some unique aspect of the product delivery. However, in the crowded markets of the 1990s, many brands have little genuine product differentiation. The most successful brands have managed to take some aspect of their product performance and make it a perceived advantage, or to develop distinctive brand personalities and positioning that give them a perceived consumer advantage in the market. The results of this are that they can command a price premium not justified purely on the basis of the "ingredients."

Advertising is likely to influence perceived product performance in two ways: first, by guiding expectations about the product experience (a process I call *product enhancement*); and second, by creating a halo of superiority around the brand (through a mechanism I have termed *interest-status*).

Creation of Product Advantages
Through Product Enhancement

The Red Mountain coffee case study from the late 1980s (published in a 1988 IPA advertising effectiveness paper) is an excellent example of the enhancement process at work. The advertising successfully set up the taste expectations for Red Mountain as the coffee with the "ground coffee taste without the grind." Previously, consumers had been inclined to interpret the slightly bitter taste of the coffee as a negative—due in part to advertising imagery showing cowboys drinking Red Mountain around a campfire. However, in the light of the new advertising, the bitterness was interpreted positively as the ground coffee taste. This change was apparent in an increase in conversion from trial to repeat. But the full effects of this advertising were not apparent until retrial had been encouraged via a low-priced trial-sized jar. The advertising in itself was not sufficiently motivating to generate retrial, but the message was capable of influencing perceptions at trial.

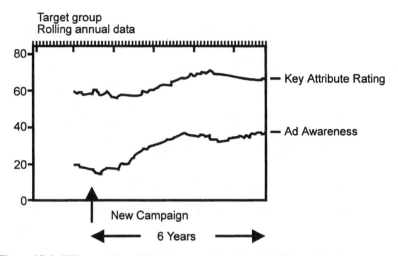

Figure 15.6. Effect on Advertising Awareness Leading the Effect on Product Attribute Perceptions

Proof That Advertising Is
Creating Product Advantage

An experiment conducted by Millward Brown in 1993 confirmed the magnitude of the enhancement effect and showed that advertising increased the conversion from "trial" to "definite purchase intent" from 19% to 30%.[3] However, in real market conditions proof that advertising is having a positive enhancement effect is not straightforward, because much of the influence works at the point of trial, rather than when the ad was viewed.

For example, the effectiveness of a sampling exercise following advertising with an enhancing element is likely to be much greater, but it could be ascribed to the below-the-line activity and not the multiplier effect of the advertising working with everything building trial. If there is no specific trial-building activity, then the enhancement effect of advertising on the product perceptions may become apparent only gradually over time.

This pattern is shown quite clearly in Figure 15.6. The campaign here generated considerable advertising presence, but the effect on product percep-tions and on underlying sales became apparent only over several years. If the advertising is working effectively with the product, then over time we would expect to see increases in the extent to which the brand is associated with specific product advantages, as shown in the figure. However, because of the

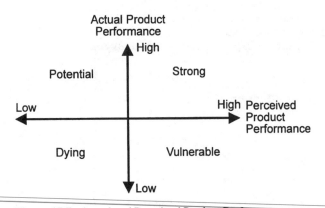

Figure 15.7. Actual and Perceived Product Performance

interaction with the product experience, we need to have a clear understanding of the strength of the product in order to be able to evaluate this fully.

Linking Actual and Perceived Product Performance

Because of the effects of product and enhancement on perceived product delivery, it is an important aid to marketing decision making to consider how the perceived and actual product performance match, as illustrated in Figure 15.7. Brands in the top right quadrant of the figure, where both perceived and actual performance are *strong,* are able to command a premium. Brands in the bottom right quadrant are *vulnerable*; branding is providing insulation for the brand, but ultimately this cannot be sustained. The brand is not able to justify its premium in the long term. Brands in the top left quadrant have *potential* and are worthy of support, in particular a combination of advertising focusing on the product strengths and trial-building below-the-line activity. And the viability of brands in the bottom left quadrant must be in doubt. Unless considerable resources are devoted to product improvement, followed by sustained above- and below-the-line investment, the brand will die.

Leading Indicators of Advertising's Effect on Product Advantage

Because the enhancement effect is delayed until product experience, we need to be able to anticipate whether advertising has the potential to work

TABLE 15.2   Brand Preference in Named Tests

	PG Tips	*Tetley*	*Typhoo*
Best-tasting cup of tea (indexed against PG)	100	85	40

SOURCE: Data from IPA studies and Millward Brown, March 1990.

through this mechanism in the short term. There are two key advertising-related factors: First, the advertising needs to be remembered—important because its main influence is at the point of trial; and second, the message should relate in some way to the experience of "using" the product—does it create any expectations of what the product would "feel like to eat"? And are they in line with what the product can actually deliver? There is therefore a strong argument for undertaking product testing alongside the advertising development work to understand how the synergies between the two can be maximized.

The role of the advertising in this context is to take some aspect of the product's performance and channel consumers toward that benefit.

Creation of Product Advantage Through Interest Status or Brand Advertising

Advertising's role in creating emotional pulls for the brand is discussed more fully below. However, it is clear that successful brand advertising can create a halo of product advantage. Perhaps the best-documented example is the case of PG Tips, the brand leader in the British tea category. The data from blind tests in 1983 showed that there was very little to distinguish among brands of tea, including the two leading store brands, Tesco and Sainsbury. However, in named tests, PG enjoyed the greatest preference (see Table 15.2).

In other words, the brand was able to create a level of perceived product advantage not wholly supported by the actual product offering. If this places PG Tips in a vulnerable position in the long term, then it would be doubly true for any brand that failed to maintain its perceived brand advantage. PG Tips continued to be supported by the much-loved advertising campaign featuring chimpanzees, and this offered some insulation against the threat from retailers' brands, but this was not true of the market as a whole. At the time of the blind taste test, store brands' share of the market was about 20%; it is now approaching 40%. Whereas the strength of retailer brands in general has increased over

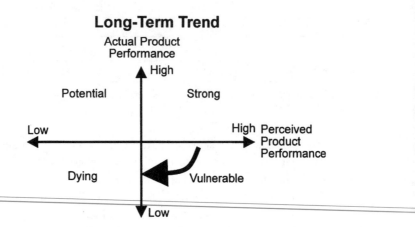

Figure 15.8. Actual and Perceived Product Performance: Long-Term Trend

the past 20 years, the lack of genuine product differentiation in this market is likely to have made the process more rapid. The trend is hypothesized in Figure 15.8.

Within the tea market as a whole, the lack of differentiation is such that for two of the three main consumer segments—the repertoire buyers and the nondiscriminators—the retailers' own brands are felt to meet the consumer's needs equally with the manufacturer brands.

Loss of Advantage Through Competitive Pressure

A brand can also lose its market advantage through the launch of competitive products. Figure 15.9 shows the effect that the launch of a new competitor had on a U.S. analgesic brand. Absolute endorsements on the key effectiveness measure did not decline, but the extent to which this perception was a unique property dropped considerably, followed by market share.

Emotional Brand Advantages

Brands can have perceived advantages that are unrelated to the physical or sensory aspects of the product delivery and relate more to the emotional appeal of the brand and the sense of belonging that comes from being a buyer of that brand. In many respects this is an extension of brand presence, except that that

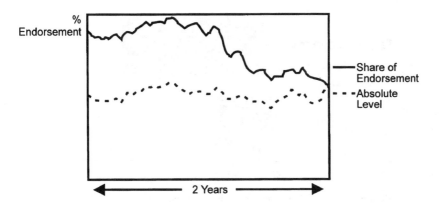

Figure 15.9. The Effect of Competitive Activity

presence is converted into a relevant advantage only if it fits with the consumer's emotional needs. Levi's would simply be another well-made pair of trousers without the Americana images from the advertising that give it stature and identity. It is these that provide Levi's wearers with the additional value that makes the brand worthy of its price tag.

Swindells and Branthwaite argue that advertising creates a halo in the viewer's mind—a halo of excitement, uniqueness, and supremacy. Such advertising creates interest in and status for the brand.[4] However, a key point is that it is not the brand that is interesting, but the "consumable" advertising. If this is the case, and I think there is strong evidence that it is, then in order to anticipate the effects of such campaigns, we should be looking to the target group for its level of involvement with the campaign. For example, with the extremely successful British campaign for Tango orange soda, 16- to 34-year-olds found the advertising actively involving to a much greater extent than most advertising (see Figure 15.10).

Swindells and Branthwaite also argue that this type of advertising is not actively processed at the time of viewing, but rather is stored as an audiovisual memory. This is then assimilated onto the brand by association and repetition. Hence it is imperative that advertising working in this way should be uniquely associated with the brand in creative terms, because there is no unique product feature or benefit to provide the link. And again, for example, this was true of the Tango campaign, with 95% of 16- to 34-year-olds saying that they "couldn't fail to realize it was an ad for Tango."

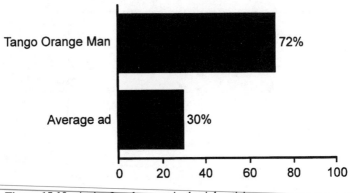

Figure 15.10. Active Involvement in the Advertising
SOURCE: Millward Brown 1995 calibration data.

It is no surprise that the advertising that is effective via this mechanism almost always has an above-average ability to cut through and generate branded advertising associations, both short- and long-term. An analysis of IPA campaign award-winning papers devoted to longer and broader effects reveals that all cases publishing research on advertising awareness achieved above-average awareness levels.

There may be a direct link between the two processes, with advertising associations acting as the vehicle for storing and encoding the message. However, the link does not have to be a direct one. The correlation may result because the factors that generate a high level of advertising memorability and cut-through are the same as those that ensure that the advertising is capable of creating a halo of excitement, uniqueness, and supremacy about the brand in the viewer's mind. The advertising is actively involving, distinctive, often enjoyable (but not exclusively—advertising may be effective by being highly challenging), and linked to the brand.

Leading Indicators of Advertising's Effect on Brand Advantage

The proof that the advertising is creating emotional brand advantages will be increases in brand appeal or affinity in the long term and measures of high brand opinion such as quality, trust, and worth, coupled with a growth in long-term brand associations. However, in the short term we can anticipate

TABLE 15.3   Consumer Choice for First Brands Versus Others

	Brand Leader	Second Brand	Other Brands
Percentage considering buying the brand exclusively	36	22	17

the effects of such advertising by understanding the relationship between the target group and the advertising. Measures of advertising cut-through such as the Awareness Index can act as a barometer for the advertising's creative power and hence potential long-term effectiveness.

Bonding

Ultimately, the trust and affinity derived from the brand's advantages can result in some consumers' becoming bonded to the brand to such an extent that they do not actively consider any other brands for purchase. This state does not preclude a consumer's trying new products for a change, but it is likely to provide insulation from the activity of competitors. For example, an analysis of the brand leaders in the tea, coffee, toothpaste, and yellow fats markets demonstrates that, on average, more than one-third of consumers would only consider these brands for purchase. In contrast, for the second and other brands in the market, the figure falls to one-fifth or less (see Table 15.3).

Students of the Dirichlet model would argue that this is purely a function of brand size. Although I would not disagree that big brands will have more bonded or loyal consumers, this ignores the fact that many consumers do have genuine emotional bonds with the brand they buy. These more loyal or bonded consumers represent the future profit stream for the brand. Work in the United States by the Coalition for Brand Equity has demonstrated that, in some cases, all of a brand's profits are derived from the 10% of consumers who are most loyal—and hence less likely to switch on the basis of price promotion.[5]

Proving That Advertising Is Driving
Consumer Brand Bonding

As a measure of the effectiveness of the advertising, we should look to see trends in brand affinity and consumer commitment—the degree to which the brand has attained the status in the consumer's repertoire where no other brand is being actively considered for purchase. However, in mature markets these movements are likely to be slow trends rather than rapid uplifts, and as such are likely to follow the creation of brand presence and advantages—or the introduction of a unique product innovation.

Conclusions

In this chapter I have attempted to set out a framework within which we can evaluate the likely short- and long-term effects of advertising that is capable of long-term brand building. Although such a framework is not definitive, it is the case that increases and declines on dimensions relating to the brand's presence, its relevance to the marketplace, its perceived product and emotional advantages, and ultimately brand preference, status, and commitment will be indicative of a brand's strength or weakness.

However, because by its nature a long-term effect occurs only over a 1- to 5-year period, we need to consider what short-term measures are precursors to long-term brand building. These fall into two categories. First, there are the effects on a brand from the immediate challenge effect of innovation, which should produce immediate changes in awareness, trial or consideration, and sales, or definite purchase intent in longer purchase cycle markets. And second, there are effects from advertising that is working via the mechanics of product enhancement or interest/status. Therefore, an understanding of the response to the advertising is key.

In the case of enhancement, it is important that the advertising is accurate about what the brand/product can deliver, and that the images, messages and claims from advertising are remembered and linked with the brand. In the case of interest and status brand advertising, because the effect is driven by "consumable" advertising, we should be looking to the target group for the level of involvement with the creativity, and because the advertising is the element creating brand differentiation, it is imperative that it is uniquely linked to the brand. In both of these latter two circumstances, the role for involving advertising creativity is key for long-term effects. However, this needs to be harnessed to the brand in order to be effective.

Notes

1. Nigel Hollis, *Persuasion: The Millward Brown Perspective* (London: Millward Brown International, 1995).

2. Paul Feldwick and Françoise Bonnal, "Reports of the Death of Brands Have Been Greatly Exaggerated," paper presented at the ESOMAR Conference, November 1993.

3. Andy Farr and Gordon Brown, "Persuasion or Enhancement? An Experiment," in *Market Research Society Conference Proceedings* (Birmingham, UK: Market Research Society, 1994), 69-77.

4. Alan Swindells and Alan Branthwaite, "Capturing the Complexity of Advertising Perceptions," paper presented at the ESOMAR Conference, Paris, December 1995.

5. Larry Light and Richard Morgan, *Brand Loyalty Marketing* (New York: Coalition for Brand Equity, 1994).

Part III

Mature Brands

16

Life-Cycle Theory

John Philip Jones

One of the most widely taught and equally widely believed marketing doctrines is that of the life cycle, sometimes described as the *product life cycle* or the *brand life cycle*. The second of these is the more dangerous description.

The central tenet of life-cycle theory is that brands resemble those things studied by zoologists and botanists; they inevitably go through the stages of birth, growth, maturity, and decline. We are talking here about long-term irreversible decline, not the short-term controllable cyclical movements that I describe in Chapter 12 of this volume. There is no shortage of examples of brands that have gone through these various stages from birth to final decline and extinction, although the actual shape of the curve up and down has varied a good deal in particular cases.[1] The empirical evidence for life cycles is, however, dangerous and misleading, for two closely related reasons.

For a start, there is also a good deal of evidence pointing the other way: to brands that have reached maturity and maintained relatively constant permanent levels of market share in the face of competition. The large number of examples I could quote includes the leading brands in 19 American consumer goods markets, brands that have kept their leadership for 50 years.[2] But this is not really the central point, because the question cannot be decided by weighting the examples on both sides, with so many demonstrating the existence of a life cycle and so many not, for the simple reason that any manufacturer can cause a brand to go into decline through simple inaction. Decline is very much within the manufacturer's control; it is not by any means entirely governed by external influences. Brands are managed.

This leads to the second and key point: The life cycle is a self-fulfilling concept, which is what makes it so dangerous.

Not long ago, a leading manufacturer was promoting a brand of floor wax. After a steady period of growth, the sales of the product had reached a plateau. Marketing research suggested that an increase in spot television advertising, backed by a change in copy, would help the brand to regain its momentum. Feeling that the funds could be better spent in launching a new product, management vetoed the proposal. But the new product failed to move off the shelf despite heavy marketing support. At the same time, the old brand, with its props pulled out from under it, went into a sales decline from which it never recovered. The company had two losers on its hands.[3]

In this instance, the manufacturer was clearly torn by a typical conflict of priorities. There is also a sometimes obsessive fear of the competition. When, in the late 1960s, Warner-Lambert was faced in Canada with aggressive new competitors (including Procter & Gamble) whose activities reduced the market share of Warner-Lambert's mouthwash Listerine, the company seriously considered removing advertising support from the brand and milking it for profit, although Listerine was still significantly the market leader, was still used on the most recent occasion by a third of all mouthwash users, and still kept a clear lead over all its competitors in virtually all image attributes when the various competitive brands were rated by consumers. Warner-Lambert's attitude toward the brand gives a remarkable insight into the psychological pressures of oligopolistic competition, although here wiser counsel prevailed. Support for the brand was increased and not decreased, with generally beneficial results.[4]

Much of the difficulty regarding life cycles stems from a failure to distinguish between a product and a brand. Products can become obsolete, but brands need not become obsolete if they are adapted functionally to remain competitive. This always requires continuous product improvement and generally also the launch of new varieties. (The leading laundry detergent Tide comes in eight different versions.)

It is, however, only too common to find examples of the opposite—of once-substantial brands that have dwindled. This should immediately prompt us to ask how many reductions in the market shares of existing brands following the launch of new brands are caused by conscious transfer of resources from the old to the new. This often represents tragic misjudgment, because the growth of added values in an old brand represents a genuine investment and source of quantifiable scale economies all too often sacrificed through a misled belief in the inevitability of the brand's decline. To make matters worse, the new investment for which so much is sacrificed produces in many cases an unsuccessful or mediocre new brand. Remember that most new brands are unsuccessful.

One of the temptations to milk a brand (to turn it into a "cash cow") is the fact that the withdrawal of support means an immediate increase in profit. But this is temporary, because sales invariably decline, so that the brand after a time yields not only a much-reduced profit, but also often a drastically reduced contribution to the general overhead.

Observation of oligopolistic markets demonstrates unambiguously the rapid pace of innovation. But for oligopolists to survive, the qualities of balance and judgment that should lead them to nurture the old and extract the maximum return from past investments are second only in importance to the urge to participate in the forward thrust of innovation that the competitive nature of the market demands. Some 20%-30% of the brands of most established manufacturers were not on the market 5 years before.[5] But the intelligent manufacturer who plans for the long term invariably accompanies this internal shift with a rising total market share, so as not to pay for new successes by undersupporting established and almost certainly more profitable brand properties. Based on the firm's observed behavior in the marketplace, Procter & Gamble is clearly an organization that accepts this philosophy. One former P&G brand manager has noted, "The first thing they tell you is, 'Forget product life cycles and cash cows!' One of the soaps has been reformulated over eight times and is thriving." [6]

Procter & Gamble's main competitor, Unilever, shares the same view. Sir David Orr, who was chairman of Unilever for 8 years, has stated:

> Just as major brands collectively have shown that they can survive and prosper, so have individual brands refuted the concept of life cycles for products. The

decline, or "milking" phase of the life cycle exists only as a self-fulfilling prophecy. A brand is a wasting asset, one that must be replaced and rejuvenated if it is to thrive. Provided that it is kept up-to-date as a product, by technical innovation and updating, and that its communication is kept relevant, it can be sustained for decades or more.[7]

Notes

1. R. Polli and V. J. Cook, "Validity of the Product Life Cycle," *Journal of Business,* October 1969, 385-400; R. Polli, *A Test of the Classical Product Life Cycle by Means of Actual Sales Histories* (privately published, Philadelphia, 1968).

2. Estimates based on the statements of Murray Lubliner, president of Lubliner/Saltz, in the feature article " 'Old Standbys' Hold Their Own," *Advertising Age,* September 19, 1983, 32.

3. Nariman K. Dhalla and Sonia Yuspeh, "Forget the Product Life Cycle Concept," *Harvard Business Review,* January/February 1976, 102.

4. Stephen A. Greyser and Robert J. Kopp, *Cases in Advertising and Communications Management,* 3rd ed. (Englewood Cliffs, NJ: Prentice Hall, 1992), 85-86.

5. James O. Peckham, Sr., *The Wheel of Marketing,* 2nd ed. (privately published, 1981; available from A. C. Nielsen, New York), 80. The 3M Company requires each of its 40 operating divisions to generate 25% of any year's sales with brands introduced during the previous 5 years. See Thomas J. Peters and Robert H. Waterman, Jr., *In Search of Excellence: Lessons From America's Best-Run Companies* (New York: Harper & Row, 1982), 233.

6. Quoted in Peters and Waterman, *In Search of Excellence,* 233.

7. Sir David Orr, "Foreword," in John Philip Jones, *Does It Pay to Advertise? Cases Illustrating Successful Brand Advertising* (New York: Simon & Schuster-Lexington, 1989), xx.

17

The Defensive Role of Advertising

Paul Feldwick

Can Advertising Pay for Itself by Incremental Sales?

In 1983, a new television campaign for Hofmeister lager beer in the United Kingdom produced impressive sales results.[1] Analysis showed fairly conclusively that an advertising expenditure of £1.7 million sterling had been responsible, within the same year, for additional profit to the client of £1.9 million sterling.

This case conforms to the popular expectation of a successful advertising campaign. The client spent a pound and got more than a pound back. Claude Hopkins wrote, "The only purpose of advertising is to make sales. It is profitable or unprofitable according to its actual sales. Treat it as a salesman. Force it to justify itself."[2] The Hofmeister campaign was a salesman who had earned his wage.

The trouble is, cases like Hofmeister are very rare. Part of the reason for this, of course, is that not all advertising succeeds in meeting its objectives—a point that is too often forgotten. But this type of short-term payback is unusual even among successful campaigns. Hofmeister was a very large brand already, due to its exclusive distribution in most Courage pubs; it was worth more than £100 million sterling. And the new campaign—not its first advertising, but its first effective advertising, so in a way still a launch campaign—suddenly stepped up its rate of sale by 13%. A large brand, a dramatic movement in sales—the combination of these two elements is very unusual.

Consider the arithmetic. An advertiser might spend £1 million sterling on advertising. If the gross profit margin on sales is 33%, the company will need to see an increase of around £3 million sterling in net revenue before it even gets its money back. On a £15 million sterling brand, this is an extra 20%, and not just for a month or two but sustained across a whole year. This might just happen in a growing market, but then that growth could not be attributed entirely to advertising. In a mature market it means that growth must come at a competitor's expense. To sustain a modest budget of £1 million sterling per annum, this rate of growth would have to take place every year.

If advertisers are spending their money in the expectation of a short-term sales increase big enough to return their investments with interest, the vast majority are almost bound to be disappointed. Extensive analyses of advertising elasticities show that they average around 0.2; that is, a 1% increase in advertising will create an increase in revenue of 0.2%.[3] For most brands with established budgets, this calculation will show that they would be more profitable if they reduced their ad spending.

Either major advertisers such as Mars Pedigree and Unilever are sadly misled or there is some other reason for continuing to advertise established brands at the weights they do. One way of explaining the benefits they get is to talk of "long-term effects." In other words, the advertising cost not covered by immediate revenue increases will be paid for out of revenue increases in years to come. This is nearly right, but not totally convincing, because the expectation is that similar advertising budgets will also be spent in years to come, with similar modest sales effects—so that even if the hypothetical long-term effects materialize, they will never result in payback from incremental revenue.

But we need to be clear about what the word *incremental* means. Any financial appraisal of a business cost should start not with a straight-line projection, but with a realistic base-case scenario of *what would happen if the investment were not made.* The assumption made in the preceding paragraph is that the base-case scenario (for sales without advertising) would be a straight line. Some people will argue and more people will simply assume that this is more or less correct—that once advertising has built a brand, its sales will continue at the same rate almost indefinitely. And if this were the case, the continued investment in advertising would never pay back. It makes financial sense only when we can assume that without advertising, revenue would sooner or later suffer.

A Defensive Role for Advertising

It therefore makes sense to talk of the major justification for advertising of established products as defensive. Although advertising may continue to build volume and revenue over time, and although, in particular circumstances, it may achieve startling and dramatic results, the majority of the money is being spent, as Tom Corlett said a long time ago, to protect the 90% of sales the brand already has, rather than to gain a possible extra 10%.[4]

In any given case, the hypothesis that revenue would decline without advertising is notoriously difficult to prove. A year or two without advertising often has little clear effect on sales, giving encouragement to those who think sustained advertising is unnecessary. It is possible that during this time the brand is living off a reservoir of goodwill built up with the help of advertising over previous years, which will be difficult to replenish once it is empty. The only way to test this hypothesis is to withdraw advertising until the brand visibly suffers, by which time it is often too late. Even when we observe that the withdrawal of advertising over a period of time accompanies the decline or death of a brand, there is usually some room for debate over which was cause and which was effect.

There is a good deal of evidence that the defensive hypothesis will often hold true. Analyses published by PIMS show correlations between advertising/sales ratios, perceived quality, and profitability.[5] The *Advertising Works* series published by the British Institute of Practitioners in Advertising (IPA) has included some detailed examples of the "longer and broader" effects of advertising, particularly the cases of PG Tips and Andrex.[6] What has been discussed less, however, is the process by which these so-called long-term effects occur.

Advertising agencies have not always been their own best advocates in this matter. "Long-term effects" or "brand effects" are talked about as if they work in mysterious ways that have little connection with short-term sales effects. At worst, agencies can use the rhetoric of "long-term effects" or "brand imagery" as an attempt to justify any piece of advertising that is failing to show results in the marketplace. If advertisers are to accept the defensive role of advertising, they deserve a rather more reasoned explanation of how it works.

We know from experiments conducted years ago by Colin McDonald that advertising has immediate effects on the probability of an individual's buying the advertised brand at the next purchase occasion.[7] These immediate effects, because small, have often been disregarded by ad agencies as irrelevant. It seems most likely, however, that these small influences on behavior have a powerful cumulative effect over time, and that consumers' attitudes and behavior (both modified by advertising) are mutually reinforcing. Established behavior and the attitudes that go with it will persist for a considerable time in the absence of advertising, but will sooner or later be eroded by other influences—not least of these being competitors' advertising. Although it is possible to find examples of genuine "long-term effects"—in the sense of advertising memories that persist over a number of months or years and continue to affect behavior—we also know that most advertising memories decay in a more or less predictable manner. The majority of advertising's effects on the individual consumer should therefore be apparent relatively soon after exposure, and these short-term effects are likely to constitute the building blocks of how long-term effects on brand performance are built up. To make sense of this, however, we need to go beyond the commonly held notion that advertising works by "persuasion."

The historical model of how advertising works is something like this:

Prospect sees/hears advertisement → prospect buys product.

This sequence of events is elaborated in well-known "linear-sequential" models such as "Awareness–Interest–Desire–Action" (AIDA) and "Defining Advertising Goals for Measured Advertising Results" (DAGMAR). It sounds obvious; in fact, Russell Colley (the author of DAGMAR) felt he needed to justify his hierarchical model only by saying that it is "applied common sense." [8]

And this is what the public, on the whole, thinks advertising is meant to do. However, the interesting thing is that no members of the public think it does it to them. They say, "Advertising doesn't make me buy the product."

This model is highly pervasive, but it can probably be dated back to the influence of Claude Hopkins in the 1920s. What we tend to forget is that all of Hopkins's experience was in direct-response advertising. And this is a fair model for direct response. Direct response could be evaluated as if it were a salesman. The ad was supposed to take the prospect from ignorance, to conviction, and then to a sale; the sale was the end of the sequence.

This is very different from what we expect, say, television advertising to do for an established packaged goods brand. In the case of television advertising, there is very little ignorance. Most of our potential customers have bought our brand many times before. They have formed their own opinions about it from experience, and they are unlikely to take seriously anything we say that conflicts at all with that experience. And the sale, as far as they and we are concerned, is far from being the end of the process. We want them to go on buying the brand, again and again.

In this repeat-purchase situation, it is far harder to change people's minds about things. However, we have evidence that advertising can still influence their behavior in a number of ways:

- Through memories and associations accessed during the purchase decision
- Through reinforcement of existing behavior
- Through transformation or enhancement of the experience of the product itself

Memories and Associations Accessed During the Purchase Decision

First of all, it is important to remember that most people are not brand loyal in any absolute sense; they buy within a repertoire of brands, and their decisions about which of the repertoire to choose on particular occasions are often trivial—driven by habit, desire for a change, or a penny or two price difference (or, of course, availability, a particular need, and so on). Given the essential triviality of the choice, memories and associations created by advertising, perhaps even the fact of advertising itself, can be enough to nudge the shopper toward one brand or another. It is important to note that ideas or images created in this way need not amount to conviction on the part of the consumer in order to affect behavior, contrary to models like DAGMAR, which posit conviction as a necessary stage before purchase.

Reinforcement of Existing Behavior

It is difficult (although by no means impossible) to change people's minds with advertising. What advertising does very well, however, is reinforce their existing beliefs and patterns of behavior. A consumer will not only be inclined to believe an advertisement for a product that she has bought and found satisfactory, she will be positively encouraged that she made the right decision and that her judgment of it has been endorsed. All of which leads to an increased probability of her buying it again in the future. This notion of reinforcement has been much talked about in connection with the so-called weak theory of advertising—giving rise, perhaps, to the belief that re-inforcement is itself a weak force. But as anyone who has been involved in behavior modification knows (training dogs to obey commands, or children to pick up their clothes), regular positive reinforcement of the desired behavior is far more effective than threats or punishment. Reinforcement is in fact a powerful way of affecting, and indeed modifying, behavior.

Transformation or Enhancement of the Experience of the Product Itself

There is, however, a third mechanism by which advertising has an effect on consumer behavior. This mechanism has been called *transformation* by Wells, and more recently has been demonstrated in a valuable experiment carried out in 1994 by the research organization Millward Brown, which calls it *enhancement.*[9] Millward Brown's experiment showed that exposure to advertising had no positive effect on people's intention to buy a new product, but that among those who had tried the product, exposure to advertising substantially increased their satisfaction with the product and their intention to repurchase subsequently. In other words, people are very suggestible: Their experience of the product itself will be enhanced, or transformed, by images or messages received via advertising. All of which will come as no surprise to those who have seen the usual results of blind versus branded product tests, or Alan Branthwaite and Peter Cooper's experiment on analgesics (reported in the *British Medical Journal*), which demonstrated that a preferred brand of painkiller was 25% more effective than a chemically identical, unbranded product.[10] It can therefore be argued that advertising actually creates a part of the satisfaction that the user derives from the brand.

In place of the traditional "persuasion" model, then, which depicts advertising creating conviction that leads to a sale, the consumer should be seen as buying repeatedly from a repertoire of brands. At a number of stages in this continuous process—while buying, after buying, and while using the product—advertising has the potential to increase the probability that the consumer will choose the advertised brand either at that time or on a future occasion. Repeated over time, these processes will build up a strongly reinforced pattern of purchasing behavior that will resist competitive activity or price dealing and so create the phenomenon we refer to as a "strong brand."

The implications of the defensive role of advertising should be taken seriously. Although much in this chapter is far from new, in real life many clients, agencies, and researchers still continue to talk and behave as if advertising were all about conquest. For one thing, the politics of business encourage brand managers to set growth objectives every year, however unrealistic these may be, and however often they fail to attain them. This may in itself be a fairly harmless bit of self-delusion. But the assumption that advertising is all about growth can lead to a number of inappropriate choices when it comes to planning, testing, and evaluating the campaign.

At the planning stage, how much emphasis is put on understanding existing users' attitudes toward the brand and its competitors, compared with peripheral or nonusers?

Although marketing people will always rightly consider barriers to purchase and opportunities for growth, it can be easy to include a disproportionate number of nonusers in research samples, in both qualitative and quantitative work. Perhaps the worst example of this is the continued use of the persuasion test for established brands—a design that explicitly sets out the ability of the ad to "convert" nonusers and tells us nothing about the reactions of users.

And sales evaluation, in the absence of clearly specified objectives, still starts from an unspoken assumption that the evidence of a successful campaign will be a sales increase.

So some implications for advertisers might be as follows:

- Budgets should be planned on a strategic, rather than tactical, basis. Either advertising is a key factor for success of the brand or it is not. It cannot be a luxury to be indulged in when there is spare money around or a reserve that can be raided to make up profit targets.

- In planning creative strategy, the primary focus should be on existing users and an understanding of the core values of the brand.

- In evaluative research, the emphasis should be on measures of involvement with the advertising and of closeness to the brand, not persuasion. Econometrics can be used to look not just at short-term effects but at relative brand strength as shown by price elasticity. Overall, the long-term success of the advertising should be evaluated using a brand audit approach.

Conclusion

Does it pay to advertise? It depends on the corporate objective. If the objective is to maximize this year's profit, it may be hard to justify advertising. But if the business is to be flourishing in 10 years' time, advertising may be a valuable and even a necessary investment.

Most managers will complain that the pressure to short-termism is forced on them by the stock market and the demand for frequent reporting of profit figures. Yet the price of stock, theoretically at least, is based on a prospect of long-term earnings. Analysts should be astute enough to see where companies are artificially inflating their profit figures by cutting back on advertising, and such a failure to invest for the future in marketing expenses, as with research and development, should set alarm bells ringing.

Notes

1. C. Channon, "Hofmeister Lager," in C. Channon (ed.), *Advertising Works 3* (London: Holt, Rinehart & Winston, 1985), 70-83.

2. Claude Hopkins, *Scientific Advertising* (Chicago: Crain, 1966), 220.

3. See John Philip Jones, *How Much Is Enough? Getting the Most From Your Advertising Dollar* (New York: Simon & Schuster-Lexington, 1992), 110, for references.

4. Tom Corlett, "How We Should Measure the Longer-Term Effects of Advertising on Purchasing," *Admap,* September 1976, 422-433.

5. Alexander L. Biel, "Strong Brand, High Spend: Tracking Relationships Between the Marketing Mix and Brand Values," *Admap,* November 1990, 35-40.

6. See Paul Feldwick (ed.), *Advertising Works 6* (Henley-on-Thames, UK: NTC, 1991), 3-24; and C. Baker (ed.), *Advertising Works 7* (Henley-on-Thames, UK: NTC, 1993), 53-74.

7. Colin McDonald, "What Is the Short-Term Effect of Advertising?" paper presented at the ESOMAR Conference, Barcelona, 1970; reprinted in Simon Broadbent (ed.), *Market Researchers*

Look at Advertising (Amsterdam: Sigmatext for the European Society for Opinion and Marketing Research, 1980), 39-50.

8. Russell Colley, *Defining Advertising Goals for Measured Advertising Results* (New York: Association of National Advertisers, 1961), 53.

9. See William D. Wells, John Burnett, and Sandra Moriarty, *Advertising: Principles and Practice* (Englewood Cliffs, NJ: Prentice Hall, 1992), 258; and Andy Farr and Gordon Brown, "Persuasion or Enhancement? An Experiment," in *Market Research Society Conference Proceedings* (Birmingham, UK: Market Research Society, 1994), 69-77.

10. Alan Branthwaite and Peter Cooper, "Analgesic Effects of Branding in Treatment of Headaches," *British Medical Journal,* no. 2821.

18

Are All Consumers Equal?

Segmentation: The Statute of Limitations

Mark Stockdale

Once upon a time, there was a toiletries and cosmetics client. One day, during a discussion about the launch of a new hair-care brand, he made an impassioned case for targeting "anyone with hair." The agency team thought it best to share with him some of their concerns. Might it be difficult to put together a cogent media plan against such a broad and vaguely defined target audience? Might they encounter some difficulty in identifying a coherent proposition for such a variety of people?

Yet the more they all talked, the more entrenched the client became. The agency became alarmed that he may even decide to add "anyone without hair" so as not to exclude anybody from his target audience.

The brand was eventually launched (by another agency) and, despite a significant advertising investment, was never heard of again. The media budget was dissipated across such a range of viewers that few people got to see much of the brand's advertising, and even if they did, being so blandly generic, it had very little of interest to say to anyone.

A fairy tale? Sadly not—a true story. This may be an extreme example, but it is not an isolated one.

The erstwhile client in this story represents a school of thought that believes that to segment is to limit. And, of course, it is. The question is whether such limits on target audience definition are desirable. Those who feel uncomfortable with segmentation see any limitation as unnecessary and undesirable.

Add to this doubt the misery that can accompany the implementation of segmentation studies, and it is no wonder this is often a contentious topic. There are three Miserable Ps of implementation: politics, principles, and practicalities:

- Politics can be messy, to say the least. Segmentation by its very nature cuts across most functional areas of the company, and turf wars can break out. Individual functions may even feel forced into suboptimal plans of action as companywide target audiences are "imposed" upon them.

- Agreeing on the principles of how to conduct a segmentation is often difficult. Should we use systems derived from demographics (such as SAGACITY), or values (such as VALS), or needs/benefit clustering, or lifestyles, or attitudes, or pure behavior, or something else? (A recent issue of the *Journal of Marketing Management* even included an article that discussed the use of astrological star signs as a basis for segmentation.) There are so many approaches and so much conflicting advice, it should not be surprising that many studies struggle even to get to an agreed-upon initial proposal.

- Segmentation studies typically confront a number of practical problems. In particular, they can be very expensive (data collection can necessitate significant primary research) and involve highly complex analyses (teasing meaningful segments from a multivariate data soup is rarely easy).

And it is not just down here on the ground among us practitioners that segmentation faces some resistance. It also finds detractors in the more rarefied high altitude of academia. In a recent article, Ned Anscheutz concludes that segmenting is not in the interests of brand growth: "The mantra to segment . . . leads ironically in a direction that is *opposite* of what is really needed. . . . [What is needed] is the *opposite* of segmentation." This argument is based largely on Ehrenberg's analysis of repeat buying. Ehrenberg has demonstrated that the profile of heavy/medium/light buyers of any brand can be estimated using a common distribution function, which he calls the *nega-*

tive binomial distribution (NBD). If you know a brand's penetration, average weight of purchase, and interpurchase interval, you can predict the shape of its NBD and hence its profile of light/medium/heavy buyers.

Anscheutz argues that this implies the primary aim of all marketing activity must be—above all else—to drive penetration: If the profile of heavy/medium/light buyers always fits a "preordained" distribution, surely, he suggests, the only thing we can control is penetration. In other words, segmentation is wrong because it prevents us from expanding our target audience to include as many people as possible, thus undesirably limiting potential penetration gains. Anscheutz goes on to argue, "Advertising is one of the few elements of the marketing mix that can build broadly appealing popularity for a brand."

To put this another way, in the 1970s Paul Stevens—then a somewhat disillusioned copywriter with a New York advertising agency—wrote a book titled *I Can Sell You Anything.* In it, he asserted that the central ethical problem with advertising is that it is capable of selling anything to anyone, regardless of how good or bad the thing is. Stevens may not have realized it then, but his views have much in common with those of Anscheutz. In order for advertising to do what Anscheutz describes—generating broadly popular appeal for any brand—it must be innately capable of talking to (and ultimately, if it is to succeed, selling to) as near to an almost universal cross section of people as possible.

I disagree with both Anscheutz and Stevens. I believe that segmentation matters because targeting matters, and that good targeting increases advertising effectiveness. It may not always be easy in practice, but understanding market segmentation is a prerequisite of success—just as targeting "anyone with hair" is a prerequisite of failure.

How Good Targeting Improves Advertising Effectiveness

Let me start with the easiest point of all: Good targeting through segmentation improves advertising effectiveness. This is easy not least because there is available a wealth of published case study material that shows how advertising has made a contribution to business success. One of the most valuable sources is the "Advertising Effectiveness" database maintained by the United Kingdom's Institute of Practitioners in Advertising (IPA).

The IPA Effectiveness Awards have been running biennially since 1980. Written papers are judged and awards made not only by advertising and marketing practitioners, but also by university academics, management consultants, financial and accountancy professionals, and others. In short, the competition is tough, and submissions are required to present rigorous proof, using hard results and quantitative data, of the contribution made by advertising to business success. To date, the IPA database comprises nearly 1,000 case studies covering more than 20 product categories. The winning cases tell us a great deal about how advertising works—indeed, the IPA has published a number of guides to best practice.

From the IPA database, it is clear that effective advertising begins with a clear understanding of who is being talked to. A few brands, generally because of their sheer size, have to address very wide target audiences, but—crucially—none seeks to talk to absolutely everyone; every brand deliberately limits its audience to some extent. Moreover, the vast majority of brands target very specific consumer segments, generally determined by factors specific to the product category or brand, or on the basis of relevant consumer attributes.

I could present case after case to illustrate how segmented targeting helps to maximize advertising effectiveness, but that could take up a book in itself. So instead I will go through one case in particular, simply because it is such a pure demonstration of the power of appropriately defined segmentation.

Security Pacific Bank used to market loans to upmarket British customers who had reasonable disposable incomes and substantial net assets. Put more simply, the bank targeted safe, profitable customers. Then, during the massive spending and credit boom of the mid-1980s, the so-called Big Four U.K. banks decided to drive their loans business more aggressively. And so Security Pacific found its core business under serious threat from the largest of its advertising competitors. That there was little or no difference between the products made matters worse.

Security Pacific used advertising to sell direct off-the-page and measured performance through an "effectiveness ratio"—the ratio of the amount of money loaned to advertising expenditure. From a peak of 200:1 in the early 1980s, this fell to 20:1. Breakeven was 100:1.

The bank was in dire straits and so considered its options carefully. It ruled out the possibility of taking on the Big Four banks head-to-head, because it was hard to see how Security Pacific could possibly win. So instead the bank took a fresh look at segmentation.

After some careful research, it was decided that Security Pacific would target one very specific segment: "enthusiasts," or people with strong particular interests, such as vintage car collectors, yachtsmen, and hang gliders. The research told Security Pacific that people in this segment felt insecure about going to their normal bank managers for loans to finance their hobbies. The British have always had an uneasy relationship with money in general and financiers in particular, and many enthusiasts believed major banks would feel that wanting to buy a 1930s Bentley sports car, for example, would be a poor justification for a £60,000 personal loan.

So Security Pacific used specialist press to reach the various types of enthusiasts and talk to them sympathetically about their hobbies, their need for financing, and their insecurities regarding the Big Banks. As a result, the bank's effectiveness ratio rose to 450:1—its highest ever. And this was achieved with less media expenditure because the segments were so easy to target and reach, with a product that was entirely unchanged and against a general background of vastly increased competitive activity from the Big Four banks.

The use of segmentation was the one and only thing that dramatically improved Security Pacific's advertising effectiveness.

Why Does Segmentation Help to Maximize Advertising Effectiveness?

Ned Anscheutz would be particularly dismayed by the way in which Leo Burnett approaches segmentation: Not only does the agency believe in segmentation, but it thinks in terms of two layers of segmentation. On the one hand, we need to understand who the brand is for—who has or could have need of it? This is called the *target group segment,* and it is generally a core output from developing the overall brand strategy. On the other hand, within this overall target group there are likely to be a range of possible subsegments—perhaps people with very different relationships with the brand, or differing patterns of usage. By understanding these *target group subsegments,* we can construct more effective communications plans that, as far as possible, target the right messages to each sort of person who makes up the overall target for the brand.

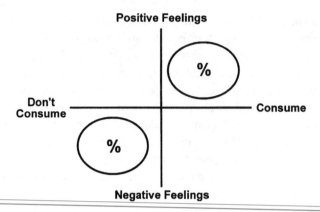

Figure 18.1. Attitudinal/Behavioral Consumer Quadrants: 1

The agency's experience shows that the key to effective target group (sub)segmentation is understanding patterns of consumer behavior—not attitude or values, but behavior. It may be that attitudinal data or values groupings add color to our description of the various target segments, but first and foremost they are defined in terms of behavior.

Take McDonald's, for example. The overall target group segment is extremely broad, by nature of the breadth of the brand's functional roles for lots of different people. But within this target group, advertising has been produced to target specific subsegments according to the time of the day/meal occasion, life stage/age group, and product/service benefit. Each of these strands of subsegmentation receives communications tailored specifically to ensure that it receives the most relevant message.

Gordon's Gin faces a slightly more complex targeting issue. The brand, although market leader, has been in long-term decline in the United Kingdom. Its existing drinkers are older (and somewhat upmarket), and the brand needs to recruit a new generation of younger drinkers if it is to survive into the next century. At first sight, one may be forgiven for thinking that such a split target audience is irreconcilable—that the brand needs to target all adults, young and old. Perhaps, then, this is a case that supports Anscheutz's thesis.

Not so. At Leo Burnett we have developed a range of segmentation tools, one of which segments people according to the relationships they have with brands—behaviorally and emotionally.

There is a commonly held belief that all consumers of a brand feel positively predisposed to it, and that nonconsumers do not—a situation

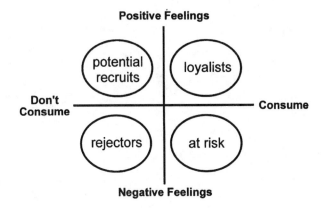

Figure 18.2. Attitudinal/Behavioral Consumer Quadrants: 2

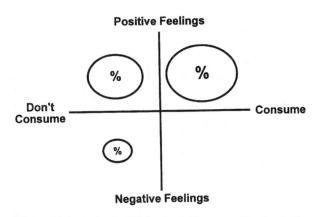

Figure 18.3. Attitudinal/Behavioral Consumer Quadrants: 3

illustrated in Figure 18.1. The reality is less clear-cut, as anyone familiar with tracking or usage and attitudes data will have observed. Every brand has a proportion of consumers who do not feel entirely positive about it—some may feel merely ambivalent, but some will actually feel slightly negative. Conversely, there are people who feel relatively good about a brand but do not consume it—even though they consume other brands from within the same category. This means that we can identify four key types of consumers according to how they behave and how they feel about a brand (see Figure 18.2).

Importantly, different brands within the same category exhibit different profiles. Clearly, a brand is in a healthy position if the majority of category

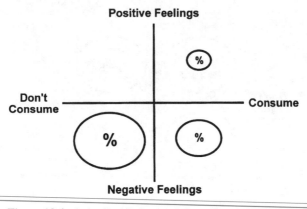

Figure 18.4. Attitudinal/Behavioral Consumer Quadrants: 4

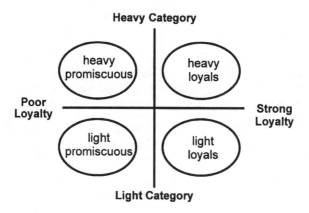

Figure 18.5. Behavioral Consumer Quadrants: 1

consumers feel positive about it (see Figure 18.3). And, conversely, it is in an unhealthy position if the majority of a category's consumers feel negative about it (Figure 18.4).

We can take our understanding of consumer behavior further by looking at each consumer's loyalty and weight of category consumption. This is a widely used method of segmenting databases, for example, and it allows us to identify different patterns of consumer behavior (see Figure 18.5).

Again, different brands tend to exhibit very different profiles. Clearly, a healthy brand will have a lot of heavy loyals (see Figure 18.6), and an

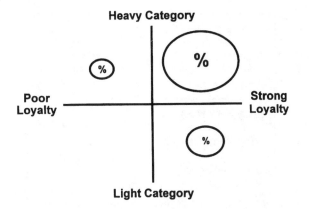

Figure 18.6. Behavioral Consumer Quadrants: 2

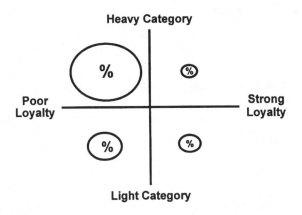

Figure 18.7. Behavioral Consumer Quadrants: 3

unhealthy brand will have poor loyalty and/or a high proportion of light consumers (see Figure 18.7).

We combine these various behavioral and emotional relationships to analyze how close people are to the brand—segmentation via "brand proximity" (see Figure 18.8). In the case of Gordon's, we identified a series of such subsegments (see Figure 18.9).

The older existing "heavy loyal" drinkers and the younger potential "hot recruits" are in psychological terms very close to the Gordon's brand. Indeed, they share remarkably similar perceptions, and this enables us to use a

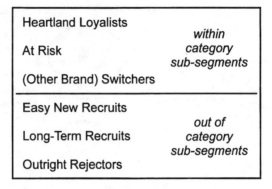

Figure 18.8. Segmentation via "Brand Proximity"

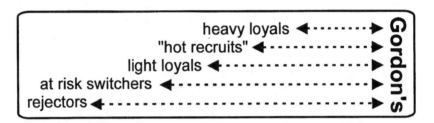

Figure 18.9. Segmentation for Gordon's Gin

common creative approach to speak to them both. So instead of targeting all adults, young and old, we target people on the basis of their closeness to the brand.

Moreover, understanding the relationships different types of people have with Gordon's allows us to identify appropriate roles for communications—such as reinforcing perceptions of product quality for "at-risk switchers," dramatizing the brand benefit for "light loyals," or explaining how to mix a perfect Gordon's and tonic for "hot recruits." And because for each of these roles we know exactly whom we are targeting, we also know precisely what media to use.

In the United States, Leo Burnett was one of the sponsors of the Information Resources Inc. (IRI) single-source study that was originally published in 1992. As part of Burnett's involvement, the agency took on a number of key analysis projects under the guidance of Josh McQueen, global head of planning. In particular, the agency was interested in looking at those brands that had exhibited consistent growth.

One way in which we analyzed these brands was to use another Leo Burnett segmentation tool: Buyer Strategy Detection. This technique classifies consumers using consumer panel data according to their patterns of purchasing. We identify five types of purchasing behavior:

1. Long-term brand "loyals"

2. "Deal selectives," who chase promotional offers (but generally buy the brand leaders and not the discount brands/cheapest on display)

3. "Rotators," who are typically heavy consumers of the category, but who spread their purchases around (again, generally buying the brand leaders and not the discount brands/cheapest on display)

4. The "price driven," who promiscuously buy the cheap brands and anything on price offer

5. "Light users" of the category (whose purchasing is too light to exhibit any loyalty)

Different brands have differing mixes of the various buyer types. This is why, in the "proximity" analysis described in Figure 18.8, we find such variations in positive versus negative feelings among a brand's purchasers and such different patterns of buying behavior. Indeed, the difference between brands we might consider healthy and unhealthy can often be explained by Buyer Strategy profiles.

In the IRI study, the dominant Buyer Strategy type was identified for each of the brands that had shown long-term growth, and the brand's purchasing time series revealed whether this growth came from new purchasers (i.e., penetration growth) or from the same purchasers (i.e., increased buying rate). The source of brand growth was then compared with the buyer type (see Figure 18.10).

What is apparent is that brands with a lot of loyals tend, as one might expect, to gain most growth from buying rate (these brands also tend to be the bigger brands). And at the other extreme, brands with a lot of light users tend to get most of their growth from penetration gains. This is again as one might expect, because light users' purchases are so light that they show little or no loyalty to any brand, so as the brand begins to grow, by definition, every incremental purchase appears to have come from a new user.

TYPES OF CONSUMERS	CONTRIBUTION TO GROWTH		% OF BRANDS
	Penetration	Buying Rate	
Loyals	15%	85%	15%
Deal Selectives	50%	50%	17%
Rotators	68%	32%	20%
Price Driven	75%	25%	29%
Light Users	100%	0%	19%

Figure 18.10. Deconstruction of Brand Growth

Brands Develop in Different Ways

What Ned Anscheutz seems to have failed to understand is that not all brands grow in the same way. Each brand has a slightly different pattern of purchasing behavior, and the types of consumers who buy a brand will determine how best to make it grow.

Does this invalidate Ehrenberg's work? No—the negative binomial distribution is calculated using penetration, average weight of purchase, and interpurchase interval. The NBD is not some kind of curious, preordained, almost metaphysical law of marketing. It is simply derived from an arithmetical relationship among three related variables (e.g., if penetration goes up because light users have been recruited, the average purchase weight will obviously fall; plug the new figures into the model and it will generate a differently shaped distribution curve).

Paul Stevens's assertion that "I can sell you anything" is patently untrue. Gordon's Gin will never appeal to absolutely every adult in the United Kingdom—some will not like its taste, others will reject its imagery, and vast numbers of people eschew the delights of gin. In practice we have to understand all this, and doing so leads us to think about how best to limit our target audience to those most likely to buy. In other words, we have no choice but to segment.

And when we develop detailed strategies for growth, we need as much insight as possible into the "levers" we can use to grow the brand. Gordon's faces different issues and has different opportunities than the number-two gin brand. Similarly, not everyone is interested in a McDonald's breakfast. How different consumers relate to the brand—how they feel about it, how they use it now or could use it in the future—is the source of our insight. People are different, and so there are opportunities to grow the brand by addressing the specific characteristics of each type of person. Segmentation enables us to do this by giving us the insights we need into a brand's current and potential market.

So segmentation drives best practice. It facilitates targeting, and targeting is fundamental to implementing the most apposite communications plan. And this maximizes advertising effectiveness because segmentation is how brands grow. Advertising effectiveness is maximized because segmentation connects individual communications activities to the right target audiences, and the overall communications plan to the brand's underlying purchasing dynamics—the dynamics that will ultimately drive the brand's long-term growth.

19

Relationship Marketing

John Dalla Costa

The marketers of national brands recently have struggled to serve the increased value demands of consumers while thwarting the inroads of ever-more-astute retailers. Some businesspeople have questioned the very viability of brands, slashing investment in advertising and selling on price. This of course has only accelerated the demise of some brands. As consumer loyalty has declined, it seems that many in business have mistakenly assigned blame to the concept of branding rather than to the practice of marketing.

If marketing were a product, we would plot its life-cycle trajectory as a mature one. In the vernacular of the Boston Consulting Group, marketing would be more of a "cash cow" than a "star." Hence the attitude of so many businesspeople that marketing is an activity for "harvesting" rather than "investing."

The Streetwise Consumer

The decline and growing irrelevance of conventional marketing are understandable. In many ways the consumers at whom marketing activity is targeted are really no longer consumers. The harsh, enduring effects of the continuous

225

restructuring of the now-global economy have undermined the confidence and job security upon which attitudes toward consumption are based. People are generally more demanding, more discerning—not just "street-smart" but increasingly "streetwise." Inherent in this wisdom is an appreciation that a product's value goes beyond function and price, to include the broader issues of shared values, environmental accountability, job creation, and support for community causes.

That the interaction between an individual and a product now carries such broadened expectations has also diminished the role of the traditional marketing function within many companies. During the 1980s, managers learned that the only way to achieve continuous improvement was to make quality a preoccupation for every discipline within an organization. Relationships are the concern of this chapter. Now that the management of such relationships is the new priority for competitive differentiation, many companies are using the same principle to spread the understanding of customer needs throughout their structures. The insights into relationships, once the exclusive domain of marketers, are now the common currency of design, engineering, research and development, manufacturing, distribution, sales, and service.

Retailer Revitalization

If national marketers need tangible proof of their declining authority, they need look no further than the resurgence of retailers. Store brands, once the poor-quality, low-price cousins of the national entries, have in many product categories become the new badges of the smart consumer. Food retailers such as Loblaws in Canada and Sainsbury's in the United Kingdom have turned the value relationship upside down. In offering more of what the consumer values, retailers have not only increased their own relevance to their customers, they have effected a fundamental repositioning of national brands.

Grant McCracken, a market researcher and anthropologist at Toronto's Royal Ontario Museum, has observed that the new store brands have "successfully co-opted the cynicism" that consumers felt toward traditional marketers.[1] That they could buy a better product for less money confirmed consumers' impressions that national brands—with their not-very-significant improvements and continuous discounting—were really not all they claimed to be.

Many marketers attribute the new power of modern retailers to the instantaneous tracking provided by scanner data. Such information certainly makes possible greater insight and understanding. Yet the success of retailers has come not from the data, but from their actions. Whereas many marketers plan and communicate to "the lowest common denominator," Loblaws assumes that its customers are curious, experimental, smart, and hungry for variety. The retailer does not buy the conventional wisdom that food is a low-involvement item, needing only cursory communication of its "taste benefits." Instead, Loblaws provides copious detail, using brochures, videos, infomercials, and a quarterly magazine titled *Insider's Report*. Loblaws has become expert in selling knowledge, capability, and confidence, as well as food.

Whereas many marketers moved away from image building in deference to the pragmatism of the 1990s, Loblaws simply built a more relevant image. The many people who stock the retailer's "President's Choice" products in their kitchens are appreciating the greater value, but are also making an important statement. They are saying, "Look how smart and self-confident I am, buying antibrands."

Store brands have often been seen as a cyclical phenomenon. Now that the economy is not so much cyclical as continuously chaotic, the value of store brands seems to be entrenched. With this enduring mainstream acceptance, store brands are redefining the expectations of consumers toward all marketers. People want more variety, more flexibility, more knowledge, more innovation, and more interaction. Conventional product planning, conventional marketing, and conventional advertising are too limited to carry the full bandwidth of these new consumer expectations.

Relationship Marketing

To connect with a more restless franchise, and to catch up with more aggressive retailers, many brand managers have begun to worship at the new altar of relationship marketing. Developing a multidimensional connection with individual consumers is seen as the way to revitalize tired brands, so in virtually every product category there have been new programs for listening, service, responding, and following up after sales. These are important initiatives. However, in most cases, the essential basis of marketing is still directed toward a transaction. Plans and objectives continue to focus almost exclusively on the product. Despite the growing use of toll-free telephone numbers for inquiries and sales, it seems as if the language and sensibilities of relationships have been co-opted by many marketers only as the latest ruse against an ever-more sophisticated and marketing-hardened target audience.

Human relationship building cannot work as a tactical embellishment to existing strategies; the very principles, obligations, and processes of marketing must change. As the initiators of this relationship, marketers are seeking to engage customers over their lifetimes, offering for their brands a combination of hard and soft attributes that encompass performance, added values, service, and a broader affinity with values and interests. Interconnecting on this higher plane with consumers involves creating ever-stronger bonds of trust, through what researcher Max Blackston calls "intimacy." [2] Marketers must listen better, respond more personally, give more of themselves, and understand individuals for more than their purchase behavior or preference criteria.

Extending marketing thinking to this realm of intimacy increases the opportunity for mutual exchange between a brand and a consumer. However, it also adds considerably to the responsibility of the marketer. To disappoint as a product risks losing a sale—to disappoint within a trusting relationship risks a far deeper and more damaging disrespect to the consumer.

Whether or not companies manage relationships, some consumers are already applying standards of relationship to the products and services they buy. One of the reasons Intel bungled its response to the flaw in its Pentium chip was that it totally underestimated the intimacy its users already extended to its product. Computers are not simply processors—for many people, they are extensions of their personal capabilities and creativity. That the flaw would not affect operations, as Intel initially protested, was irrelevant, because consumers were not judging their computers for their mathematical accuracy. The issue for many users was not the product issue of performance, but the relationship issue of integrity.

Relationship standards are being applied by consumers against virtually all brands, at all price points, in all categories. And even the most sophisticated marketers can stumble. Coke, the quintessential multinational, offended many Islamic believers by displaying the Saudi flag in a World Cup promotion, without realizing that this national emblem is inscribed with sacred text from the Koran. Archrival Pepsi fell victim to its own religious insensitivity by beaming a laser advertisement for a touring rock show on the bell tower of a medieval church in England. No harm was meant in either case. Apologies

Figure 19.1. Positioning Spectrum

and acts of contrition were quickly delivered. But the question remains, how could companies with so much research available to them, and with so many international resources supporting them, make such disrespectful transgressions?

Part of the answer is a limitation in the often-used concept of positioning. Marketers have used positioning since the mid-1970s to carve distinct, singular, and unique places for their brands within the often-jumbled perceptions, beliefs, and understanding of consumers. The focus of positioning has been competitive differentiation, creating the circumstances for brands like Coke and Pepsi to focus so much attention on each other that they occasionally miss talking to their own consumers. The orientation of positioning as a fixed, precise strategy is illustrated by a hypothetical brand in Figure 19.1.

As competition has intensified, and as consumers have grown more savvy, the rigidity of a fixed position has become more of a liability than an asset. Henry Mintzberg, business professor at McGill University, has argued that a strategic perspective is more relevant and effective than a strategic positioning.[3] Perspective is active, malleable, and adaptable; positioning is static and inflexible. Perspective embraces the consumer, whereas positioning deflects the competition.

In a world of relationships, brands must be more dynamic in order to grow and evolve with their changing consumers. In addition to providing the key performance and value variables, brands must have the breadth of character, responsibility, flexibility, insights, and interests to warrant their intimacy with their consumers. As shown in Figure 19.2, this requires that marketers create not so much a strategic position as a strategic space.

Occupying a strategic space affords a brand the latitude to expand the scope of stimulus to consumers. For more than 30 years, Dove has positioned itself as a beauty bar that contains "one-quarter cleansing cream." Each advertisement used a now classic mnemonic visual of the cream being poured into the Dove bar. Several years ago, the marketing group at Lever in Canada experimented with a new advertising approach—an idea that the Canadian com-

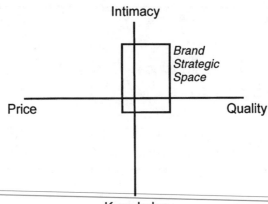

Figure 19.2. Relationship Spectrum

pany's president, Peter Ellwood, admitted was "technically off-strategy."[4] Using a litmus paper demonstration, the brand compared its mildness to that of others in its segment. In a brave departure, Dove's advertising contained no reference to its functional discriminator of one-quarter cleansing cream, nor did it resort to any of the traditional pouring shots.

Consumers responded immediately. The market share for Dove, which had been static, quickly grew several points. As a bonus, the litmus demonstration not only reinforced Dove's mildness, but also negatively repositioned brands such as Ivory and Neutrogena. Dove began to operate within a broader strategic space than before. Many marketers who resist such strategic flexibility are often confusing single-minded with simpleminded. Dove's experience shows that consumers, far from being disoriented, are smart enough to process more than one piece of information about a brand. The only requirements for this renewing stretch are relevance and respect.

Introducing: A "New and Improved" Approach

The interest in relationship marketing reflects a growing appreciation for two business fundamentals of today. First, companies are now viewing customers as assets who represent not individual transactions but lifetime values. This acknowledges that it is easier and more cost-efficient to grow with an existing consumer than to attract a new one. Second, companies now recognize that the equity of a brand is given value only by its consumer. Researchers such as Alexander Biel explain that marketers may engineer a certain value into a brand, but its equity is realized only in the interaction with a satisfied and willing buyer.[5] Because equity resides outside the brand, because it depends on interaction with consumers, relationship building is not a discretionary nicety, but a financial imperative.

To provide a structured approach to developing this more expansive marketing, we can compare the disciplines widely used for products with those that are needed for relationships:

Product Marketing Model	Relationship Marketing Model
Focus on the product.	Focus on the process for serving customers.
Define the target group.	Feed and nourish the relationship.
Set brand objectives.	Extend respect and value to customers.
Gain opportunity from analysis.	Gain opportunity from synergy.
Focus on brand benefit.	Develop and refresh relevance.
Create strategic advertising.	Open the doors for dialogue.
Operate against a brand plan.	Improvise to sustain the relationship.
Operate as driven by a marketing group.	Operate under a pervasive interdisciplinary attitude.

The purpose for suggesting such a radical change in the fundamental disciplines and language of marketing is to overcome the product bias within most companies. Product strategies remain valuable, but they are not complete. Following are some examples of companies that have begun to evolve their brand-centric marketing to focus more on the interaction and exchange required by relationships.

Marketing as Service

IKEA, the world's largest furniture retailer, sells a product that is not the least expensive, not the most convenient, and not the highest quality. It requires customers to drive to a single location, to design and choose their own room settings, to pull boxes out of the adjacent warehouse, and to take the materials home and assemble the furniture themselves. In the context of traditional marketing practice, this approach would seem to be a recipe for failure. In fact, the whole process involves interaction and respects the customer, and is therefore creating its own value. Marketing provides the information, the measuring tape, and a play area for the children. These are not so much selling tools as services that allow customers to use their own imagination and creativity.

Extending the Relationship

During the 1980s and 1990s, Chrysler completed a remarkable turnaround in North America and now boasts one of the most stylish and exciting model lineups in the automotive industry. In a recent advertising campaign, Chrysler chose to focus not on its cars, but on the jobs that its investments were creating in the local community. At the time, North America was in the third year of a jobless economic recovery, so Chrysler's message had significance for its relationships as well as its image.

Respecting the Consumer

Gillette has been enjoying considerable profitability since its Sensor brand preempted all the other wet shaving systems with a superior, floating-blade technology. In 1994, Gillette introduced yet another innovation: rubber fins on each blade that provide an even smoother shave. Wall Street analysts questioned why the company had launched yet another improvement when consumers were so satisfied and competitors so far behind. Gillette executives answered that it was their job "to amaze their customers." Such respect for the user leads to momentum for the brand.

Opportunities From Synergy

Molson, the largest brewer in Canada, started supporting small, local fund-raising efforts for AIDS research. Over the past 5 years, this involvement has grown, helping to raise more than $5.5 million (Canadian) in the Toronto market alone. This tactical program ultimately had strategic implications. In its market research, Molson learned that the majority of its core franchise supported its involvement in such community initiatives, preferring them even to the sports sponsorships that had been the traditional vehicles for beer marketing. Such community involvement, often regarded as tangential to business, has become essential.

Renewing Relevance

Nestlé's Taster's Choice developed a worldwide following for its advertising campaign featuring a romance between mature and sophisticated people. Most marketers believe that the way to break through clutter is repetition, but the opposite is true. In clutter, people have many options, so they will not sit through communication that is repetitive or boring. The saga used by Taster's Choice refreshed the message, involving the audience and giving them a reason to stay tuned. The campaign has been used in seven countries worldwide.

Strategic Improvisation

IBM found itself outflanked by competitors in large part because of the constraints of an overly developed, highly rigid strategic planning system. Bill Etherington, head of North American operations, compared IBM's old planning approach to a very deliberate and thoughtful chess game. While IBM plotted its next move on the strategic chess board, the marketplace transformed into an entirely different genre, becoming a real-time video game in which the competitors were firing live ammunition. In the urgent struggle for survival there was little time for strategic modeling. The company and its employees were forced to improvise to do whatever it took to secure customers and rebuild their trust. Success in such improvisation went a long way toward helping to restore the much-battered confidence of employees and to rebuild IBM's brand reputation and sales.

Interdisciplinary Trust

Canadian Airlines International (CAI) faced bankruptcy during the recession of the early 1990s. To reassure passengers who were watching reports in the business press of the company's life-and-death struggle, CAI developed a testimonial campaign that aired interviews with passengers and employees on television within hours of the footage being shot. People addressed the issues honestly, and the topicality of the dialogue impressed upon customers that CAI was not only still flying, but was very clever and resourceful. Achieving such immediacy required the client and the agency to ignore totally traditional roles and procedures. Employees and customers served as "creative directors," the agency producer served as "the client," the TV station that did the editing served as the "production house," and, within the time constraints of the exercise, the client was as powerless as a "junior account executive." Such interdisciplinary trust in the creation of the marketing program helped reestablish the company's trust with its jittery customers.

Process Changes

The process changes demanded by relationships challenge some of the most cherished beliefs of marketers. For instance, most of us who gained our experience in packaged goods marketing have been influenced by the doctrine of singularity: Find a single benefit, then repeat it single-mindedly. The literature about positioning emphasizes the importance of standing for a single value in the minds and hearts of consumers. Strategic counselors teach processes for arriving at a single basic stance. And creative people, after digesting the buzzwords of strategy documents, usually ask, "So, what's the hook?" The discipline of such focus is important, but the competitive chaos in most markets does not lend itself to single solutions.

Traditionalists will argue that it is exactly the complexity of the highly cluttered business environment that makes single-mindedness even more important. However, consumers and customers are far more marketing literate than we usually give them credit for. They can process more than one message. They can keep track of brand news, inducements, and extensions. The key is not complexity but relevance. If it means something to them, if it demonstrates both understanding and respect, consumers can and do keep track.

The fuzziness of the marketplace and the imprecise nature of relationships require marketers to look beyond a single selling benefit for their brands and to create a variety of relevant and synergistic inducements. Instead of a hook, modern advertisers need a Velcro-like approach:

Hook	Velcro
Single benefit	Multiple benefits
Single-minded	Many-sided
Repeats consistently	Consistently surprises
Fixed for the long term	Flexible for the short term
Differentiates versus competitor	Engages the customer
Presents a positioning	Surrounds with inducements
Focuses on transaction	Builds toward relationship
Simple for memorability	Complex for involvement

Conclusions

In an information economy, the creation of value depends more on knowledge than on "things." Marketing involves a packaging of knowledge—a bundling of "meaning"—so its importance to companies and brands will only increase. However, the practice and disciplines of marketing, which were designed to sell things, must change to reflect the importance of knowledge and understanding in the new value equation.

Business structures have been through endless waves of reengineering. The pressure for such process renewal is now affecting marketing departments as well. Rather than reengineer systems, it is far more important for marketers to "rehumanize" practices. Relationships with customers and consumers are tricky and messy. They force marketers to surrender the principles of control to achieve reciprocity, mutuality, and ongoing interaction. Strategic planning and market research have a place in this world of interaction, not as sources of definitive doctrine, but as tools for perspective and learning and for creating the space in which relationships between brands and consumers flourish.

Notes

1. Remarks made during a presentation given in June 1995.

2. Max Blackston, "Beyond Brand Personality: Building Brand Relationships," in David A. Aaker and Alexander L. Biel (eds.), *Brand Equity and Advertising* (Hillsdale, NJ: Lawrence Erlbaum, 1993), 121.

3. See Henry Mintzberg, *The Rise and Fall of Strategic Planning* (Toronto: Maxwell Macmillan, 1994).

4. Quoted from a personal interview in John Dalla Costa, *Working Wisdom: The Ultimate Value in the New Economy* (Toronto: Stoddart, 1995), 230.

5. Alexander L. Biel, "Converting Image Into Equity," in David A. Aaker and Alexander L. Biel (eds.), *Brand Equity and Advertising* (Hillsdale, NJ: Lawrence Erlbaum, 1993).

A Picture of a Brand

Campbell's Soup

Carla V. Lloyd

The Campbell Soup Company

The Campbell Soup Company of Camden, New Jersey, is a classical manufacturer of repeat-purchase packaged goods. The company's business is concentrated in the food trade. Its leading line, and the category in which it holds
a commanding position, is canned soup. Other branches of the company's
business trade under separate brand names, such as Pepperidge Farm for
cookies (and upmarket soups), Godiva for chocolate, and Prego for spaghetti
sauce. This is a policy that avoids dilution of Campbell's core franchise.

Campbell's strong position in the soup category is secured by a number of
well-established and successful policies:

1. *A focus of the product line on soup:* The only other products that also carry the Campbell's name are a small number of related lines (e.g., baked beans and vegetable juices).

2. *Maintenance of high product quality:* The company's quality standards are based on tested recipes and excellent natural ingredients.

3. *A wide range of varieties:* The average supermarket carries on its shelves at least 50 flavors of Campbell's (standard) condensed soup.

4. *Controlled segmentation:* Campbell's condensed soups account for two-thirds of the brand's total sales, but the brand name embraces a number of specialist lines of condensed soup in addition to its standard range, and also half a dozen separate lines of full-strength soup, each differing from the others in functional terms. Campbell's overall position is so strong that the competition is confined to a limited number of (mainly specialist) canned soups, plus the packet and cube "dry" segment, where Campbell is not represented.

5. *Strong and consistent advertising:* Not least in importance is the powerful battery of added values that Campbell has built over the years through strong and consistent consumer advertising. This is the main theme of this chapter.

When consumers are asked to describe the personality of the Campbell's brand as if it were a human being, the descriptions give evidence of unusually favorable attitudes that are the cumulative sum of consumers' long experience of using the brand plus their absorption of the added values created and nurtured by the advertising:

Mrs. Campbell is kind of grandma, you know, a place to go eat on Sunday. Lots of kids around all the time. Table is always ready; a lot of food in the refrigerator.

Oh, I don't think she has much leisure time. I don't think there's another minute left in the day for all the things that perhaps she'd like to do, but she's just so busy.

Everybody goes when they're invited to Mrs. Campbell's house.[1]

Campbell's is indeed a power brand. Power brands are the real giants of the marketplace. Their names are as familiar as members of our families—Coca-Cola, Kellogg's cereal, Ivory soap. Many of them have been around for more than 100 years, yet they are as strong today as they were 10, 20, or even 50 years ago. They have flexed their muscles abroad and have won legions of fans in countries far from home. They have triumphed over competition and have become the real heroes of industry. And as heroes, these brands are worshiped. "Power brands have established a strong 'pact' with consumers," says Paul Stobart, director of Interbrand Group.[2] Consumers are devoted and loyal to power brands. Power brands work hard to maintain the bonds that tie them to their consumers. Campbell's red-and-white label soup is a power brand.

A Ubiquitous Presence

Campbell's soups dominate American pantries. They can be found in 93% of American households, which is a higher proportion than that for cold cereals, coffee, or bathroom tissue, according to a recent Campbell study.[3] The average American household has 8 to 10 cans of Campbell's soup tucked away in its pantry.[4] The Campbell Soup Company views Chicken Noodle, Tomato, and Cream of Mushroom as its "icon soups." These three soups are among the top 10 best-selling items in the grocery store.[5] This is the situation in a day and age when the grocery store is more cluttered than ever, with 30,000 different items crowding the shelves of an average supermarket,[6] and with competition reaching a feverish pitch. In 1997, for example, there were a record 25,261 new consumer packaged goods introductions.[7]

Shoppers buy canned soups on average once every 29 days,[8] and when they do, they reach for Campbell's soup. Campbell is currently the number-one liquid soup company in the world. Americans purchase more than 70 cans of Campbell's soup every second, with 100 cans purchased per second worldwide.[9] In the United States, Campbell's soup controls two-thirds of the multi-billion canned soup market.[10] This accounts for 38% of all soup servings in America—including homemade. Power brands tend to be market leaders. The red-and-white label's strong combination of penetration and purchase frequency has made the brand a market leader both nationally and internationally.

What It Means to Be a Power Brand

Besides a strong pact with consumers and a top leadership position, there are other characteristics that separate brand powerhouses from ordinary brands. According to Paul Stobart, power brands

1. have been established for a long time;
2. are equally at home in any country in the world;
3. appeal to all kinds of consumers regardless of age, color, or background;
4. have demonstrated that they can influence the markets in which they operate;
5. are very valuable;
6. are particularly well adapted to the environments in which they operate;
7. have strong, visually distinctive identities; and
8. are generally supported consistently and powerfully by advertising and promotional initiatives.[11]

Using this list of characteristics, we can now examine why we can call Campbell's soup a power brand—and, more important, how Campbell's soup has evolved into the power brand that it is today.

Power Brands Have Staying Power

Power brands are long-lived. The Campbell Soup Company is 130 years old and employs 41,000 people worldwide at 100 facilities in 22 countries over 6 continents. The red-and-white label soup is more than 100 years old. If one of the distinguishing qualities of a power brand is longevity, then the Campbell Soup Company and its famous red-and-white label soup have met the test of time.

Power Brands Are Welcome Anywhere

Power brands prosper in any country in the world, according to Stobart. Besides its red-and-white label soup, Campbell has 12 other brands. These products are sold in 120 countries around the world, yet soup is the most important product Campbell makes. "Soup is our middle name, and the heart of our powerful brand portfolio," states Campbell's 1997 Annual Report. Campbell focuses on soups and sauces because "they have the highest growth potential and provide the most attractive returns on investments." Soup also crosses borders with ease—it is one of the world's favorite foods. And if a real sign of a power brand is its ability to feel as comfortable at home as it does abroad, then Campbell's soup excels here. Campbell's chief executive officer, Dale F. Morrison, says that "soup is a central element in the diets of most of the people on the planet. . . . Soup is the perfect food because of its convenience, value, variety and 'good for you' qualities." [12] People from all corners of the globe agree. Around the world, people consume more servings of soup than of Coke—a phenomenon driven by particularly high consumption levels in some countries (e.g., Germans consume six times more soup per capita than do Americans).

Power Brands Have a Massive Consumer Franchise

Power brands also appeal to everyone. People of all ages, colors, and backgrounds like power brands. Campbell's soup has this mass appeal. According to Morrison, "Our opportunity is to sell Campbell's soup in more places in more forms to consumers of every age." [13] In Hong Kong and China, Campbell's make special varieties of Chinese soup, such as Fig, Date, and Duck Gizzard. In Australia, Campbell produces a Pumpkin soup that is one of the nation's top sellers.

Power brands also have a proven track record of influencing the markets in which they operate. This is at present happening in Japan, where Campbell is trying to gain a foothold for condensed soup. The company's goal in Japan is to "transform an American icon into an international symbol of quality, convenience and value." Campbell hopes to achieve this goal by tailoring a unique range of soups that will appeal to local tastes, such as Corn Pottage and Tappuri Yasai (a cream of vegetable).

To begin changing Japanese consumers' perceptions of condensed soup, Campbell has created "innovative advertising featuring an animated Mr. Campbell character." The commercial is educational, with Mr. Campbell teaching viewers "the delicious and simple ways to enjoy Campbell's soup."

Power brands are valuable. The Campbell Soup Company, with its meticulously managed portfolio of brands, had sales in 1997 worth $6.7 billion.

What separates average brands from power brands is that power brands are particularly good at adapting to the marketplaces in which they operate. Power brands have been around for a long time and continue to survive and prosper because the managers of these companies are focused and skilled. What distinguishes the world's leading brands, on both the international and national playing fields, is the "care and attention which are lavished on these brands by their owners. . . . Good brand management requires single-mindedness, even a streak of fanaticism." [14] All the great power brands "display an attention to detail which sets them apart from the normal [brands]." [15]

This takes strong management, and Campbell's managers are routinely recognized for outstanding leadership. In 1997, *Fortune* named Campbell the

"Most Admired Food Company" in its first year of eligibility. In his 1997 Annual Report letter, Campbell's chairman, David W. Johnson, cited this honor as "a testament to our brand power and our people power." Talented people have helped adapt the Campbell's red-and-white label soup for more than 100 years to suit the ever-changing needs of consumers.

Power Brands Are Supported With Strong Marketing

The final three characteristics of power brands involve marketing. Power brands adapt to market changes, and as such are particularly well suited to the markets where they operate. Power brands have strong and distinctive visual identities. They also are generally supported consistently and powerfully by advertising and promotion. We shall now look at some details.

A Historical Perspective

Before the Campbell Soup Company started canning soup in Camden, New Jersey, in 1869, grocery shopping was a far cry from what it is today. There were no branded goods on the shelf. Everything was shipped, stored, and sold in bulk. Shoppers grabbed crackers out of barrels, scooped peanut butter out of crocks, fished pickles out of huge jars, and spooned beans out of boxes. They asked grocers to cut them slabs of bacon. It was essentially hand service by the grocer. This all changed when prepackaging and trademarks came onto the scene. The way Americans ate and shopped changed radically with the invention of the can opener in 1858.[16]

Tin cans were actually invented in 1815, with the first U.S. patent application for canning taking place in 1825. Corn, tomatoes, and seafood were the first canned foods to find limited markets in the Northeast. Then came the California gold rush, the invention of the can opener, and then the Civil War. With these historic events, the canning industry began to take off, with the tin can becoming a familiar part of the American landscape. But widespread acceptance of canned foods was slow. It wasn't until big businesses entered the canning scene around 1890, bringing with them technological and industrial innovations like the open-top seamed container, that canned convenience foods became staples in people's cupboards and on grocers' shelves.

At the turn of the century, industrial and other innovation brought major advances in the canning industry. There were new and more efficient farm machinery, improved transportation systems, the invention of refrigerated railroad cars, safe and attractive methods of packaging, the development of modern advertising and trademarking, and shifts in family behavior.

At first, canning was a seasonal business, with canneries packaging whatever was available at the time.[17] Canneries produced batches of canned items and concentrated on selling each of these batches. Thomas Hine recounts how these early canners approached branding:

> For a very long time, food canners did not use packaging and advertising to establish brands. The multiplicity of interesting trade names on the can labels, with their illustrations of fruits and vegetables, country scenes, and canneries, had unmistakable nostalgic appeal. Moreover, they were in general more attractive than the branded lines that followed them. But most canners concentrated on selling each batch, rather than establishing a clear, year-round identity for their products.[18]

The early labels, although artistic, were cluttered. Even Campbell had a cluttered label and a number of brand names. From 1869 to 1899, Campbell was a regional canner that bought produce from southern New Jersey farms to can and sell to the Philadelphia area. In 1889, Campbell invented the idea of taking water out of soup, calling it condensed soup.[19] Just one year later, the company decided to go national with its new condensed soup. The incentives were that condensed soup would save the company money in shipping costs, save grocers space on their shelves, and save homemakers room in their cupboards.

Business no longer needed to be seasonal. Consumers could now buy canned goods year-round—something they had never been able to do before. The goal became to convince people to buy all of the new canned goods. Campbell would have to teach people not just to buy soup, but to buy Campbell's soup.

Creating a New Look in Red and White

One can scarcely discuss Campbell's soup and branding without exploring the soup's famous label. Many packaging experts believe that Campbell's soup is "probably the most successful use of a package to establish brand identity for a canned good."[20]

To help establish a new and distinctive identity for its new condensed soup, Campbell simplified its ornate packaging to a much more streamlined design. This design would stand apart from the highly embellished and picturesque labels used by the company's competitors. "Just as the soups were concentrated . . . so was the expression of the can."[21]

The red-and-white color combination was recommended by someone from the firm who had attended a football game between Cornell University and the University of Pennsylvania. He was so taken by Cornell's striking red-and-white uniforms that they became the inspiration for the now classic can.[22] In 1900, Campbell's soup won the Gold Medallion at the Paris Exposition. A rendering of this medallion was placed in the center of the new label. All pictures were stripped from the can and the brand name was highlighted. The simple red-and-white can stood in stark contrast to the more elaborate labels used by Campbell's competitors.

Advertising's Kick Start

With a strong, distinctive new package, the Campbell Soup Company, like many American businesses of the time, began using continuous advertising. By 1900, "it was now routine for any new product to be introduced by a wave of advertising."[23]

As early as 1899, the Campbell Soup Company spent $10,000 on advertising. Two years later, the ad budget increased to $50,000. A decade later, in 1911, Campbell increased its ad budget eightfold, to $400,000. By 1920, Campbell's ad expenditures hit the $1 million mark, accounting for 5% of the company's total sales. Today, Campbell spends $130 million annually on its soups alone.

Campbell's soup has made it a common marketing practice to test and eventually adopt each new kind of advertising medium available. Thus the brand's advertising moved from the printed page to the airwaves, and most recently to computer screens.

In 1905, Campbell's advertising committee, the internal management group, decided to try out a relatively new type of advertising: streetcar cards. After analyzing all the media choices of the day, the firm's ad committee members decided to place cards in streetcars splashed, for the first time, with the "Campbell Kids," together with a newly created illustration of the red-

and-white soup can. At the bottom of the cards were slogans such as "6 plates 10¢" and "Just add hot water and serve." The first contract called for cards to be used in a third of all New York City streetcars. The initial streetcar campaign boosted sales by 100%, and by the end of 1905, Campbell had renegotiated its contract to include every streetcar in New York City. The streetcar cards were so successful that Campbell's advertising committee expanded its poster media campaign to 372 cities and towns throughout the United States. This called for 35,000 cards to blanket all the streetcars in these regions.[24]

The Campbell Soup Kids

The chubby, apple-cheeked Campbell Soup Kids made their first appearance in Campbell's soup advertisements in 1904. Campbell was among the first manufacturers to use human characters in its advertising as well as one of the first companies to understand that "packaged branded products had to establish a relationship with the consumer." [25] Before canned and packaged foods, shoppers had enjoyed close relationships with their grocers, who had helped them scoop and shovel out quantities from barrels and jars. The relationship Campbell forged with consumers with its Soup Kids helped "replace or supplement any relationship buyers might have had with the shopkeeper." [26]

And the relationship between the Campbell Soup Kids and real kids was strong: "In the days before Saturday morning television, cutting out Campbell's Kids and making scrapbooks was at the top of youngsters' free- (and sick-) time amusement."[27]

The Real Target Consumers

American women, who did the majority of the cooking, were at first slow to fill their shopping baskets with canned goods. Their resistance persisted well into the 1920s. Relying on canned food to provide the family dinner—the most important and elaborate meal of the day—was unthinkable. As early as 1907, Campbell published books and meal planners designed to show homemakers how to use canned soups. These books and planners were the brainchild of John Dorrance, and they caused a major change in American eating habits. Campbell provided further incentives for using its soups through sales promotion premiums that featured the popular Soup Kid dolls. In 1916, Campbell introduced the idea of cooking with condensed soup by publishing its first cookbook, *Helps for the Hostess.*

The first national magazine advertisement for Campbell's soup appeared in 1905 in *Good Housekeeping.* By 1914, Campbell dropped newspapers completely from its advertising schedule, throwing the bulk of its advertising dollars into mass-market magazines such as the *Saturday Evening Post* and *Ladies' Home Journal.* The first color ad appeared in 1926. This provided a new dimension of appetite appeal. Until full-color printing was available, early food advertisers operated under a general "understanding that food sales seem to depend as much upon color as taste. . . . Campbell's reputedly supplied printers with its own tomato-red ink."[28] Campbell also found that with magazines, there were few wasted advertising dollars; the women reading the magazines were also the ones purchasing the soup. Campbell also contributed articles to magazines in which expert cooks gave homemakers helpful advice about using soup as part of main meals.

Audiovisual Media

Campbell first used radio for advertising in 1931, when it sponsored an early-morning jazz show. This produced disappointing sales, however, and radio was put on hold for 2 years. But by 1934, Campbell was back on the air, this time sponsoring two of the most popular radio shows of the day: *The George Burns and Gracie Allen Show* and *Amos 'n' Andy.* The advertising on the latter show played a significant role in the success of one of Campbell's most popular soups.

In 1934, Campbell's introduced a new soup: Chicken with Noodles. Sales were lackluster despite the high quality of the product. After much discussion, the company decided that Chicken with Noodles would be featured prominently on the popular *Amos 'n' Andy* show. The commercial was written and handed to Freeman Gosden, who played Amos, to read live on the air. His tongue slipped, and what went out to millions of listeners was "Chicken Noodle Soup," not "Chicken with Noodles." The Amos gaffe was providential and was shown within days to be the key to the success of this particular variety of soup.

During the mid-1950s, Campbell reshuffled its advertising dollars to give television a major chunk of its total budget. In 1954, the company spent $11.5 million on advertising, with TV receiving $4.5 million (39% of the total). The first television sets had screens that were no bigger than 12 to 14 inches. Families had to huddle around to get a glimpse of the blurry, black-and-white, flickering images of their favorite shows. They needed a quick food that was easy to prepare, convenient, and—perhaps most important—compact, so that it could be eaten in front of the TV on a lap or a small tray. "Television really transformed the American domestic center of gravity, moving it from the kitchen to the living room." [29] Seeing a need for meals tailor-made for TV viewing, Campbell bought out the Swanson Company of Omaha, Nebraska, manufacturer of TV dinners and other frozen-food items. But with the arrival of big-screen television sets, TV dinners began to lose much of their relevance, and Campbell sold off its Swanson line.

Changing Lifestyles

Americans still crowd around their television sets, but they also spend time in front of their computers, surfing the Web and playing CD-ROM games. When they do watch television, it is increasingly an individual experience rather than a family event. Americans now watch cable TV, talk on portable and cellular phones, and feel stressed out because they are working so hard. Campbell is adapting its soup and its advertising to meet the needs of working people who currently live in a more complex media world.

Campbell's real challenge is to convince harried working people to take time out and cook. Fewer and fewer Americans cook at home. It is easier to buy fast food, grab a ready-made meal from a take-out restaurant, or pick up prepared food from the supermarket. And when they do cook a meal, they want shortcuts. "By 2005, many Americans will have never cooked a meal from scratch," according to a study by McKinsey & Company.[30] Campbell is having to convince people to buck this trend and is communicating this message to consumers via the grocery shelf. In the mid-1990s, Campbell changed both the front and the back of its famous label. The front of the label promotes soup consumption by including an appetizing picture of the bowl of soup. The back of the label stresses how Campbell's soup can be used to prepare quick and easy meals by including a recipe and a four-color photo illustration of the finished meal.

Other ways that Campbell's soup is adapting to help its users include a telephone hot line: 1-888-MM-MM-GOOD. By calling this number, people who are at a loss about what to cook for dinner are able to talk to a live representative who provides recipe ideas. Campbell's soup was one of the first big consumer goods companies to take advantage of the World Wide Web. Part of Campbell's comprehensive Web site includes an interactive on-line recipe service. The company is also including recipes on freestanding "pantries" set up in supermarkets.

Campbell is also adapting its soup to appeal to younger users, and recently created a new, pourable tomato soup that comes in a clear plastic half-gallon bottle. The bottle is easy to grip, and kids don't have to add water to the soup. They merely pour it out and pop it into the microwave. Campbell was the first packaged goods marketer to cooperate with Disney Interactive to create a promotional tie-in. With the purchase of eight cans of Campbell's soup, kids could receive a free sampler of three Winnie-the-Pooh CD-ROM educational titles. The promotion was advertised on the soup package and through a national freestanding newspaper insert. According to Kevin Lowery, director of public information at Campbell, "The promotion already has yielded incredible results." [31]

Campbell's soups are also being modified to attract high school and college students. The company has created a new line of microwavable single-serving soups called Soup to Go. These seem particularly well suited to high school and college students who have ready access to microwave ovens.

Perhaps the real power behind the Campbell's soup brand is its ability to change and adapt yet stay the same. For more than a hundred years, the image of quality has remained constant, yet the soup itself has evolved to fit the changing lifestyles and preferences of consumers. Campbell has carefully adapted its soup, making it more convenient, relevant, and easy to use. And this is what keeps people buying 70 cans of the red-and-white label every second.

Notes

1. All quoted in John Philip Jones, *How Much Is Enough? Getting the Most From Your Advertising Dollar* (New York: Simon & Schuster-Lexington, 1992), 164.

2. Paul Stobart, "Introduction," in Paul Stobart (ed.), *Brand Power* (New York: Macmillan, 1994), 5.

3. Campbell's Community Center—Around the World, 1997 (on-line: http://www.campbell soup.com/center/around_world/index). This is the source of much of the information in this chapter.

4. Marcia Mogelonsky, "Soup Is Good Food," *American Demographics,* March 1998, 34.

5. Campbell's Soup 1997 Annual Report (on-line: http://www.campbellsoup.com/financial center/1997AR/pages/soup_sauces).

6. Thomas Hine, *The Total Package: The Evolution and Secret Meanings of Boxes, Bottles, Cans, and Tubes* (Toronto: Little, Brown, 1995), back cover.

7. Nancy Ten Kate, "New and Improved," *American Demographics,* March 1998, 32.

8. Mogelonsky, "Soup Is Good Food," 34.

9. Campbell's Community Center, 1997.

10. Constance L. Hays, "Campbell Soup Hopes a New Campaign Aimed at Children Will Help Bolster Sagging Sales," *New York Times,* May 20, 1998.

11. Stobart, "Introduction," 5-7.

12. Dale F. Morrison, CEO letter, in Campbell's Soup 1997 Annual Report (on-line: http://www.campbellsoup.com/financialcenter/1997AR/page/letter_ceo/html).

13. Ibid. The quotes in the following two paragraphs are also from this source.

14. Stobart, "Introduction," 12.

15. Ibid.

16. Robert Atwan, Donald McQuade, and John W. Wright, "The American Diet," in *Edsels, Luckies and Frigidaires: Advertising the American Way* (New York: Dell, 1979), 186.

17. Hine, *The Total Package,* 86.

18. Ibid.

19. Charles Goodrum and Helen Dalrymple, *Advertising in America* (New York: Harry N. Abrams, 1990), 23.

20. Hine, *The Total Package,* 86.

21. Ibid.

22. Ibid.

23. Stephen Fox, *The Mirror Makers: A History of American Advertising and Its Creators* (New York: Vintage, 1984), 38.

24. Douglas Collins, *America's Favorite Food: The Story of Campbell Soup Company* (New York: Harry N. Abrams, 1994), 44.

25. Hine, *The Total Package,* 88.

26. Ibid.

27. Goodrum and Dalrymple, *Advertising in America,* 88.

28. Atwan et al., "The American Diet," 188.

29. Robert Thompson, director, Center for the Study of Popular Television, Syracuse University, personal communication, 1998.

30. McKinsey report, as cited in Kate, "New and Improved."

31. Quoted in Kate Fitzgerald, "See the CD-ROMs," *Advertising Age,* September 29, 1997, 50.

21

The Case for Collectible Brands

Jan S. Slater

A mericans love to collect things—anything—from stamps, coins, Coca-Cola bottles, cars, books, and toys to Beanie Babies and sneakers. Therefore, it should be no surprise that one in three Americans collects something—meaning that one-third of the population are willing to call themselves "collectors" and participate in a continuous pursuit of objects that are mostly deemed "inessential."

The collecting industry is exploding. Because of the public's infatuation with things they don't need, the collectibles industry posted $9.2 billion in sales in 1997. This included everything from plush collectibles (e.g., Beanie Babies) to figurines (e.g., Cherished Teddies and Hummels), to Christmas ornaments (manufactured by Hallmark, Christopher Radko, and Kurt Adler, to name a few), to an array of Elvis and Princess Diana plates from the leading direct-response marketer of collectibles, the Franklin Mint.

Why has collecting—an activity that has existed for centuries—suddenly
become such a phenomenon in 20th-century America? Part of the growth is
attributed to a redefinition of what is collectible. Historically, collecting has
been an activity for the rich, who used disposable income to invest in fine art,
china, books, coins, and furniture. These were items considered to be antiques
(already more than 100 years old), whose value increased with age. Today,
many collectibles are items that have been mass-produced in the 20th century
and most often cost less than $200 at the time of production. These collectibles
are often deemed "old trivia," having been produced in the past 15 to 20 years.
Such items include Barbie® dolls, McDonald's Happy Meal toys, baseball
cards, Beanie Babies, and TV show memorabilia.

The alteration in perceptions of what is collectible has created the avenues
for Beanie Babies and the like. It has also led to the merchandising of products
associated with specialized brands, such as Coca-Cola, Mattel, Campbell's
soup, Hershey, Hallmark, and McDonald's. This merchandise has become
known as *brand collectibles.* Because of this shift, more and more brands are
entering the collectible business, developing collectible items with brand
names emblazoned on glassware, clothing, toys, Christmas ornaments, dolls,
watches, and figurines. The collecting activity has been prepackaged, with
manufacturing, marketing, and distribution controlled by some of the most
prominent *Fortune* 500 companies as well as some of the most recognizable
brands in the United States.

Collectible Brands

Brand collectibles are big business. Mattel currently manufactures a collectible line of Barbie dolls, some in clothes by famous designers (e.g., Donna
Karan) and others dressed as movie characters (e.g., Scarlett O'Hara), as well
as brands such as Got Milk? Barbie, Harley-Davidson Barbie, Coca-Cola
Barbie, and The Gap Barbie. Hallmark makes collectible Christmas ornaments, the Keepsake Ornament line. McDonald's is selling Ronald McDonald
cookie jars on QVC and hand-beaded designer evening purses in the shapes
of burgers and fries for $2,000 on Rodeo Drive. Franklin Mint, the leading
manufacturer of mass-produced collectibles, has forged partnerships with a
variety of corporate marketers to create collectible products for some of the
top commercial brands. Coca-Cola, Walt Disney, Planters, Pillsbury, LifeSav-
ers, Ralston Purina, McDonald's, Harley-Davidson, and Campbell are just a

few of the corporations that have signed agreements to tie their brands to collectible dolls, plates, sculptures, and Christmas ornaments.[1] These mass-merchandising efforts have extended the individual brands by making them collectible, and the companies are using marketing strategies to attract new collectors and increase purchase frequency among current collectors—two classic strategies for building a brand's business.[2]

Brands are most often thought of as products, products that are consumed or used. The typical textbook definition of a brand is "a distinguishing name and/or symbol (such as a logo, trademark, or package design) intended to identify the goods or services of either one seller or a group of sellers, and to differentiate those goods or services from those of competitors."[3] But this technical explanation does not encompass the emotional element of brands. According to John Philip Jones of Syracuse University, although all brands are products, not all products are brands. A brand is imbued with personality characteristics; a brand is unique; a brand is timeless. Consumers purchase a brand not just because of what it will do or how it will taste, but because of how they feel about the brand, the emotional or psychological rewards they gain from using it. A brand, then, encompasses both tangible and intangible benefits, a combination of "functional benefits plus added values that some consumers value enough to buy."[4]

Most consumers purchase brands because of some superior functionality—whiter wash, moister cake, lower calories, less fat, quicker delivery, better gas mileage. In addition to these tangible deliverable benefits, consumers also purchase brands because of the feelings or emotional attachments or psychological rewards they gain by using them—feeling better about themselves, providing for their families better, or simply having fun. These "added values" defined by Jones are important in how consumers feel about brands.[5] Therefore, branding is about the way customers perceive and buy.[6] So what is it that makes brands collectible, and why are so many brand market leaders moving into the collectibles market?

In reviewing the collectible brands listed above that have been identified by *Advertising Age* as entering the collectible market, three similarities are immediately evident:

1. All are relatively old brands, ranging from 40 to more than 100 years in production.
2. Each brand is the leader in its product category (e.g., soft drinks, soup, entertainment, fast food, greeting cards).

3. Each brand is in a mature product category, meaning that there is little opportunity for extensive natural growth.

Coca-Cola and Pepsi-Cola control the soft drink category with more than 70% of the market. Campbell controls approximately 70% of the canned soup category. Large groups of new consumers are not entering these categories; most people already use these established brands. Therefore, the only opportunity to grow the categories, as well as the brands, is to increase purchase frequency among current users. Mature product categories such as these have relatively slow growth potential.

It is likely that these brands and many others have reached maximum market penetration; that is, consumers are already using the products, and consumer purchase frequency is saturated. For example, the per capita consumption of Coca-Cola is 297 eight-ounce servings in the United States.[7] If that is the case, the only means to grow the brand is through a "defensive strategy" that advocates retaining existing users and slightly boosting their purchase frequency.[8] Collectible marketing may be viewed as a brand extension that capitalizes on the added values of these brands and strengthens relationships with consumers by making the brands collectible. Extending a brand, using the brand name on new products to enter new product categories, such as the collectible category, is a key ingredient in maximizing the value of the brand in terms of profit as well as brand loyalty.[9]

Keeping existing customers and keeping them brand loyal is more difficult today for many reasons. Product proliferation is a primary concern. It is not uncommon for current supermarkets to stock upward of 20,000 lines. In addition, more than 3,000 brands (excluding extensions) are introduced each year for supermarket distribution.[10] According to data from Mediamark Research, Inc., there are 93 cat food brands, 80 different brands of soft drinks, 76 brands of beer, 73 brands of dog food, 23 brands of toilet paper, 30 brands of margarine, and 119 different brands of ready-to-eat cereal overflowing supermarket shelves.[11] In addition to these nationally distributed brands, supermarkets have begun to add to the fray by developing their own brands of soft drinks, margarine, toilet paper, and cereal to compete with the national brands on the shelf. Now that is proliferation. This saturation only provides more choices for the consumer and, in some cases, more confusion. With this brand overload, coupled with the slowing growth of mature product categories, collectibles may be a strategy through which brands can maintain existing users and a means to reinforce loyalty. In the following sections, I offer profiles of two prominent collectible brands.

Collecting Coca-Cola: It's the Real Thing

Considered by many to be the quintessential international brand, Coca-Cola transcends ethnicity, gender, age, education, and social class. True to its current advertising slogan, it seems there has "always" been Coca-Cola. Almost no one alive today can remember a time when the famous soft drink was not available in restaurants, supermarkets, convenience stores, and vending machines (and, of course, at soda fountains). Not only is Coca-Cola the best-selling soft drink in the world, it is the world's number-one brand.[12]

The history of this American icon is a textbook case study in building, managing, and maintaining a brand. Since its beginning in 1886, Coca-Cola has built a powerful brand image. The brand is imbued with added values: the discriminating benefits that go beyond the functionality of a refreshing soft drink.[13] Coke is seen as traditional, patriotic, friendly, and American. The brand has become a part of the rituals of many American consumers' everyday lives, at ball games, barbecues, family reunions, and so on. In fact, internationally and at home, Coca-Cola is America.[14]

Although the brand dates back to the late 1880s, the basic brand proposition—Coca-Cola satisfies; Coca-Cola is a delightful, refreshing beverage—has remained virtually unchanged, as have the brand name and its distinctive logo. Early on, the company developed a strong support system for the brand by building lifelong partnerships with its distribution franchises and by creating a distinctive personality that appealed emotionally to consumers. Furthermore, the company has consistently supported the brand and its identity with powerful advertising messages and substantial investment, along with shelf-stopping package designs. Yet all the while, Coca-Cola has been at the forefront of change—adapting to suit changing tastes and conditions. New forms of packaging and special versions of the logo have been produced to suit a wide range of languages, and different flavors have been introduced to fit a variety of tastes and lifestyles.

When the "Always Coca-Cola" slogan was introduced in 1993, Don Keough, former president and chief operating officer of the Coca-Cola Company proclaimed, "Coca-Cola must be reinterpreted for each new generation.

The essential promise must be kept fresh and contemporary, because Coca-Cola itself must remain timeless and yet new at the same time." [15] Indeed, within the soft drink industry, and among worldwide businesses, consumers, and collectors of advertising memorabilia, there is no substitute for Coca-Cola.

The story behind Coca-Cola, a product that is 99% sugar and water, and its ascent to an $18 billion business marketed in 195 countries is an American phenomenon. But almost as remarkable is the Coca-Cola Collector's Club, which boasts 7,300 members worldwide who collect Coca-Cola memorabilia, from bottles and cans to delivery uniforms, old advertisements, vending machines, and coolers.

Coca-Cola is not only the largest brand in the world, it is also the largest brand collectible in the world. From the time the secret formula for Coca-Cola led to a marketable product in the late 1800s, the Coca-Cola Company has been producing a wide range of promotional materials to encourage the consumption of the drink. Even the company admits that one of the reasons for its success has been a strong commitment to a consistent and long-term investment in advertising.[16] From its first ad budget, in 1901, of $100,000 to its current $100 million "Always Coca-Cola" campaign, Coca-Cola has been heavily advertised using virtually every possible message channel.[17] Long before today's mass media, the Coca-Cola Company used millions of promotional items to advertise and sell its product to the masses. These items ranged from utilitarian merchandising items such as bottles and coolers to traditional and also familiar advertising items such as signs and print advertisements, from point-of-purchase items such as trays and calendars to complimentary novelties such as toys and bookmarks.[18] Today these items are considered antiques, and many are rare and extremely valuable. For example, Coca-Cola calendars from 1891 and 1892 are valued at $10,000 or more,[19] and a 1903 metal Coca-Cola sign was recently sold at auction for $12,000.

These items form the basis for today's collections of Coca-Cola memorabilia. Part of the charm of these items for the collector is that their original purpose was to promote the sale of Coca-Cola, not to be collected. Unlike other collectibles that are essentially traditional (e.g., Hallmark Christmas ornaments, salt and pepper shakers, stamps), Coca-Cola collectibles literally span the full range of artifacts manufactured to merchandise and advertise consumer products since the 1880s. These include, among many other items, fans, chewing gum, pocket mirrors, pocket knives, wallets, cuff links, thimbles, pins, clocks, ashtrays, pens, matchbooks, and even match safes.

Today, Coca-Cola is building a new line of collectibles with the Franklin Mint, the Hamilton Collection, and Cavanaugh Productions, all manufacturers of collectible merchandise. For example, the Franklin Mint is well-known for its production and promotion of collectible plates and coins. The ubiquitous Coca-Cola logo is showing up on plates, calendar and tray reproductions, clothing, glassware, commemorative bottles, and Christmas ornaments. The considerable interest in collecting older Coca-Cola memorabilia has created a secondary level of new collectibles manufactured strictly to be collected. This new line of products, which includes polar bear ornaments, glassware, trays, posters, and kitchenware, has been developed to feed the appetites of the collectors of Coca-Cola artifacts.

The Coca-Cola Company became interested in the memorabilia craze as the nation was engulfed in a nostalgia wave during the 1970s. Before that time, Coca-Cola paid little attention to items being manufactured with the company logo but without company approval. But the 1970s nostalgia movement changed all that. People were frantic for any piece of Coca-Cola merchandise that reminded them of their childhood or of simpler times, and the company was determined not to disappoint these loyalists. It is believed that the interest generated during this period was responsible for the growth in memorabilia collecting that continues today.[20]

Beginning in the 1970s, the company offered reproductions of early trays, calendars, glasses, and other items to this growing number of new enthusiasts for Coca-Cola collectibles. These products were sold in specialty and gift shops primarily, although some were available in mass-market outlets. Amid this activity, many pieces were manufactured without Coca-Cola's permission, and large quantities of "fake collectibles" emerged during this time as well. Even today, it is difficult to convince some collectors that these illegal items are not original Coca-Cola pieces.[21]

Basically, there are three types of new Coca-Cola collectibles: reproductions, fantasy products, and licensed products.[22] A reproduction is a copy of an original Coca-Cola item—in many cases an exact copy. To many new collectors, the differences between these pieces and the originals are undetectable. But the discerning eye of a well-educated Coca-Cola collector can usually spot a reproduction.

A fantasy product is one that appears to be old, but is not. In this case, the item looks like an old Coca-Cola piece, but in fact no such piece was ever previously produced. Unlike a reproduction, for which there is an original version, a fantasy item has no original counterpart.[23] For instance, a fantasy serving tray may depict a Victorian-looking lady drinking Coca-Cola, and may be reminiscent of actual trays manufactured in the early 1900s. However, the picture on the tray was never used by the company. Fantasy goods are easily sold to novice collectors, but they frustrate and anger experienced collectors. As Allan Petretti, a dealer in Coca-Cola collectibles, clearly points out, "The joy of Coca-Cola collecting is collecting memorabilia of The Coca-Cola Company."[24] Fantasy items are not pieces from the Coca-Cola Company.

Since the mid-1980s, the Coca-Cola Company has had a licensing program that has put the well-known logo on Christmas ornaments, watches, clothing, commemorative bottles, puzzles, towels, dolls—the list goes on. Up to that point, the company had not maintained control of the use of its famous script logo on products. Today, more than 250 companies worldwide are issued licenses to manufacture more than 10,000 different products bearing the Coca-Cola trademark. More than 50 million Coca-Cola items were sold in 1997 in various mass-merchandising retail outlets as well as through the Coca-Cola Catalog and Coca-Cola's own retail outlets in Atlanta, New York City, and Las Vegas. The Coca-Cola Company receives annual licensing fees from the manufacturers of the collectibles as well as an estimated 8%-10% of the manufacturers' gross sales value.[25] So, although Coca-Cola's main business remains soft drinks, the income generated from collectibles and the added value the collectibles provide, add to Coca-Cola's bottom line while enhancing brand equity.

Hallmark Collecting: When You Care Enough

According to independent research provided to Hallmark, "When You Care Enough to Send the Very Best" is one of the most trusted and believed advertising slogans in the United States, because it associates the product with the experience of Hallmark. Not only has the slogan been in use for more than 50 years, it is the philosophy of the Hallmark company as well. Founder Joyce C. Hall has written: "While we thought we had only established a good advertising slogan, we soon found out we had made a business commitment. The slogan constantly puts pressure on us to make Hallmark cards *the very best.*"[26]

Hallmark Cards, Inc., claims to be "the world's largest manufacturer of greeting cards and other personal expression products."[27] The "personal expression" line of products includes cards, ornaments, mugs, T-shirts, gift wrap, and stationery items. The products are manufactured under the brand names of Hallmark, Ambassador, Crayola, Hallmark Connections, Heartline, Keepsake Ornaments, Liquitex, Magic Marker, Party Express, Revell-Monogram, Shoebox Greetings, Springbok, and Verkerke.[28] The greeting cards and ornaments are, respectively, the two top sales-producing product lines, and Hallmark is considered the domestic market leader in both categories. Hallmark is one of three companies that share 85% of the greeting card market: Hallmark holds the largest share with 42%, American Greetings has 35%, and Gibson is a distant third with only 8%.[29] The remaining 15% is split among many small companies, most with less than 1% share.

In 1973, Hallmark introduced the Keepsake line of Christmas ornaments. The company was looking for a way to expand its product line while staying within the guidelines of manufacturing what it does best: "personal expression" items.[30] It was the annual Hallmark employee gift to founder Joyce C. Hall that marked the company's entry into the ornament line. The tradition of crafting a special greeting for Hall began in 1938. Hallmark artists would create a card and it would be signed by every Hallmark employee. Each year the card became more sophisticated, until 1966, when the card became a Christmas tree. This tradition continued until Hall's death in 1982. It was these immense, ornate, theme-designed trees that provided the idea, as well as some of the designs, for Hallmark's Christmas ornament product line. The first offering included six decorated balls and 12 yarn figures as Christmas decorations. Today, Hallmark manufactures more than 250 ornaments per year under the Hallmark Keepsake Ornament umbrella.

According to industry experts, ornament collecting has grown very fast since Hallmark's introduction into the marketplace.[31] Total annual sales volume of the ornament industry was $2.4 billion for 1996, an increase of 25% over 1995. Today, more than 22 million households collect Christmas ornaments, and it is estimated that 75% of those households collect Hallmark Keepsake Ornaments.[32]

Because of this increased interest in collecting, the company launched the Hallmark Keepsake Ornament Collector's Club in 1987, which is now the largest collector's club in the nation, with a membership of more than 300,000. It is one of the few clubs, if not the only one, that is completely managed and maintained by a manufacturing company. Most collectors' clubs are volunteer organizations with no company affiliations (e.g., the Coca-Cola Collector's Club, the Campbell's Soup Collector's Club, and the McDonald's Collector's Club).

In addition, there are approximately 300 local clubs nationwide, sponsored by local Hallmark retailers. According to Hallmark research, joining the national club is the first step. A recent buyer's study conducted by Hallmark showed that a noncollector purchases 1 to 3 ornaments per year. A person begins to call him- or herself a "collector" when purchases grow to 13 ornaments a year. Buying jumps to an average of 40 ornaments per year when the collector joins the national club and doubles to 80 when the collector then joins a local club. Therefore, club membership does indeed increase purchasing. Based on estimates of national membership fees, event fees, event purchasing, and annual collector purchasing, the Hallmark Collector's Club generates $128 million annually.[33]

Unlike Coca-Cola, Hallmark controls the collecting environment—actually generating the environment just as it manufactures the collectibles. The only way to obtain the "first-issue" ornaments (i.e., the new line of ornaments issued each year) is to purchase them at a local Hallmark store or another retailer that carries the Hallmark line or at special collector events. Among Hallmark's 40,000 retail outlets, only 8,360 are specialty stores, or stores that carry the Hallmark name. These are independently owned stores, not owned or franchised by Hallmark. These retailers have license agreements that basically let them use "Hallmark" in their names and sell Hallmark-branded and Hallmark-approved items. Only the Hallmark stores carry the complete line of ornaments, and only Hallmark stores offer frequent-buyer plans. By these means, Hallmark encourages collectors to purchase ornaments at Hallmark stores.

In addition, collector events are chosen each year based on which areas have the heaviest collector activity and which local clubs have the largest numbers of members. Hallmark monitors sales and conducts research via the local clubs to ascertain the collecting activity. They have ranked, by state, the top 10 markets for Hallmark Ornament collecting; in order, from first to tenth, these are California, New York, Illinois, Pennsylvania, Florida, Texas, Michigan, New Jersey, Ohio, and Missouri.

Hallmark's marketing strategy, including products, events, and communications to collectors, serves to enhance a strong brand association with this special group of consumers. This translates into the retention of a consumer/collector over a long period of time, and this relationship provides Hallmark a competitive advantage in the marketplace.

Brand loyalty has long been a central construct in marketing. It has been defined as "a measure of the attachment that a customer has to a brand."[34]

Basically, brand loyalty is a measure of how easily a customer will switch to another brand. Loyalty has often been thought of as a barrier to substitutability—if the customer is loyal, he or she will buy the brand more than 50% of the time. But in today's marketplace, brand loyalty is difficult to develop and maintain, for reasons discussed in the earlier description of product proliferation and competition in retail environments. Most consumers are not loyal to just one brand, but most often have a repertoire of brands, usually three in any one product category. Brand loyalty is still the ultimate desire, as it does reflect future sales. However, the process of building brand loyalty is time-consuming and difficult.

In order to create and maintain brand loyalty, Hallmark and Coca-Cola must build an association between the brand and the consumer, and in the process stay close to the customer. This association becomes the link to the consumer's attitude about the brand. And that link is strengthened when it is based on positive and/or reinforcing experiences with the brand.[35] With both Coca-Cola and Hallmark, the act of collecting these brands is seen as a very positive, very powerful experience with the brand.

Building Brand Loyalty

Two key elements in brand growth are penetration and purchase frequency.[36] *Penetration* refers to the number of people who buy the brand and *purchase frequency* refers to how many times those people buy it. Penetration must come first. Once the consumer has tried the brand, the next step is to get him or her to repurchase and eventually buy more.

This same strategy is apparent in the collectibles market—first, get the person to buy a collectible, then get him or her hooked by buying more. People start collecting for various reasons. The first purchase is driven by something internal: a desire, a want, a need. But the next purchase and the next purchase can be driven not only by something internal, but also by something external.

The internal drive is what Muensterberger terms *replenishment.*[37] There is no rational need for anyone to have 200,000 Christmas ornaments when the average Christmas tree holds perhaps 100; nor does anyone need to have 60 metal Coca-Cola serving trays that are never used to serve anything. It is an emotional need that causes the collector to be in a "constant replenishment" mode. The need, according to Muensterberger and Belk et al., can vary from one of excitement to one of approval, acceptance, security, control, power, comfort, or escape.[38] Such emotional needs are fulfilled through the collecting of Hallmark ornaments or Coca-Cola metal trays. As these needs surface, replenishment is necessary. Muensterberger relates it to the recurring state of hunger: "Regardless of how often and how much one ingests, within a few hours hunger returns and one must eat again."[39] So it is with collectors. According to many of the collectors I have interviewed, they call it the "collector's mentality." As one collector admitted: "It is like a mistress, or a habit like drugs. Every so often, you have to have a fix."[40] Hallmark and Coca-Cola capitalize on that "collector's mentality" to build brand loyalty.

As defined by Aaker, brand extensions use the brand name to enter new product classes.[41] Naturally, a key element in a successful brand extension is a strong brand. Both Hallmark and Coca-Cola have capitalized on that strength to move into the collectibles product category. Hallmark did so intentionally. Recall that Hallmark was looking to expand its product line in the early 1970s, and decided ornaments were a good "fit." About the same time, Coca-Cola realized that the marketplace was littered with unlicensed Coca-Cola merchandise and people couldn't get enough of it. The company capitalized on the situation and developed a licensing program that allowed it to control and benefit from the collectibles. Whether opportunistic or intentional, there is little doubt that collectibles extend the brands of Hallmark and Coca-Cola, and little doubt that these extensions are profitable.

Although Hallmark does not release ornament sales figures, it has been estimated that the membership and purchasing power of the collectors club add more than $128 million to the company's volume. This income is just from club members. Hallmark's research has revealed that noncollectors purchase 1 to 3 ornaments per year and collectors who are not yet club members purchase 13 ornaments a year. Using Hallmark's data on the number of households collecting Hallmark ornaments, this estimated purchasing power generates approximately $1.4 billion in ornament sales from non-club members alone.[42] If this is true, the sale of ornaments would account for more than 40% of Hallmark's $3.6 billion in overall sales.

Coca-Cola has licensing agreements with more than 250 companies in the United States alone. The licensing fees generate more than $50 million. In addition, Coca-Cola receives a royalty on the sale of each licensed item that is estimated to be between 8% and 10% of the sale price of the item. For example, when Coca-Cola teamed with Mattel to create a collectible vintage

Coca-Cola Barbie, Mattel paid a licensing fee and also provided Coca-Cola with approximately 8% of the sales of the doll. Some 10,000 dolls were sold for $130 each, garnering Coca-Cola more than $104,000. It is estimated that the other three dolls in the series will generate even more sales, making Coca-Cola Barbie worth half a million dollars. That is just one licensed product; Coca-Cola licenses thousands more.

An interesting aspect of brand loyalty is that, with Coca-Cola and Hallmark, the name of the product and the company are one and the same. This is rare, especially among packaged goods. For instance, Procter & Gamble manufactures Pert, Folgers, Tide, Crest, Cheer, Cascade, and many other brands. But the company name does not appear as a branded product. Larry Light, a branding expert, believes the potential for creating and sustaining brand loyalty is increased when the product name and the company name are the same. This allows the consumer, or collector, as the case may be, the opportunity to have positive associations with the product as well as with the company. The brand image is created by sets of these positive associations. The strength of these associations links the collector to the brand, building a relationship of trust, likability, and loyalty.

Linking the product and the company is especially important for these collectible brands. Both Hallmark and Coca-Cola have contact with their collectors beyond the retail shelf. Hallmark and Coca-Cola must provide positive associations for collectors in many instances: in the retail environment, during collector-only events, in the products they manufacture or license, in collector-only communications, and in mass-media communications as well. According to Light, this marketing environment of multiple contacts positions the brand as a "trustmark" instead of a trademark, and that becomes the point of differentiating the brand in the marketplace.[43] Therefore, Coca-Cola isn't just a big company that manufactures a refreshing soft drink. It becomes a friend who is trustworthy, likable, and welcome in your home. The Hallmark Keepsake Ornament is not just a resin decoration for the Christmas tree; it is a memory, a tradition, a part of the family, part of celebrating the holiday.

Light claims that brands such as Hallmark and Coca-Cola are moving from a "transaction mentality" (sell the product off the shelf) to a "relationship mentality" (building an affinity for the brand that is positive and long lasting). Brand loyalty, as defined by Light, is "a factually grounded, positive, suitable, mutually beneficial relationship" between the consumer and the brand.[44] In the case of Hallmark and Coca-Cola collectibles, the relationship extends beyond the brand.

Conclusion

There is no question that brands are under siege. Supermarkets house more than 20,000 products; hypermarkets stock more than 30,000. Store brands continue to lure the price-conscious consumer, and grocers such as Wegmans and Kroger stock their own brands in more than 40 product categories. In addition, hundreds of new products are introduced each year, 90% of which may fail. Product proliferation, product parity, price-conscious consumers, mature product categories, and saturated markets make it very difficult for old brands as well as new brands to survive in the marketplace. Consumers of the millennium have so many choices and so many incentives to switch brands that brand loyalty is being diminished. Mature brands, such as Coca-Cola, McDonald's, Hallmark, and Campbell, find themselves adopting a defensive strategy as a means of retaining current customers. The brand collectible acts as a retention mechanism not only to keep the customer, but also to enhance brand loyalty. The consumer ultimately becomes a collector, and the attachment to the brand is not only enhanced psychologically, but fortified in behavioral terms.

Notes

1. Laura Loro, "Nostalgia for Sale at Franklin Mint," *Advertising Age,* May 15, 1995, 33.

2. John Philip Jones, *How Much Is Enough? Getting the Most From Your Advertising Dollar* (New York: Simon & Schuster-Lexington, 1992).

3. David A. Aaker, *Managing Brand Equity: Capitalizing on the Value of a Brand Name* (New York: Free Press, 1991), 7.

4. Jones, *How Much Is Enough?* 29.

5. Ibid.

6. David Arnold, *The Handbook of Brand Management* (Reading, MA: Addison-Wesley, 1992).

7. "Coca-Cola: Into the 21st Century," *Beverage World,* vol. 112, 1993, 6-207.

8. Jones, *How Much Is Enough?*

9. Aaker, *Managing Brand Equity.*

10. Ibid.

11. Mediamark Research, Inc., data reported spring 1995.

12. Frederick Allen, *Secret Formula: How Brilliant Marketing and Relentless Salesmanship Made Coca-Cola the Best-Known Product in the World* (New York: HarperCollins, 1994).

13. John Philip Jones, *What's in a Name? Advertising and the Concept of Brands* (New York: Simon & Schuster-Lexington, 1986).

14. Allen, *Secret Formula.*

15. "Coca-Cola," 32.

16. Phil Mooney, Coca-Cola archivist, interview, April 3, 1997.

17. Mark Gleason, "Sprite Leads the Pack in Soft Drink Growth," *Advertising Age,* February 12, 1996, 14.

18. Randy Schaeffer and Bill Bateman, *Coca-Cola: A Collector's Guide* (London: Quintet, 1995).

19. Allan Petretti, *Coca-Cola Collectibles Price Guide,* 9th ed. (Hackensack, NJ: Nostalgia, 1994).

20. Schaeffer and Bateman, *Coca-Cola.*

21. Ibid.

22. Ibid.

23. Ibid.

24. Petretti, *Coca-Cola Collectibles Price Guide,* 10.

25. Mooney, interview.

26. Joyce C. Hall, *When You Care Enough* (Kansas City, MO: Hallmark Cards, Inc., 1979), 211.

27. Hallmark press release, July 1, 1995.

28. Hallmark fact sheet, 1996.

29. Ibid.

30. Linda Fewell, Hallmark marketing specialist, personal communication, September 16, 1995.

31. Unity Marketing, *Annual Collectible Industry Research* (Steven, PA: Unity Marketing, 1997).

32. Ibid.

33. This figure is based on membership fees of $20 for 300,000 members, 10 special collector events sold out at 2,000 for $10 registration each, the purchase of 2,000 special-event ornaments at all 10 events at $60 each, and the average collector spending $400 annually.

34. Aaker, *Managing Brand Equity,* 39.

35. Ibid.

36. Jones, *How Much Is Enough?*

37. Werner Muensterberger, *Collecting, an Unruly Passion: Psychological Perspectives* (Orlando, FL: Harcourt Brace, 1994).

38. Ibid.; and Russell W. Belk, Melanie Wallendorf, John Sherry, and Morris B. Holbrook, "Collecting in a Consumer Culture," in Russell W. Belk (ed.), *Highways and Buyways: Naturalistic Research From the Consumer Behavior Odyssey* (Provo, UT: Association for Consumer Research, 1991), 178-215.

39. Muensterberger, *Collecting,* 16.

40. Jan S. Slater, "Trash to Treasures: A Qualitative Study of the Relationship Between Collectors and Collectible Brands," unpublished doctoral dissertation, Syracuse University, 1997, 113.

41. Aaker, *Managing Brand Equity.*

42. Hallmark estimates that of the 22 million households that collect ornaments, half collect Hallmark ornaments. Deducting club membership from that figure, it is estimated that nonmember collectors total 10.7 million households. Hallmark's research estimates that nonmembers who collect buy, on average, 13 ornaments per year. The average Hallmark ornament costs $10, therefore the spending would approximate to $130 annually. Multiplied by the 10.7 million households, the nonmember collectors generate $1.4 billion in ornament sales. See Hallmark fact sheet, 1996.

43. Larry Light, *The Fourth Wave: Brand Loyalty* (New York: American Association of Advertising Agencies, 1996).

44. Quoted in Ryan Matthews, "Branding the Store," *Progressive Grocer,* vol. 74, November 1995, B4.

Part IV

Brand Concepts in Unexpected Fields

John Philip Jones

In Chapter 1 of this volume, I introduced the idea of extensions of the brand concept into untraditional product and service categories. I started with the more obvious extensions beyond the field of repeat-purchase packaged goods (listed in Table 1.1), but I also discussed briefly the topic of this part of the book, which examines the use of branding in more unexpected territory. The fields described in the chapters that follow are at the outer frontiers of branding.

These frontiers are not covered comprehensively here, although the next five chapters describe a representative selection of the new fields. Chapters 22 (politicians as brands), 23 (cable television stations as brands) and 26 (arts organizations as brands) are devoted to services of various types. Chapters 24 (green brands) and 25 (brands directed at elderly consumers) are concerned with specialist types of consumer goods. The authors of these chapters discuss fully the techniques of branding and marketing in their fields, but these should be seen in a broader context. There are branding signposts exemplified by each of these five cases.

The first signpost is the basic fact that all brands, if they are to be successful, must offer what can be broadly described as effective functional performance in a competitive marketplace. For a politician, does he or she offer policies that the electorate regards as both in the public interest and cost-effective? Does the cable television station broadcast programs that consumers look forward to watching? Do the brands targeted at the green market genuinely protect the environment as well as carry out their primary jobs to the satisfaction of consumers? Do the brands directed at older consumers respond to these consumers' specific needs? And do the arts organizations produce shows that have a strong audience appeal?

The point about functionality is well expressed by Palda and Palda in Chapter 22, in their discussion of political advertising: "There is a parallel here with the advertising for brands of consumer goods. Underlying successful campaigns for the latter is efficient product performance, otherwise repurchase becomes impossible."

The second point is that all brands—again, if they are to be successful—will be enriched with added values. How attractive literally is the personality of the politician? (However, to what degree is his or her physical appearance and personality being consciously manipulated to enhance television appeal?)[1] Does the cable television station reflect the tastes and attitudes of its heavy users? Do the brands directed at the green market and at elderly consumers speak to these respective groups with appropriate tone of voice—in the one case honest and caring, and in the other case lucid and unpatronizing? Does the arts organization have a "necktie" quality? Are its patrons connected together by invisible bonds, in the way that male members of a particular club will wear neckties bearing the club's emblem?

Mary Baumgartner Jones makes this point neatly in Chapter 23, when she describes how one cable television station builds a relationship with consumers: "A&E's successful print magazine *Biography* . . . does devote a reasonable amount of space to promoting upcoming A&E shows. . . . the magazine's editorial decisions help to reinforce the 'classy, smart, and intelligent' personality the channel has created for itself."

An intimate and creative synthesis of functionality and added values drives repeat purchase, and this is just as important in the fields described in the next five chapters as it is for breakfast cereals, soap, cars, or credit cards.

As with brands of all types, the effectiveness of the marketing in each of the untraditional branded fields discussed in these chapters depends on the precision of the consumer targeting. Note the importance of targeting current users to boost repeat business (e.g., arts organizations), targeting consumers defined by psychographic criteria (e.g., brands directed at green consumers), and, obviously, targeting consumers based on demographics (e.g., brands targeted at elderly consumers).

In all circumstances, strong branding is a result of reinforcement: working with the grain of consumer habits and attitudes, a process in which consumers' satisfaction with the brand is gradually underscored by the added values built by the advertising. As Palda and Palda describe the marketing of political candidates in Chapter 22: "What advertising does is strengthen the tendencies and beliefs that people already have and clarify which candidates share those beliefs." These purposes of advertising are also totally appropriate for such marketing practitioners as Procter & Gamble and American Express. Indeed the commercial organizations were the pioneers in using advertising in these ways.

Note

1. An example of such manipulation is found in the notorious case of Richard Nixon's presidential candidacy. See Joe McGinniss, *The Selling of the President, 1968* (New York: Trident, 1969).

Political Advertising

How It Works and Who Benefits

Filip Palda
Kristian Palda

I n 1972, politicians at all levels of government in the United States spent $425 million on their election campaigns. By 1988 the sum had risen to $2.7 billion. The 1990s have seen a seeming explosion of congressional campaign spending. These trends have excited great passion in the media and among election reformers. They lament the explosion in campaign costs and the waste they see in lavish political advertising. The amount of money expended in election campaigns is painted as an evil that corrupts politicians and twists the minds of voters.

The academic research that has been building on this topic since the early 1970s paints a more cautious and optimistic picture. Political advertising is an important source of information for voters. Voters prefer candidates who speak about the issues. Money of itself cannot buy an election. Campaign spending has force only if the ideas of the candidate reflect the basic beliefs of members of the community. Campaign spending allows candidates to learn what their constituents want and to package their platforms in a manner that voters can understand. The increasing sums spent on campaigns reflect the increasing importance of the issues being discussed. Political advertising is a cost we must pay for resolving uncertainty about issues that matter to large numbers of people.

The view of advertising as a conduit for information is well-known and accepted in commercial markets. Many of the same principles carry over to politics. Our purpose in this chapter is to explain how political advertising in a democracy informs voters about election issues and how information helps voters to choose between competing candidates. Our understanding of these issues comes from two branches of empirical research into politics. One branch uses surveys and laboratory experiments to measure how well voters retain information from election advertisements. The other uses data on campaign spending and vote totals to isolate and measure how many extra votes a candidate can win for every extra dollar of advertising. We survey both branches below and show that they point to a richer and less one-sided role for advertising in politics than the one we are used to hearing about in public debates.

Size and Nature of Election Advertising

There are two popular impressions of the size of campaign spending. One is exemplified by this statement made by Congressman Charles Rose (D-NC):

> No one can deny that their constituents are fed up with high-priced campaigns. These campaigns . . . involve enough spending to feed the residents of some of the smaller countries in the world for one year.

The other viewpoint has been expressed by Senator Robert Packwood (R-OR):

> [The United States does not spend] anywhere near what other democratic countries do in their elections. We do not come near to spending what we do in this country on . . . advertising for pet food. So, in terms of priorities and importance, let us not get things out of scale. I would like to think that the value

TABLE 22.1   Total Political Spending at Federal, State, and Local Levels, 1952-1988

Year	Spending ($)	Percentage Increase
1952	140,000,000	NA
1956	155,000,000	10.7
1960	175,000,000	12.9
1964	200,000,000	14.2
1968	300,000,000	50.0
1972	425,000,000	41.6
1976	540,000,000	36.4
1980	1,200,000,000	122.0
1984	1,800,000,000	50.0
1988	2,700,000,000	50.0

SOURCES: Data from Herbert A. Alexander, *Financing the 1972 Election* (Lexington, MA: Lexington, 1976); Herbert A. Alexander, *Financing the 1980 Election* (Lexington, MA: Lexington, 1983); Herbert A. Alexander and Brian A. Haggerty, *Financing the 1984 Election* (Lexington, MA: Lexington, 1987).
NOTE: NA = not applicable. Figures are rounded.

of an election for Congress or the Senate is worth as much as a can of cat food or dog food.[1]

The truth falls somewhere between these two extremes. As Table 22.1 shows, the sum total of campaign spending appears large and has obviously been growing rapidly. However, as Robert Packwood has advised, we should look at things in perspective. The $2.7 billion spent on elections in 1988 is roughly the same amount the two leading U.S. commercial advertisers—Procter & Gamble and Philip Morris—spent in 1987 to promote their products. As Table 22.2 shows, spending in congressional campaigns as a fraction of voting-age population shows no clear trend until the early 1990s, when it begins to rise. Perhaps even more telling is that spending as a percentage of gross national product has been at times as high in the late 1970s and early 1980s as in the early 1990s, a period of supposedly unprecedented campaign spending.

Simple figures such as these can give us only rough clues to the influence advertising has come to have on election outcomes. These figures do not hint at the technological changes that every year make the advertising dollar reach more voters with messages of greater potency. To start forming an idea of how political advertising influences voters, we must turn our attention away from these raw figures and ask what exactly advertising is and how it is used in election campaigns.

TABLE 22.2   Nominal and Real Congressional Campaign Spending and Its
Relation to Voting Age Population, and GNP, 1972-1996

Year	Campaign Spending in Thousands of Current $	Campaign Spending in Thousands of 1991 $	Campaign Spending in 1991 $ Spent per Adult of Voting Age	Campaign Spending in Current $ as % of GNP
1972	77,300	252,074	1.79	0.00652
1974	88,200	243,847	1.73	0.00615
1976	115,500	276,672	1.89	0.00672
1978	194,800	407,228	2.67	0.00900
1980	239,000	395,336	2.52	0.00875
1982	342,400	483,618	2.92	0.01090
1984	374,100	491,232	2.87	0.00992
1986	450,900	560,234	3.24	0.01060
1988	457,700	526,896	2.96	0.00038
1990	445,200	464,275	2.56	0.00806
1992	679,700	700,161	3.66	0.01090
1994	726,000	789,964	3.81	0.01050
1996	765,300	881,612	3.95	0.01010

SOURCES: Compiled from FEC press releases, *Statistical Abstract of the United States 1997*, U.S. Survey of Current Business.

Election advertising is a broad term. It covers the highly visible efforts of candidates to present themselves to the public through the paid media, but it also includes putting out lawn posters, going from door to door, and having volunteers call potential supporters. Candidates for minor offices advertise less in the media than do candidates for major offices. Sometimes minor candidates will not even advertise. Instead they rely on word of mouth, meetings with constituents, and their party's reputation. This is why most research has focused on high-level campaigns, such as congressional and presidential races. In such contests media advertising is one of the major determinants of election outcomes, and its effects are more obvious to the researcher. Unmeasurable forces such as word of mouth have less influence on outcomes and hence do not cloud the meaning of results as might happen in smaller campaigns, where uncontrolled variables may play a larger part.

Even in high-level campaigns, advertising is seldom a major part of the budget. In 1990 Senate races, candidates spent 35% of their budgets on advertising. Fixed costs make up a large part of their outlays. Before any information flows between candidate and public, the candidate must pay for office, staff, and the production of advertisements. Salaries and commissions to pollsters are a large part of the expenses because the candidate needs expert help to find out what voters want and how to answer those wants. In other words, the candidate's optimal "expenditure mix" includes more than just advertising.

Information in campaigns runs in many directions. Before candidates can inform voters of their platforms, they must have platforms. Candidates have beliefs, but to market those beliefs they need to know what interests the public and how to reach them. As Kotler writes, "The very essence of a candidate's interface with voters is a marketing one. . . . The structure of business marketing and political marketing is basically the same."[2]

There are many facets to this interface. Opinion polls are an important gauge of public sentiment; so are direct-mail techniques in which candidates send letters to possible supporters asking them what issues concern them. Candidates also learn what matters to special interest groups by raising funds from these groups. Candidates who represent a party cannot take any position simply to assure their majority. They must use their market information to emphasize the issues on which their opinions appeal to the most voters. Once a candidate knows his or her market, he or she can mount an advertising campaign that targets those voters who are most likely to be swayed by the candidate's platform.

Whether an exchange of information helps the candidate to win depends on the following fundamental forces:

1. Constituents' characteristics, such as age, income, education, and sex
2. The candidate's personal characteristics (sex, party, incumbency status)
3. Variables that are hard to control, such as GNP and the unemployment rate, for which voters may blame or praise the incumbent
4. Other sources of information, such as media coverage and advertising by independent interest groups

How Election Advertising Works

Stating the forces that matter is not the same as understanding how they work. Social scientists differ in their views about how information spreads and what rules consumers and voters use to make sense of that information. A view that went unchallenged until recently is that voters are passive recipients of information and that this makes them vulnerable to campaign propaganda. Candidates and interest groups with large budgets can tilt the electoral playing field to impose their agendas. For proof that voters are easily swayed, we are told to look at the many sensational 30-second political advertisements that dwell on images and ignore issues; voters seem to respond to superficial advertising that keeps the candidate's ideas and platform in a haze, so that through advertisements candidates can increase voter demand for their services.

To the surprisingly large number of reporters and political pundits who believe the above argument, advertising is either a tool for manipulating the public or at best an expense that conveys little useful information. Many incumbent politicians also speak of advertising as a necessary evil with little useful output. Senator Ernest Hollings has derided congressional elections as "mega-dollar derbies."

Informative Election Advertising

These views, however, must contend with a growing body of research that shows that election advertising is a public good that reaches voters who need it most and helps them make intelligent choices. In election campaigns that get little press coverage, such as those for the U.S. House of Representatives, advertising is the main source of information for voters. Many studies back the claim that voters get useful information from these ads. During the 1972 election campaign, Patterson and McClure collected data in four waves from a panel of 626 respondents in New York State.[3] They found that election advertising increased voters' knowledge of issues and candidates. Similar results have been found for congressional campaigns. In the 1988 Canadian federal election, 70% of people who were not exposed to either the media or political advertising could not name a single candidate in their district, whereas only 24% of those who were highly exposed to both sources of information could not name a single candidate. Nelson has shown that the political market directs information to those who need it most. His central finding is that "advertising for a candidate will be distributed most heavily among those who would be likely to vote for the candidate if they knew the candidate's position."[4]

Optimal Ignorance

Even though election advertising is useful, it cannot inform voters on all the issues. Voters must be selectively ignorant. This determines the rules voters use to process information and the effects that political advertising will have on them. What the right, or "optimal," amount of ignorance is, depends on the type of election being contested and the costs and benefits to each voter of different outcomes. Referenda are mostly about issues contested by different interest groups. On questions of great importance, such as school privatization or tax reform, voters speak with friends and rely on information from many sources. Such races are not won by charismatic leaders who rely on image advertising. The advertising in such races tends to inform voters on technical details or tells where they can find more information. There is a parallel here with the advertising for brands of consumer goods. Underlying successful campaigns for the latter is efficient product performance, otherwise repurchase becomes impossible.

Elections for public office rely more heavily on image advertising. This advertising is an intelligent response by candidates to the problem of communicating with people who do not have time to explore all the details. Voters need images to choose a candidate of ability and integrity. A candidate with these qualities does not always need to be supervised or questioned. This eases the voters' burden of exploring what the candidate thinks on every issue. Finding an able candidate is important because often no one knows what all the issues are or what they will be. It is too costly for candidates to spell out every possible choice they will face while in office, and it is too expensive for voters to form opinions on every contingency.

The search for the candidate who will on average make the right choices as situations develop is the search for an able candidate. Ultimately, voters should care only about the issues. But they may not be able to afford to believe a candidate without evidence about his or her character. Testimonials from important people and scenes of large, enthusiastic followings are a candidate's credentials. Without good credentials, a candidate cannot make credible promises. This, and the demand for a competent individual in office, is why so many political ads are a mix of image (credentials) and issue. Voters form their opinions about a candidate by combining what they know about the image of the candidate with what they know about the candidate's positions. These cannot be separated from questions of integrity and ability—that is, the candidate's image.

We can expect that as voters become more educated, they will rely less on simple cues such as images and endorsements and more on their own research on where the candidates stand. The influence and strength of U.S. parties has declined in the past 30 years in part because voters rely less on official endorsements such as party approval. The technology of communications is advancing and making it easier for many competing views from candidates and independent groups to reach voters. This is forcing candidates to place more emphasis on issues and to take explicit stands. For example, Joslyn found that issues surfaced in 77% of the television political ads he analyzed.[5] Patterson and McClure found issues in 70% of television advertisements in the 1972 presidential campaign.[6] Faber and Storey discovered that in the 1984 Texas contest for governor, voters were more likely to remember issues than images.[7]

Talking About the Issues Pays

Talking about the issues is not the same thing as taking a stand on them. One view, supported by some research, is that by sending vague messages candidates may avoid alienating certain voters, while at the same time projecting an image of seriousness and sincerity. However, there is growing evidence that taking a stand on issues may be a better campaign strategy than being vague. Comparisons of candidates who did not take stands with those who did suggest that those who took no stand were not highly rated by voters. There is also evidence that voters consider candidates who do not take a stand to be less honest, less direct, and less well-informed than their opponents who did take a stand. Experiments with volunteers show that voters give higher ratings to candidates who take more precise positions on the issues.

Information and Choice

Having more information may not necessarily change the voter's choice of candidate. To study the effect of information on choice, Rothschild gathered some people from a shopping mall and asked them to look at political advertisements for presidential candidates and for candidates in state congressional races.[8] He found that advertising could sway the choice of state congressional candidate but had little effect on the choice of presidential candidate. He concluded that in "low-involvement" races such as state elections, voters could be more easily swayed by advertising than in "high-involvement" races, where voters had a great deal of intellectual capital already invested in who could best represent them.

Rothschild's finding made researchers question whether advertising sways only low-involvement voters—voters who feel the election is not important or who have little personal stake in the outcome. Such voters will not have thought much about the issues and can be easily convinced. The evidence to date on this question tentatively suggests that advertising changes the minds of more than just low-involvement voters. After incumbency and party iden- tification, election advertising is the third best predictor of whether voters will change their minds. There is broad evidence that both high- and low-involve- ment voters are especially receptive to messages by challenging candidates. Little is usually known about challengers, so voters have the most to learn from hearing about them.

None of this suggests that money can buy elections. Poor challengers routinely defeat rich incumbents, and millionaires are never easy victors. What advertising does is strengthen the tendencies and beliefs that people already have and clarify which candidates share those beliefs. The information changes the minds of some and encourages others to vote instead of staying home to abstain. How well money transmits information and sways voters depends on the spender and the context. Is the candidate female, an incumbent, a good speaker? Is the constituency wealthy, educated, religious? A female candidate may spend a fortune in a traditional constituency and get nowhere, or might spend little in a liberal constituency and do quite well. In other words, money alone does not determine election outcomes; there are many other forces that interact subtly with spending. In the next section we describe the efforts of researchers to pin down these subtle effects and to answer the question, How many votes does a dollar buy?

The Effect of Money on Election Outcomes

Surveys can uncover how voters use campaign information, but surveys cannot say precisely what effect money has on election outcomes. Measuring this effect is the golden fleece of empirical election studies because it lies at the heart of the debate on candidate spending limits. The data needed for this undertaking became available only in the early 1970s, an era of intense campaign reforms throughout the Western world. Because of these reforms, the U.S. Federal Election Commission (FEC) and similar organizations in Canada and Europe now publish detailed information on how much advertis- ing candidates buy.

Researchers try to relate these data on advertising to the votes candidates receive, using the statistical procedure known as regression. If you believe a variable, such as votes, depends on many different forces, such as incumbency, the demographic details of a district, and the amount of money the incumbent and the challenger spend, then regression lets you gauge the separate impacts of these independent variables on votes. Jacobson estimated the following regression equation for 1972 House challengers:[9]

Challenger Share of Votes = 20.7
+ 0.112 (Challenger Spending in Thousands of Dollars)
(9.42)
− 0.002 (Incumbent Spending in Thousands of Dollars)
(−0.14)
− 0.47 (Party Dummy Variable)
(−0.61)
+ 0.299 (Challenger Voteshare in Last Election)
(6.49)
Number of candidates = 296; R^2 = 49%

The numbers attached to each variable are the estimated coefficients, which show by how much an increase in the variable will change challenger vote share. The numbers in parentheses are t statistics, which give an idea of whether the estimated coefficients are statistically significant. The R^2 value says that the explanatory variables can account for 49% of the variation in the dependent variable. The remaining 51% variation in vote share is due either to randomness or to some variables that should have been but were not included in the regression. The party dummy variable takes on a value of 1 if the candidate is a Democrat and a value of 0 if the candidate is a Republican.

The coefficient attached to challenger spending says that challengers could expect 1.12% of the share of the popular vote for every extra $10,000 they spent. The t statistics indicate that incumbent spending did not even have a statistically discernible effect on the incumbent's vote share (neither did the challenger's party affiliation). This confirms the survey results mentioned earlier, which showed that voters learn more from challenger advertising than from incumbent advertising.

Regressions have also shown that incumbents start the race out with an advantage in votes simply by virtue of being incumbents. This is very different from saying that incumbents win more votes. If we simply compared the vote totals of incumbents and challengers, we would find that on average incumbents do better. This finding is of limited interest, because many factors may account for the difference. Incumbents may advertise more, or quality challengers may prefer to run in districts where there is no incumbent. To isolate the pure effect that being an incumbent has on votes, we could take challengers and incumbents who are identical in every way—in their campaign spending, in the districts where they compete, and so on—and compare their vote · difference. This way we would have "controlled" for the many varying factors that can explain why they perform differently at the polls. Regression is another way of controlling for these other influences. It allows us to isolate the effect of incumbency status on electoral outcomes.

In Canadian federal constituencies it was discovered that incumbency status gives incumbents an advantage of between 6% and 19% of the popular vote.[10] This advantage probably flows from the government-paid mailings incumbents are allowed and from the media exposure they receive. It is the goodwill capital the incumbent has banked with constituents. In commercial enterprises such goodwill is also referred to as the advertising's cumulative effect, or as brand-name recognition. Businesses consider goodwill capital to be as important a part of producing their final good as the physical capital in their factories. The situation is no different in politics.

Incumbents can protect their name capital in several ways. One of them is to spend money during elections to reinforce what constituents have learned about them during their stay in office. Such spending may not gain incumbents many extra votes, but it can preserve their initial advantage. This is perhaps why we find that the marginal product of incumbent spending is lower than that of challengers. Few people, however, know about challengers. This may explain their very high marginal product of spending.

Incumbents can also protect their capital with regulations. Campaign spending limits, limits on contributions, short elections, complicated and costly candidate registration requirements—all keep challengers from becoming recognized by constituents. These laws resemble strong antiadvertising regulations within the professional associations of medical practitioners and others. Incumbents in most democracies have passed variations on these laws. The most recent trend in campaign finance regulation has been to restrict election advertising by public interest groups. Advances in communications technology, inexpensive desktop publishing systems, and cheap computer mailing lists now make it easy for small, independent groups of citizens to criticize officeholders. This technological shift perhaps explains the urgency and surprising unanimity with which incumbents pass laws to silence these outside critics.

In a fascinating study of incumbent self-protection, Bender measured the marginal productivity of campaign spending by members of Congress.[11] He found that members of Congress with the lowest productivity of spending were the likeliest to vote for the 1974 amendments to the Federal Election Campaign Act. These amendments included campaign spending limits on candidates for Congress. Bender's study is only one example of the uses to which measures of election advertising potency are being put. Such measurements figured heavily in a major Canadian government report on election reform published in 1991. These estimates have also been used in court cases challenging the constitutional validity of campaign spending limits.

Reading Too Much Into the Results

Understanding of this field has come far, but in making pronouncements about election regulation, care should be taken not to read too much into a simple number such as the marginal product of campaign spending (i.e., the incremental votes generated by a stated increase in expenditure). Three examples illustrate the problems in the interpretation and use of estimated marginal products.

1. As Filip Palda has suggested, researchers do not yet know how much skill incumbents have to affect their own marginal products.[12] If an incumbent chooses to change his or her platform significantly to meet the threat of a popular challenger, this may convince voters that he or she is a remade candidate, worth a second hearing. The renewed incumbent's marginal product of spending is suddenly higher because of the changed platform. If many incumbents adopted this strategy, estimates would show that incumbent marginal products are not low. This might tempt researchers to conclude that campaign spending limits will not hurt incumbents any less than they will hurt challengers. This inference, however, would be wrong. Incumbent products in this example are high because incumbents change their stances to ward off popular challengers. If spending limits were in place, innovative challengers, handicapped by spending restrictions, could not make incumbents move in this way. We would then find that incumbents have very low marginal products.

2. High challenger marginal products do not necessarily mean that voters prefer the challenger to the incumbent. Many challengers who have come close to winning say that a few thousand more dollars would have taken them over the top. If one looks at how productive their small campaign funds are, this argument is hard to refute. But productivity of funds is only half the picture, because productivity gives only a "local" idea of the candidate's strength. Even untalented, unappealing candidates may get great mileage from the first few thousand dollars they spend. Once they have won over the small number who are willing to support them, a further increase in spending may not get them very far. It is not clear how much more competitive elections would be if challengers received subsidies, or even that the majority of voters would be served by such artificial promotion.

3. As we have shown in previous work, the context in which candidates advertise determines how productive that advertising will be.[13] We cannot simply estimate the marginal product of spending and then predict how many extra votes a dollar will buy. The power of campaign spending to win votes depends in part on where candidates raise their money. A thousand dollars spent on advertising will have a greater effect if the money was raised from many small contributors who are representative of the constituency than if it was raised from a single eccentric contributor. A candidate who must rely on an eccentric for funding is less likely to reflect the will of the constituency. For the same reason, candidates who rely on subsidies may find that subsidy money is less productive than money raised from constituents. Although Emperor Vespasian's dictum that money has no odor holds true in commercial advertising, it may not in the political kind.

Beneficiaries of Public Advertising

Commercial advertising lowers the consumer's cost of searching for goods. Advertising can also be a part of the product. Commercials for fashion products promise the consumers of the products membership in a lifestyle shared only by special people. Political advertising serves a similar function for voters. However, the difference between politics and commerce is that voters cannot directly buy the "good" being offered in the political market-place. This makes it hard to see what direct benefit a voter can get from political advertising. Having learned that one candidate is better than the other, the voter cannot simply decide which candidate will step into office. The voter is constrained by the opinions of all other voters. Even a voter's favored candidate may not come close to satisfying his or her demands.

The key difference between political markets and commercial markets is that most exchanges in politics are zero- or negative-sum, whereas most exchanges in commerce increase the welfare of all participants. In Western democracies, roughly 70% of government spending is a transfer of resources from one group of citizens to secure resources for another group. Political advertising may be used by one group of citizens to secure resources from another group. Such advertising does not add value to the economy or increase the sum of voter wealth. It is simply a cost of redistributing resources the economy has already produced. This cost is often referred to as *rent seeking*, an erudite-sounding expression for waste.[14]

We can better see how political advertising increases the welfare of all voters by taking a broader perspective of politics. How to redistribute resources is not the only issue in elections. Government efficiency is important. Everyone can benefit from advertising that forces officeholders to follow sound macroeconomic policies and to keep a close eye on government bureaucracy. Political advertising can prevent government from growing. There is evidence that at the state level, voters are fiscal conservatives. They punish gubernatorial candidates who increase government spending just before elections. Such increases come to light with the help of campaign advertising.

Conclusion

In this chapter we have described how political advertising in a democracy works to inform voters about issues and how such information helps voters to choose between candidates. The evidence suggests that political advertising informs voters in ways in which the news media cannot. Candidates behave remarkably like firms. They survey the political market to learn the wishes of their constituents. They then transmit their messages to those voters most likely to agree. In this way information finds its way to those who value it most. Political advertising therefore serves to enhance the political process in a democracy by increasing the efficiency of voter decision making, even while it falls short of being the decisive influence on the electoral outcome.

Notes

1. Quotes from Ross and Packwood are both from *Congressional Record,* June 3, 1987, 7548.

2. Philip Kotler, "Overview of Political Candidate Marketing," *Advances in Consumer Research,* vol. 2, 1975, 762.

3. Thomas E. Patterson and Robert D. McClure, *The Unseeing Eye* (New York: G. P. Putnam's Sons, 1976).

4. Phillip Nelson, "Political Information," *Journal of Law and Economics,* vol. 19, 1976, 330.

5. Richard A. Joslyn, "The Content of Political Spot Ads," *Journalism Quarterly,* vol. 57, Spring 1980, 92-98.

6. Patterson and McClure, *The Unseeing Eye.*

7. Ronald J. Faber and M. Claire Storey, "Recall of Information From Political Advertising," *Journal of Advertising,* vol. 13, 1984, 39-44.

8. Michael L. Rothschild, "Political Advertising: A Neglected Policy Issue in Marketing," *Journal of Marketing Research,* vol. 15, 1978, 58-71.

9. Gary C. Jacobson, "The Effects of Electoral Campaign Spending in Congressional Elections," *American Political Science Review,* vol. 72, 1978, 474.

10. Filip Palda and Kristian S. Palda, "The Impact of Campaign Expenditures on Political Competition in the French Legislative Elections of 1993," *Public Choice,* vol. 94, 1998, 157-174. See also Filip Palda, "The Economics of Election Campaign Spending Limits," *Economia Delle Scelte Pubbliche,* vol. 2, 1996, 113-137; Filip Palda, "Desirability and Effects of Campaign Spending Limits," *Crime, Law and Social Change,* vol. 21, 1994, 295-317; Filip Palda, *How Much Is Your Vote Worth? The Unfairness of Campaign Spending Limits* (San Francisco: ICS, 1994); Kristian S. Palda, "The Effect of Expenditure on Political Success," *Journal of Law and Economics,* vol. 18, 1975, 745-771; Filip Palda and Kristian S. Palda, "Campaign Spending and Campaign Finance Issues: An Economic View," *Journal des Economistes et des Etudes Humaines,* vol. 3, 1992, 291-314.

11. Bruce Bender, "An Analysis of Congressional Voting on Legislation Limiting Congressional Campaign Expenditures," *Journal of Political Economy,* vol. 96, 1988, 1005-1021.

12. Palda, "The Economics of Election Campaign Spending Limits."

13. Palda and Palda, "The Impact of Campaign Expenditures."

14. Gordon Tullock, "Efficient Rent-Seeking," in James B. Buchanan, Robert D. Tollison, and Gordon Tullock (eds.), *Toward a Theory of Rent-Seeking Society* (College Station: Texas A&M University Press, 1980), 97-112.

Cable Television Stations as Brands

Mary Baumgartner Jones

In 1974 the first satellite-delivered cable channel, Home Box Office (HBO), was launched. In its first year of programming, HBO was available only during prime viewing hours, and still consumers flocked to the first real alternative to network TV. The idea of being able to watch uncut, commercial-free movies in one's own home was irresistible.

In the late 1990s consumers have as many as 500 channels of cable-delivered entertainment, videos, video games, on-line services, and many other home entertainment options. This dramatically increased competition for consumers' leisure time has caused the entire cable-television industry to take a new look at its marketing objectives, strategies, and positioning to make sure it is set up to meet the competitive challenges ahead. Most of all, the differentiation of cable stations from one another is a branding phenomenon.

What Are the Industry's Challenges?

Too many choices, too little time. Recent Nielsen research looked at the number of television channels watched in households with 7 to 70 channels available. The bad news for cable channels is that the number of channels watched has not increased very much even as the number of channels available has gone up. In fact, in any given household the cap on the number of channels actually viewed seems to be between 12 and 14.[1]

No new programming news. In the old days of cable a channel's personality was simply the sum of its programming parts—HBO was a movie channel, CNN had news, and ESPN had sports. This strategy was successful as long as there was clear product differentiation among the channels. Now, with multiple "classic movie" channels, cooking shows available on any of 30 channels, and coverage of the latest news stories all over the dial, it is difficult for any cable channel to have a unique programming product.

No more cable affiliate monopolies. Consumers now have choices about how cable programming is brought into their homes. The C-band satellite dish market remains stable, and the introduction of an 18-inch satellite dish has increased the number of satellite subscribers dramatically. Additionally, in some cases communities are allowing more than one cable company to offer service to consumers. Although this change is great for customers, it means that cable affiliates are spending a lot more time telling consumers about their attributes and a lot less time talking about the cable channels they carry.

Other complications. Cable operators have channel capacity restrictions (many of which are caused by mandated "must carry" channels), which means that if a channel does not attract a big enough audience it will be dropped or migrated to a digital tier. Additionally, cable affiliates continue to grapple with federal reregulation of the industry, which distracts them from their marketing activities.

Where Does This Leave Us?

The present situation leaves cable marketers looking at other mature industries for some lessons in marketing. The tried-and-true lessons of brand manage-

TABLE 23.1   Top 10 Cable Marketers by Size of Marketing Budgets

Cable Channel	Spending (in thousands of $)	Share of Voice (%)
Category total	384,569	100
HBO	109,578	28
Starz!	28,918	8
USA	23,977	6
TNT	17,729	5
A&E	15,859	4
Fox Family Channel	15,068	4
Discovery Channel	14,657	4
Showtime	14,180	4
Lifetime	13,055	3
ESPN	10,132	3
Subtotal	263,153	68
Other	121,416	32

ment are becoming increasingly appropriate, and the industry is in the middle of a major shift in terms of marketing.

The first thing the cable industry must do is set the stage in terms of the competition. The entertainment industry spends a lot of media dollars in the marketplace, of which cable is a very small part.[2] Cable marketers' expenditures are displayed in Table 23.1. The top 10 represent 68% of total spending by all cable marketers, and HBO represents on its own 28% of the category's spending. To date, most cable marketers have not spent enough time or energy trying to brand either the cable channels themselves or the method of distribution.

It might seem that cable channels do not need to market themselves as brands—they simply need to communicate to interested consumers their programming lineups. After all, consumers do not watch a particular show because it is on CBS; they watch it because they like the show. Shouldn't that apply to cable as well?

Unfortunately, it does not. Consumers have been trained by the networks to check out their programming lineups regularly, and most consumers know a lot more about network shows than they do about any cable shows. In order to lure consumers at least to consider a cable channel's lineup (which is usually in the second or third part of the daily programming grid in a newspaper's TV listings), the channel must make the individual consumer feel that the particular channel offers the kind of programming he or she might like.

A specific example of a college-educated household might be the most effective way to explain what I mean. Programming on A&E is essentially a combination of the kind of programming found on Public Television and some older rerun network programming. On any given evening, the household in question will always check A&E's listings because the family is convinced that it is likely that there will be something on that they would like to watch.

On the other side of the equation, there are some 20 channels for which this same household has no clear idea of their programming. Given the fact that much of the programming that they like on A&E is probably available on some of those 20 other channels, it is simply the perception of the brand and its programming that keeps them loyal to A&E.

There are some quite clear steps that cable channels need to take to break through all the clutter and deliver their messages more effectively to the appropriate audiences. These are discussed in turn below.

Brand personalities. Cable channels need to determine what their brand identities are. Although a few channels have done this remarkably well (MTV and Nick at Nite are good examples), and marketers can look to them for ideas, the packaged goods arena is probably a better place to start. A classic example of very different brand personalities for competing products is toilet paper— Scott has 1,000 sheets in every roll, and Charmin is "squeezably soft." American Movie Classics (AMC) and Turner Classic Movies (which offer almost identical programming) need to find positionings for themselves to create that kind of clear brand differentiation.

Media vehicles. Today cable channels spend the majority of their marketing dollars creating interstitial advertising for their own services and tune-in vehicles (see Table 23.2 and the brief glossary at the end of this chapter). Although interstitial time is very valuable for building a brand personality, in most cases the low ratings mean that very few people ever see it. MTV and Nick at Nite are exceptions to this rule. They have used interstitial to brand their channels in a very strong way, but they accomplished this in a less competitive environment. In MTV's case, the channel had a unique product when it was launched, and in Nick at Nite's case it seems that more than half of the channel's commercial breaks are about the service—both image spots and program promotion spots.

TABLE 23.2   Percentages of Marketing Budgets Spent in Six Categories, 1997

Network[a]	*Network TV*	*Cable TV*	*Spot TV*	*Print*	*Network Radio*	*Spot Radio*	*Outdoor*
Starz!	—	54	3	—	42	1	—
USA	—	—	—	97	—	3	—
TNT	—	—	—	87	—	10	3
A&E	—	—	—	91	—	6	3
Fox Family Channel	—	—	—	100	—	—	—
Discovery Channel	—	—	—	96	—	3	1
Showtime	—	6	8	80	2	2	2
Lifetime	—	—	—	61	1	37	2
ESPN	—	—	—	74	—	26	—

SOURCE: Estimates made by Leading National Advertisers, New York, 1998.
a. Networks are listed in descending order according to the sizes of their marketing budgets.

Additionally, print and radio are very difficult media in which to create a brand personality as the foundation of a media plan. Instead, increased use of network television is probably the most effective way to answer the challenge. Although not all network affiliates will accept competitive cable advertising, enough stations will accept it that a cable channel can create some noise in the market. A few well-executed network TV advertisements that clearly define for the customer the point of differentiation for a particular channel is probably money very well spent.

Relationships. It is difficult for a television channel to develop a "relationship" with its customers; however, that should not prevent it from trying. One good example of relationship marketing is A&E's successful print magazine *Biography,* available by paid subscription. Although much of its editorial content is not specific to the channel, it does devote a reasonable amount of space to promoting upcoming A&E shows—which is very important, as much of the channel's programming comes from England, and neither the titles nor the talents are well-known in the United States. Additionally, the magazine's editorial decisions help to reinforce the "classy, smart, and intelligent" personality the channel has created for itself.

Smarter use of promotion. The limited media dollars available for almost all cable channels can be stretched with promotions executed with other advertisers. A smart partnership between a cable channel and an appropriate product can give the channel media and the kind of shelf space that is very expensive. For example, if Nickelodeon wanted to do a tie-in promotion, it might consider a children's book publisher. A line of Nickelodeon titles (much like the line of Nickelodeon toys) could increase awareness of the channel's programming and reinforce in parents' minds that Nickelodeon has a focus on education—which makes them feel better about their children's Nickelodeon viewing time. Another idea for a good joint promotion might be the Discovery Channel's sponsorship of a traveling zoo exhibit tied to one of the channel's documentary series about animals. If its "Shark Week" series were to be executed in conjunction with an educational exhibit at zoos aimed at interesting children in sharks, this would be very valuable for both the zoos and the channel.

Conversely, a promotion executed by Cinemax and Banquet frozen foods was not an overwhelming success. Cinemax has spent a lot of money creating a brand that stands for entertainment and movies. Banquet, although a category leader, was not a good fit, because frozen food is not a natural partner for television entertainment. No matter how many impressions the promotion delivered, it did nothing to enhance Cinemax's brand image.

The other part of the cable marketing equation is the cable affiliates. Historically, cable affiliates have marketed the channels that they had available, but not themselves. Because consumers had no choice but to buy from their local cable operator if they wanted the product, there was no incentive for those operators to market themselves as brands.

The local monopoly that cable operators enjoyed did not encourage them to concern themselves with serving their customers. It is likely that most cable customers will complain about their operators regardless of their own personal experience, because *everybody* looks on cable operators as awful. In a newly competitive environment building a brand image is difficult enough, but overcoming overt hostility toward the category, let alone the company itself, is a daunting task.

Like cable channels, cable operators need to sit back and decide how they want to present themselves to their customers, what they are going to offer subscribers that is different and better. Instead of advertising that tells customers only what is available, cable operators need to tell consumers why they should buy an essentially parity product from them.

Almost all the ideas presented above for marketing cable channels are applicable to cable affiliates, and there are many other marketing opportunities available to cable operators. One such opportunity is community relations and the marketing of operators' involvement in their localities. Cable operators should be a part of all local community services—they should provide special programming to schools and hospitals, offer local-access channels to broadcast local events of import, donate a portion of subscription fees to local causes, and so on. These programs will progressively entrench cable operators in their local communities.

Looking Forward

As the ability to deliver more and more channels is developed, cable marketers will have to try even harder to make their mark. They can accomplish this in two ways. First, they should continue to work on creating very strong brand identities—focusing efforts to support the stronger, better-defined channels. This will probably mean diverting attention away from some of the smaller channels, and that might lead eventually to fewer of them. However, the trend toward "multichannel" offerings of big brands such as HBO and Showtime will continue.

Second, they should participate in ongoing creation of tightly targeted "niche" channels that are not meant to attract mass audiences. These channels will have limited distribution and high viewership among the target audiences, and will command reasonably high advertising rates due to their ability to deliver well-defined audiences. Examples are an increasing number of foreign-language channels and channels devoted to money management, international business, and the like.

Cable channels, like many repeat-purchase packaged goods, are brands, and as such they must be marketed like brands. This means that cable channels will have to make more strategic use of advertising media, develop smarter creative ideas, and finally begin to think of themselves as marketers of consumer products. All of these things will require cable channels to spend a lot more money on marketing and advertising themselves to the public than they have in the past. And in their structure and use of evaluative research, they will increasingly resemble large manufacturers of brands of food, drink, and soap.

Glossary

Basic cable:	Cable service that includes channels delivered to consumers as part of a programming package, not channels for which they must pay an incremental monthly fee. Basic cable networks include CNN, A&E, and TBS.
Cable affiliate:	A company that delivers cable entertainment into consumers' homes via cables as opposed to via satellite.
Interstitial advertising:	Advertising/promotion for a particular channel that runs on that channel.
Multichannel offering:	A brand name carried on more than one cable channel.
Pay-per-view programming:	Programming available to consumers that they can access (at a fee) for one-time viewing.
Premium channel:	A channel available to consumers for a monthly fee over and above their basic cable charge. Home Box Office (HBO), Showtime, and Starz! are the biggest premium TV channels.
Tune-in vehicle:	Advertising/promotion activity that drives consumers to watch a particular show at a specific time.

Notes

1. Thomas Kalinske, "History Repeats Itself: Consumers, Technology and Entertainment," *CTAM Quarterly Journal,* Fall 1994.
2. Based on estimates made by Leading National Advertisers, New York, 1998.

Green Brands and Green Marketing

Janet DiLorenzo
Richard E. Mathisen

The 1990s saw a proliferation of "environmentally correct" new products and packaging fueled by what has been termed the *green marketing* movement. By proposing to be environmentally correct, companies are essentially offering products that are considered to be "safe" for consumers and society as a whole. Such products are unique by modern standards because they do not present hazards to the health of individual consumers and do not inflict damage upon the environment during their manufacture, use, or disposal.

For many members of the public, this environmental agenda may seem familiar. During the 1960s and 1970s, large-scale producers concentrated their environmental concerns on the disposal and waste end of production. Although the 1980s passed without the consolidation of a clear perspective or any particularly watchful eye on the progressive destruction of our environment, the decade of the 1990s has shown distinct signs of a heightened concern not only for product disposal and waste, but for the prevention of environmental harm. This concern has also been the impetus for religious groups to take an active role. In October 1998, a group of 1,000 theologians, scientists, and activists attended an environmental conference at Harvard University. As supporters of the green movement, they asserted their belief that they can influence the ways companies incorporate "green" into their mission statements.[1] Importantly, the outward expression of this impulse to protect the environment from harm is now being designed into products and packages during their manufacture. The unusual change in policy of the 1990s that falls under the umbrella of "green marketing" is evidenced by the rapid pace with which companies are moving to relabel, repackage, reposition, redesign, and recommunicate the products they currently offer to the marketplace. Their primary agenda is, as we have seen, to be environmentally correct—or to make their products "green."

The historical impetus for the green marketing movement came from consumers, who are thinking more carefully about what they buy, how much their purchases will cost, and, notably, what effects their buying decisions will have on the environment. An *Advertising Age*/Gallup Environmental Survey conducted in the early 1990s found that 79% of respondents considered themselves either "strong environmentalists" or "environmentalists." [2] In a similar survey conducted for Gerstam and Mayers, a packaging concern, 83% of respondents said they preferred buying environmentally safe products, and 61% said that they refused to purchase products they felt might pose some environmental danger.[3] Most companies have responded promptly to this kind of consumer concern by carefully communicating the degree of environmental correctness inherent in their agendas. Companies currently are making "green claims" to their consumers by way of packaging and precisely planned promotional campaigns. The language chosen to articulate environmental concerns includes, for example, such terms as *environmentally friendly, biodegradable, compostable,* and *environmentally safe.* Unfortunately, the consumer is being bombarded with multiple variations on the theme of green claims, many of which have proven to be false and/or misleading.

Green Claims and the Marketer: Procter & Gamble

As the leader in the billion-dollar disposable diaper market, Procter & Gamble (P&G) initially introduced this product in the form of the now well-known

Pampers and Luvs. The disposable diaper was developed in 1961 and promptly became the solution for parents who found the cloth diaper to be unattractive. While proving to be an innovative success in product development, disposable diapers have been criticized by environmental groups as being deleterious to the environment. *U.S. News & World Report* reported in 1989 that, on average, each baby consumes 3,000 to 4,000 diapers, and the discarded product ultimately occupies approximately 2% of available landfill space.[4] Disposable diapers also take about 500 years to decompose, thus they present an obvious environmental dilemma of some magnitude.

Waste products in diapers, to make matters worse, are known to cause health problems for sanitation workers and to contaminate groundwater, thereby affecting the surrounding communities. As word circulated concerning the negative environmental effects of a once-hailed product, Procter & Gamble actively began researching the many possible ways it could ease the environmental concerns its customers were expressing.

As a first measure, the company tested recycling. Because disposable diapers consist of plastic, paper pulp, and absorbent gel, Procter & Gamble surmised that there was no reason they could not be recycled, with the resulting materials being reincorporated into products such as drywall, insulation, cardboard, and flower pots. An important obstacle to P&G's thinking turned out to be the cost associated with collection and cleaning of the discarded product. The company next researched another possible solution—composting. In 1991, P&G's expenditure for the promotion of composting technology was approximately $20 million. Although the process had been implemented in Western Europe for decades, it was fairly new at the time to the American public. Composting occurs at a plant where waste is chopped or mashed, nondegradable materials are discarded, and the remains are converted into a substance—compost—that is an effective soil enhancer, one that assists plants in their growth and development.

Procter & Gamble chose to promote its innovative idea intensively through the use of print media. Subsequently, the company was accused of misleading and deceptive environmental claims in its advertising campaign. These justifiable accusations stemmed from the fact that there were relatively few composting plants in communities that were able to process the disposable diapers. In 1991, only 10 composting plants existed in the entire United States.

P&G's attempt to promote its environmental agenda through the use of green claims about disposable diapers represents one of the several ways in

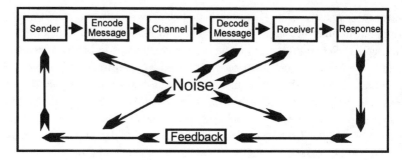

Figure 24.1. A Model of the Communication Process

which marketers have contributed to the breakdown of the communication process. The result, of course, is consumer confusion and hesitancy toward what are intended to be marketing solutions to consumer-driven issues.

The Communication Process

The communication process in its simplest form is the way that two or more people share a common thought. According to one authority, the process requires five elements: a source, a message, a receiver, and the respective processes of encoding and decoding.[5] As shown in Figure 24.1, this process can be represented in the form of a general model. Communication thus involves two parties (a sender and a receiver), specific instruments of expression (a message and a channel), and certain cognitive functions (such as encoding, decoding, and responding), as well as "feedback" and the presence of "noise." This basic model is also endorsed by the doyen of marketing academics, Philip Kotler.[6]

This model is thought to represent the fundamental elements of effective communication. If communication occurs unhindered, then the optimum expression of this model would see communication beginning with the sender, being transmitted to the receiver, and being decoded and received as initially intended. According to another authority, Berkowitz, communication is most effective when the sender and receiver have shared a "field of experience"—a concept that implies a similar understanding of and knowledge about the message conveyed.[7] Unfortunately for many companies, and for various reasons, communication has not been facilitated by a "shared consumer and company field of experience."

Breakdowns in communication may range from ambiguous to patently false claims, both of which ultimately diminish the effectiveness and degrade the integrity of the communication process. In terms of shared fields of experience, companies have generally been environmentally conscious only to the extent that their manufacturing and product offerings can be characterized as environmentally correct. Noise (e.g., claims that fail to communicate their messages clearly) has also contributed to the recent breakdown in the communication process. Consumers appear to be confused about both the number and the types of green claims made. Their confusion can be detected through the often vociferous feedback they have provided to companies about their green marketing methods.

To be fair to producers who are trying to stay in step with society's concerns, it must be noted that, though some American corporations have barraged consumers with misleading, confusing, even contradictory green claims, the federal government has failed to exploit its inherent ability to ameliorate the situation by implementing well-defined green guidelines. At present, green claims are asserted and costly product modifications are made with no certainty of government approval.

Thus inconsistencies in claims are partly the fault of companies and partly the result of too-broad, ill-defined, ambiguous, or nonexistent government standards and policies. In maintaining this position, the government sends a signal of uncertainty and lack of interest directly to the consumer, one that further enhances the increasing erosion of consumer confidence now being seen over the "greenness" of products. An extension of this argument that may offer some insight into these serious problems can be made through an analysis of the communication model, one element at a time.

Sender

The sender has a major influence on the receiver provided the communication is accepted. For effective communication, the source of the information should be credible and the communication plausible to the receiver. Conversely, one reason communication may break down is that the source is considered unbelievable and/or untrustworthy; this situation usually results in hesitancy or downright refusal to accept the message. Currently, companies such as Kraft General Foods, Mobil, Coca-Cola, Del Monte Foods, Dow

Chemical, and McDonald's, in an effort to be considered credible and responsive to the environmental needs of the marketplace, are setting discrete environmental agendas that state their missions and strategies in the green marketing movement. For example, McDonald's Corporation's "Commitment to the Environment" reads:

> McDonald's believes it has a special responsibility to protect our environment for future generations. The responsibility is derived from our unique relationship with millions of consumers worldwide—whose quality of life tomorrow will be affected by our stewardship of the environment today. We share their belief that the right to exist in an environment of clean air, clean earth and clean water is fundamental and unwavering. We realize that, in today's world, a business leader must be an environmental leader as well. Hence our determination to analyze every aspect of our business in terms of its impact on the environment, and to take actions beyond what is expected if they hold the prospect of leaving future generations an environmentally sound world. We will lead, both in word and deed.
>
> Our environmental commitment and behaviors are guided by the following principles:
>
> • Effectively managing solid waste—*Reduce-Reuse-Recycle,*
> • Conserving and protecting natural resources,
> • Encouraging environmental values and practices,
> • Ensuring accountability procedures.
>
> On all of the above, we are committed to timely, honest and forthright communications with our consumers, shareholders, suppliers and employees.[8]

This type of corporate environmental effort suggests to consumers that, in this case, McDonald's has taken a clear and explicit position on the environment. In an environmental survey conducted during the 1990s, consumers were asked to rate marketers on their concern for the environment.[9] Procter & Gamble was named the most environmentally conscious company, with the McDonald's Corporation coming in second. Ironically, 68% of the respondents believed that no one company was concerned enough about the environment.

Encoding of Message

The message is considered the most important component of the communication model: "It is the thought, idea, attitudes, image, etc., that the sender, or company, desires to transfer to the appropriate receiver." [10] The goal of the sender is to determine precisely what information is to be conveyed, for what reason, and to try to fashion its message accordingly. For many companies in the 1990s a major message being communicated to consumers is one of environmental concern. Examples include the use of green claims on packaging and in promotional campaigns. Among the terms being used today in these contexts are *biodegradable, photodegradable, degradable, recyclable, compostable, environmentally friendly, environmentally safe, ozone friendly,* and *ozone safe.*

Channel (Medium)

The channel is a variable but essential element of the communication model. It is the specific informational means by which a message is targeted to a specific audience. Companies generally select from a variety of channels, included among which are broadcasting, print, public relations, and direct mail. A particularly important medium for environmentally concerned companies has been print. Environmental features and benefits of brands expressed in the form of green claims are believed to be effectively communicated through print and have led to increased sales of such brands. For example, Mobil Corporation ran a print campaign in the early 1990s about Mobil 1 that displayed an insignia accompanied by the phrase "Environmental Awareness" and the statement "Take your used motor oil to an approved collection center." A print advertisement for Downy liquid fabric softener stated the manufacturer's commitment to the "refill." This successful advertisement could have been expected to draw much praise because refilling is economical and helps the environment by reducing the amount of trash that Downy purchasers throw out.

Receiver

Communication typically can be received as intended by companies, if the message sent is congruent with the existing opinions, attitudes, perceptions, motivations, and beliefs of the receiver. The receiver brings to the process a "field of experience" that ultimately influences the encoded message. In the case of green claims and environmental agendas, studies seem to demonstrate that the receiver's attitude is generally one of concern. Here are some examples:

- An environmental study conducted by *Reader's Digest* in 1991 suggested that 98% of respondents were personally willing to change their behavior and buying habits in order to ensure a cleaner world.[11]

- In the Third Annual Nationwide Environmental Study, conducted for the packaging company Gerstam and Mayers, 83% of respondents said they preferred buying environmentally safe products. In addition, 61% claimed they had declined to purchase certain products within the past year because of environmental concerns.[12]

- The Environment USA survey, conducted jointly by Golin/Harris Communication and Angus Reid Group, determined that 74% of those surveyed considered environmental protection a priority.[13]

- The Lempert Report noted that 50% of those surveyed felt that environmental concerns had affected their past supermarket purchases.[14]

- A survey commissioned by the British Market Research Bureau (BMRB)/Mintel, *The Green Consumer 1991*, determined that 39% of respondents had "always/nearly always" bought or used environmentally friendly products or services.

- The Leo Burnett USA survey conducted in May 1991 established that 28% of respondents were willing to make drastic changes in their lifestyles in order to help the environment.[15]

The surveys cited above substantiate the strong attitudinal concerns consumers have for the environment and their readiness to take action so that their needs will be met. Ironically, although many senders and receivers appear to have similar environmental concerns, messages have frequently failed to be decoded as intended, suggesting a complexity to the process of information exchange and of valuation in general. To date, confusion and hesitancy regarding the purchase of supposedly green products have been the norm.

Decoding

Although consumers consider most green claims to represent positive gestures on the part of companies, they are often confused about what these claims mean. One set of results, from the Environment USA survey cited above, suggested that consumers felt confident about the use of products that made such green claims as "recyclable," "recycle," or "biodegradable." They further believed that products having such claims on the packaging were safer for the environment than products without them.

When asked if these claims referred to the product or its package, however, 39% said both, 26% said product, 22% said package, and 13% were unsure about what the claims signified.[16] These results clearly indicate that although consumers may feel confident about the existence of green claims, there remains an obvious breakdown in communication—a lack of clear understanding of the message.

Noise

Noise surrounds the process and disturbs the effectiveness of encoding, the medium, decoding, and feedback. Conflicting messages from senders other than the marketer interested in making green claims, even though they flow undisturbed through the medium, can result in lessened impact of the marketer's message. These may take the form of sender(s) refuting the claims, messages from special interest groups, and messages sent by other marketers. Noise at this point in the process may also be present in conflicting messages sent by the marketer. In the medium, the intensity and volume of communications and media often result in receivers' selectively blocking messages, possibly only because of the sheer volume of messages they have to deal with.

The marketer making green claims must recognize that the attention of intended receivers is not focused solely on green issues. Noise at the decoding point may result from the receiver's inability to interpret the message or conflicting attitudes in the receiver's field of experience. The trouble and cost associated with participating in such green-related activities as recycling, reusing, and refilling may disturb the decoding and subsequent action steps. Finally, noise present in the feedback interferes with the ability of the receiver to return a clear or accurate response and the ability of the sender to receive the feedback properly.

Feedback

Communication flow from the receiver back to the sender occurs by way of feedback. Significantly, feedback has not been effective in altering the nature of recent green messages. In their efforts to portray themselves as environmentally concerned, many companies make overblown and unsubstantiated claims that do not withstand close scrutiny by consumers and environmental groups. Thus the intense motivation to be seen as environmentally conscious appears to have clouded the eyes of producers; trivial, confusing, and misleading green claims in the face of increasingly cynical reactions by consumers in the marketplace may not augur well for green marketing in general.

Procter & Gamble has modified its production and design of such brands as Pampers and Downy; Kraft General Foods has decreased packaging materials for Miracle Whip, Jell-O Pudding, and Post cereals. Other major corporations that have taken important steps include Lever Brothers, Clorox, Lehn & Fink (Lysol), Heinz, Kimberly-Clark, James River (Brawny), Johnson & Johnson, Tambrands (Tampax), and Playtex.[17] In light of the mismatch between some green marketers and some consumer groups, it is unfortunate that those corporations expressing profound sensitivity to the environment are going underappreciated owing to the strong concerns that consumers have about misleading advertising claims. This may appear to be a double-edged sword, and it may in fact be one. It is clear, nevertheless, that the core of the problem relates to the inconsistencies that currently exist among the many variant meanings of *green* as understood by consumers, companies, government agencies, and nongovernment groups. Additionally, the lack of a clear, concise communication process in green marketing circles will only, it seems, continue to deter consumers from trusting companies and accepting as valuable their brands' contributions to the green movement.

Conclusion

The success of the green marketing movement is largely determined by marketers' effective implementation of the communication process. For companies to communicate their environmental agendas, it is critical that they have sufficient knowledge and understanding of the communication process. Senders must properly encode their messages to communicate their intended ideas clearly. A message must be encoded in a form that uses the appropriate medium effectively and minimizes the impact of noise or clutter as the message is transmitted to the receiver. The communicated message must be readily decoded, so that the receiver understands it as intended by the sender and takes the desired action.

Clearly, the green movement is relevant and important today. Many companies have faced serious challenges in stimulating consumers to "buy green." The use of false, misleading, or misunderstood claims has aggravated the problem of the green marketer who is attempting to make a contribution to environmental safety. Although consumers indicate that they have concerns for the environment, their actions fall short of the expectations of green marketers. An effective communication process is imperative to reduce this disparity.

Notes

1. T. Watanabe, "The Green Movement Gets Religion," *Journal News,* February 1, 1999, 1E.

2. D. Chase, "Procter and Gamble Gets Top Marks in AA Survey," *Advertising Age,* January 29, 1991, 8.

3. J. Dagnoli, "Consciously Green Consumers Question Marketers' Commitment," *Advertising Age,* September 16, 1991, 14. See also J. Dagnoli, "Here Today, Still Here Tomorrow," *Time,* April 9, 1990, 66.

4. Wilbur Schramm, "It's Diaper City at the Landfill," *U.S. News & World Report,* July 3, 1989, 12. See also Wilbur Schramm, "Spreading a Deeper Shade of Green," *Marketing,* May 23, 1991, 16.

5. Wilbur Schramm, "How Communication Works," in Wilbur Schramm and Donald F. Roberts (eds.), *The Process and Effects of Mass Communication* (Urbana: University of Illinois Press, 1971), 4.

6. Philip Kotler, *Marketing Management: Analysis, Planning, and Control,* 2nd ed. (Englewood Cliffs, NJ: Prentice Hall, 1991).

7. See Eric N. Berkowitz, Roger A. Kerin, William Rudelius, and Steven W. Hartley, *Marketing,* 5th ed. (Homewood, IL: Irwin, 1996).

8. McDonald's Corporation, "Commitment to the Environment," in *McDonald's and the Environment* (Oak Brook, IL: McDonald's Corporation, September 1991).

9. Chase, "Procter and Gamble Gets Top Marks."

10. Leon G. Schiffman and Leslie Lazar Kanuk, *Consumer Behavior,* 4th ed. (Englewood Cliffs, NJ: Prentice Hall, 1991).

11. S. Hume, "Green Labels Good, But Confusing," *Advertising Age,* December 9, 1991, 43.

12. Dagnoli, "Consciously Green Consumers."

13. S. Hume, "Consumer Double-Talk Makes Companies Wary," *Advertising Age,* October 28, 1991, 4.

14. P. Lempert, "What's on Shoppers' Minds," *Progressive Grocer,* September 1991, 32.

15. Hume, "Green Labels Good."

16. Hume, "Consumer Double-Talk."

17. John Sinisi, *Superbrands* (New York: McGraw-Hill, 1992).

How Brands Should Be Presented to Elderly Consumers

Delight L. Omohundro

Definitions

Gerontology, the study of the elderly, is frequently confused with geriatrics, the study of diseases of the aging. But the incapacitated elderly are a true minority: Just 1.5% of Americans under age 70 are in nursing homes or hospitalized. The elderly constitute a large and growing market with possibly the highest discretionary income in the country, which may be conveniently divided into two groups: the "young-old," those aged from 65 to 85, a group usually free of work and family duties, yet in fine, energetic health, and the "old-old," those over age 85 (see Figure 25.1).

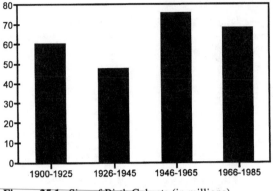

Figure 25.1. Size of Birth Cohorts (in millions)

As members of the historic "baby boom" generation born after World War II approach the age of 50, this senior adult market has escalated in importance. For decades, products that appealed to baby boomers have created a "pig-in-a-python" shape on sales charts, and national economic activities have mirrored their needs. The oldest boomers, born in 1946, are well over 50 today, and as the baby boom generation ages, the importance of developing methods of selling to the older market—of guiding brands in their direction—becomes more important with each passing year. When this group reaches 65, the mature market will surpass 30% of the U.S. population, with an even higher percentage of the buying power; it will become the dominant force in the American economy and marketplace. Therefore, the ability to communicate with the elderly in general, and with this most numerous of all generations in particular, is crucial.

In 1995, the oldest baby boomers began to qualify for membership in the American Association of Retired Persons (i.e., they were 50 or older). With their continuing progress into the realm of the young-old, changes have already begun. As is appropriate for the generation that has dominated consumer economics for five decades, their entry into a new stage in life has been welcomed with fanfare. Among the changes already visible are the following:

- *Political emphasis on senior issues:* The staggering impact wielded by the senior lobby at the polls has led both political parties to focus on such issues as nursing home costs, protection for the Social Security system, and health care funding.

- *Media coverage of "can-do" seniors:* The ultimate role model for seniors must be astronaut (and former senator) John Glenn, who returned to space at age 77. As the span of active life increases, thousands of healthy older Americans are retiring to more active lifestyles, generating a new and profitable target market for sports, hobby, and recreation gear.

- *Home design incorporating special features for more mature owners:* Items such as ramp walkways, raised countertops and eye-level appliances, large-button telephones and switches, and lever door handles instead of hard-to-grasp knobs make life easier for all.

- *More clothing available in larger sizes:* Although men's stores have always provided a range of sizes, large-size women have frequently gone wanting. Today, to accommodate the natural weight gain that comes with age, such high-fashion retailers as Bloomingdale's, Saks, and Nieman Marcus frequently incorporate size ranges up to 18/20 in the "misses" category and offer "woman's" size options for many styles.

This chapter is organized into three main sections. I first discuss the major challenges and pitfalls of communicating with the senior market, and then I delineate the key physical and psychological changes that are seen in seniors compared with younger consumers. I conclude with a discussion of the major age cohorts and the larger group referred to as senior citizens—a group that will become even larger as the baby boom generation ages.

Communicating With the Older Consumer

The elderly are like the rest of the population, but with some vital differences. Communicating with elderly consumers is a special skill, and the peculiarities of the baby boom seniors may well add some interesting twists. Although the basic principles of communication still apply, those wishing to communicate with elderly persons need to adapt these principles to the unique needs and requirements of the elderly that are attributable to the specific physical, psychological, and mental changes that occur with passing years.

Because the purpose of advertising is to sell a product or service, following are adaptations of some basic communication principles to the specific interests and needs of the elderly. This discussion follows the AIDA (Attention–Interest–Desire–Action) model, which describes the various communication processes involved in consumer purchasing (although much controversy surrounds the actual order of these processes as they are related to purchases).

Attention

The first step in the sales or advertising process is to gain the consumer's attention. In order to communicate effectively with older consumers, advertisers should follow these rules:

1. Lead off with your most convincing sales message first. Elderly readers or viewers tend to grasp meanings quickly and holistically, without complex analysis, and they make their minds up rapidly.
2. If you use graphics or illustrations, make sure they convey the same sales message as the text, so the theme is comprehensible at a glance. Whatever image is dominant will affect the elderly viewer's reaction, so your visual and verbal messages should be consistent with each other.
3. Avoid audio or visual images that are not appropriate for—or may even offend—members of this market, who have a more conservative value system than younger consumers. (Some of the symbols that reflect basic and timeless values are listed later in this chapter.)
4. Make sure that any attention device will be understood by this age group.

There are also a number of pitfalls to be avoided:

1. The use of MTV-style "noise" and images (e.g., high-decibel music, rap, rock music).
2. The use of negative images (e.g., old man with a cane, poverty, handicaps, doom and gloom).
3. Providing nothing for the mature audience to identify with or "connect with."
4. The use of unreadable type (e.g., hard to follow, too small, or scrambled).

Interest

Generating interest on the part of older people is not easy, but there are two useful guidelines to follow. First, relate your product to the real interests of your senior audience, not what a youthful copywriter might assume them to be. Marketers need to position their product benefits to relate to this new senior citizen market; today, older people's needs are frequently both broad ranging and complex. Older people are not yearning to be young again; most of them don't feel "old" in the first place. Instead, with the luxury of leisure time, many want to expand their lives in different and interesting directions. With passing years comes a shift from self-centered interests to external issues.

Second, define your brand in terms of the news it brings and its emotional or psychological rewards. Recent studies of the senior market show that seniors are interested in more products, are more "brand curious," and are more experimental in attitude than many professional advertising people had assumed. Although an elderly consumer may not "need" your product in the material sense, he or she might become very interested in the product you are selling as a means of obtaining improved performance, a psychological reward, a pleasant new experience, or a lifestyle change. Time has an impact on the body, and also upon the inner self. Once basic material needs have been satisfied, many older people become open to appeals that offer an attractive lifestyle and personal growth.

There are a number of real dangers to avoid in attempting to generate interest among elderly consumers; among these are stereotyping, condescension, and false urgency.

Stereotyping. Avoid emphasizing physical limitations in message or pictures. Changes in the traditional American family mean that some young people have never had personal experience with older relatives. They may assume that visible characteristics (e.g., bifocals, hearing aids) dominate life for the elderly. However, any concentration on the outward handicaps of the elderly is misdirected. Although many older Americans have physical ailments of some type or other, almost all seniors regard them as minor problems only and—quite literally—ignore them.

Other incorrect and damaging stereotypes include the notion of "bedridden elderly," senility, poverty, and the need for nursing care. Aside from Alzheimer's patients (about 10% of seniors over age 65), the brain does change with age, but in some key areas its functions are actually enhanced. For instance, whereas there is some slowing of verbal recall, research indicates that decision making is improved.

Condescension. Some of the casual social conventions of younger generations, such as the general use of first names, are interpreted by many older Americans as displaying a lack of respect. Other ways that marketers risk treating the elderly as inferior are by showing them in dependent situations, in need of aid or guidance, or by showing paternalistic young "caretakers" waiting to assume control. This image of dependency has led to the failure of various brands that have portrayed older consumers as decrepit. In many societies, the elderly are respected for their experience, an attitude that cannot be mistaken for condescension.

False urgency. Older audiences have learned to resist typical sales pressures. They know that time is relative, and that they can afford to wait a day or so before making up their minds.

Desire

To encourage buying, especially for the first time and, even more important, if there is a high ticket price, one must inculcate desire. Elderly consumers are generally interested in learning all about the products they buy, and they usually have plenty of time to take in all the necessary information. Be sure that you cover the vital characteristics related to performance, construction, and reliability, but keep in mind the importance of phrasing each product feature in terms of its benefit to the user.

Focus on the major personal benefits offered by your brand. Does your product offer personal improvement? A new experience? A better way of accomplishing a task? Cost savings? A solution to a continuing problem?

Position the brand in a positive manner. Show the ways in which your product enhances living. (Shampoo for "older hair" was a failure; nobody wanted to admit to having "older hair.") Does it perform better than the competition? Why is that? Does it have a strong warranty? Discuss each benefit separately, and relate it to your main sales message. Use visual sales points if you can—seniors may forget the words, but their visual recall is strong.

For instance, the adult diaper for control of bladder incontinence is a product directed almost exclusively to the older marketplace. It may be one of the most difficult product challenges ever confronted by a marketer. One major brand, Attends, chose to deliver a scientific, straightforward, biologically correct message describing the problems of bladder control. The other major brand, Depends, chose as its spokesperson June Allyson, a favorite star of the 1950s, and had her deliver an upbeat message of freedom and lifestyle improvement. By emphasizing benefits, not problems, and through association with a favorite film star of their own generation, Depends has come to dominate the adult diaper market. This demonstrates how skillful product positioning, even when dealing with a negative physical problem, can create a successful appeal to the senior market.

Use "nostalgia pegs" or symbols that your viewer or reader will relate to.[1] The following are some examples of symbols of timeless basic values:

- Flags
- Churches
- Civic buildings
- Schools and colleges
- Historical monuments
- Historic scenes
- Fireworks
- Patriots
- Homes
- Small towns and neighborhoods
- General stores
- Bandstands
- Circuses
- Mothers and children
- Fathers and children
- Grandparents and grandchildren
- Neighbors chatting
- People playing cards
- Nature scenes
- Animal friends
- People helping others

It is interesting to speculate on these traditional interest patterns as the baby boomers enter the marketplace of elderly consumers. Certainly the range of symbols will broaden to include people, places, and things from their early memories. This group began as antiestablishment rebels, turned into "yuppies," and some are now at the prosperous, low-fat-diet, "empty-nester" age. But psychologists expect baby boomers to follow the normal course of maturation and become seniors, just as "flappers" of the 1920s developed into traditional matrons. Fundamental neurological and psychological changes occur in maturity that affect a person's basic outlook and values as well as the thinking process itself (see the section on changes in the older consumer, below). Therefore, the same types of messages related to lifestyle improvements, hope, and fulfillment that have been effective with prior generations will probably be just as successful with the baby boomers.

Action

How do you encourage the senior customer to put down the newspaper and write your brand name on a shopping list? Or to call your 800 number? As noted above, the "urgency" appeal is not very credible to the experienced senior citizen. He or she knows that your used-car lot will be there next week (and next month), that the retirement community can build another section, that another "special fare" will come along next week. So the fire sale, "act now or lose out" appeals that work with a more naive audience will not be successful with these customers. On the other hand, senior consumers' breadth of experience also enables them to recognize genuine bargains, like markdowns found at a store closing, when they come along. The following are some proven ways to stimulate purchasing action among older consumers:

1. Make sure your phone number is readable! Type that is crowded, too small, in italics or some other hard-to-read style, or reversed white-on-black merely makes it harder to see the numbers and often discourages further effort.
2. Tell readers or viewers exactly what you want them to do. Don't be coy or make them guess—or worse, leave them wondering.
3. If there is a real benefit to the consumer's taking action soon, explain it clearly and believably.
4. Repeat your name and address at the end of a radio or TV commercial. Young or old, listeners will not recall it unless you repeat it.
5. Repeat your TV graphic image or message on the package and in the store. Take advantage of the reminder that leads to impulse purchases.

Communication Path for the Elderly

The basic model of communication has a unique variation for the elderly consumer. Products that are related to their health or well-being may well receive special attention. Figure 25.2 shows a communication path with two branches, the upper *scanning pathway* for products that are not related to basic

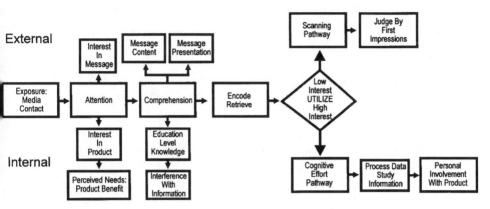

Figure 25.2. Bimodal Communication Pathway for the Mature Market[7]

health or survival needs and the lower *cognitive effort pathway* for products related to health needs, where more intensive mental effort will be expended. The more important you make your product to the elderly consumer, the more attention or cognitive effort your communication will receive.

According to the *Wall Street Journal*, Young & Rubicam invested more than $10 million in developing a model of brand building based on the sequence "Familiarity–Relevance–Esteem–Differentiation," which goes by the friendly acronym of FRED. Here is how this model can be interpreted for the gerontological marketplace:

- *Familiarity:* The more familiar your brand name, the stronger your market position. So if your brand is an old favorite, stick with it in selling to the older consumer. Do not change it because people in the manufacturing company or advertising agency want some variety. Do not monkey with the tried-and-true values it represents.
- *Relevance:* How personally important is the brand to older customers? How does the brand fit into their lifestyles?
- *Esteem:* How highly regarded is the brand by the customer? Your goal should be to preserve the positive values you have with other customers and build appropriate new ones relating to the senior market.
- *Differentiation:* Brand differentiation is a vital rung on the ladder to market success. The brand must be seen as different from the others available, with specific characteristics that appeal to the senior market. Remember the example of the Depends adult diaper.

Changes in the Older Consumer

Age-related changes or development can be either positive or negative. Positive development is growth; negative development is deterioration. Growth, which was once considered the province of children and adolescents, has now been recognized as occurring into advanced old age. Deterioration, once considered the hallmark of aging, appears to be related to cell function, nourishment, and use, and occurs in the cradle as well as in old age.[2] Both growth and decline occur at different rates, and the direction of development will reverse depending on conditions. At a given age, a person's development may be stable, growing, or in decline, and scientists are learning that much is under personal control.

The typical older American does not feel his or her age. When asked how old they feel, time and again seniors of all ages respond, "About 35," "About 40," or something similar. Not even when they pass a mirror do they feel their age. The psychological mellowing that occurs with maturity makes it possible for seniors to overlook and ignore physical deficits and to devote attention to more interesting subjects. In addition, the sense of time itself changes. Moving beyond the pressure and clock-watching that dominate much of modern life, there gradually emerges a sense of timelessness, which permits greater appreciation of the "now."[3] This compares in many ways to the brain waves generated during meditation.

Although there are some changes that occur to all human beings with the passage of time, research is narrowing the spectrum of changes that are inevitable due to aging, which are termed *primary aging. Secondary aging* refers to changes due to disease, nutrition, or abuse, which are not inevitable. The changes that occur with aging are threefold: physical, cognitive, and psychological.

Physical Changes

Different body systems age at different rates. The hair turns gray, then white, or falls out. There is some loss related to the five senses: Most senior eyes eventually require glasses. Some seniors suffer hearing loss in the higher-frequency ranges. The sense of touch may lessen to a slight degree. The skin develops wrinkles and age spots. The sense of smell may diminish, but this has not yet been definitively established. And the taste buds may lose their acuity, somewhat related to a loss in the sense of smell. For most seniors these changes represent minor shifts in the threshold of capacity.

Many other symptoms once thought to be age related have actually been traced to treatable and preventable diseases: heart failure, high blood pressure, clogged arteries, digestive problems, and so on. A decline in muscle tone, once thought inevitable, appears to be directly related to amount of exercise. In a study at Tufts University, seniors of 80 and beyond were found to build muscle from weight lifting at the same rate as younger people. Loss of calcium in bones leads to osteoporosis, which today is seen as preventable and treatable through the maintenance of magnesium levels. Dental problems may diminish as passing generations take better care of their teeth.

In fact, much of the deterioration traditionally associated with old age is actually secondary aging, symptomatic of chronic diseases that can be avoided or prevented through dietary and lifestyle changes. As more is learned about prevention and reversal of chronic conditions—cancer, diabetes, heart disease, arthritis—advances in scientific knowledge are making it possible for people to postpone if not avoid many of the signs of old age that were once thought unavoidable.

Although marketers should avoid emphasizing handicaps or physical disabilities in trying to reach elderly consumers, they should not overglamorize the senior citizen. Seniors do not expect to be portrayed as teenagers with white hair. They accept an increase in their weight, a few wrinkles, the normal accumulation of wear and tear that comes with their age. Also, just as advertisers should show diversity in races when they depict groups of people, they should show mixed ages. Elderly Americans like to associate with friends and family of all ages.

Cognitive Changes

Important studies have changed our thinking about the aging brain. Scientists once thought we were born with a fixed number of brain cells that gradually died away, leading inevitably to senility, but new research demonstrates that there is no decline in the number of active cells. Brain cells have demonstrated the ability to grow, repair themselves, and sprout new axons in individuals 80 years old and beyond. Elderly patients who stay mentally active may be encouraging this process. Other studies demonstrate that, in general, intelligence does not decline with aging.

Senility (forgetfulness, loss of mental acuity, confusion) was once thought to be an inevitable accompaniment of aging. Today these symptoms are understood to be related to the most dreaded disease of the aging brain, Alzheimer's, which afflicts 10% of Americans over 65 and as many as 50% over the age of 75. Symptoms like forgetfulness and confusion are not a laughing matter to many older consumers who live in apprehension of the onset of Alzheimer's. It is important to keep in mind that forgetfulness is not necessarily a warning sign of the disease—a person may be forgetful due to everyday stress, interaction of medications, or a treatable condition such as depression.

The thinking process itself undergoes a remarkable shift in the mature brain, from the linear, step-at-a-time logic of youth to the holistic at-a-glance comprehension of maturity. What causes this shift? Studies indicate that several factors are at work: the dense accumulation of experience, which provides an integrated perspective, and the slowing of neural processing with the accumulation over time of waste matter in the cells. This slowing may result in an overload of verbal signals in the left, linear brain lobe, causing a shift to the right, holistic lobe. (In some adults this biological change occurs simultaneously with some short-term memory loss.)

The environment and personal behavior also have impacts upon cognition. Such factors as environmental conditions, amount of stress, and social roles can accelerate deterioration or reverse it. Personal factors such as nutrition, exercise, smoking, alcoholism, and drug abuse also affect cognitive health.

Testing methods may indicate cognitive weaknesses that are actually the result of the test or testing conditions, rather than inherent in aging. Time limits often create stress, which is a handicap for many elderly test takers. Duke University recently demonstrated that many older adults performed better in the morning hours than in the afternoon. Most studies of mental prowess are conducted in the afternoon, and this may affect test scores among the elderly (note that this may also affect memory for morning communications versus afternoon communications).

Sooner or later, adults who become "mature" in the psychological sense undergo a specific cognitive change or "brain shift" that affects their entire outlook, including their perception of communications. Understanding the nature of this change will assist marketers in successfully directing their programs toward all segments of the maturity market. As adults mature, these changes affect their perceptions and how they process information as well as how they respond to communications. Because this brain shift is a switch from the segmented or linear thinking characteristic of younger adults to holistic or whole-brain thought processing, older consumers tend to grasp the overall meanings of advertising communications rather than follow step-by-step arguments. This processing shift also leads to an enhancement of the judgment process, which is part of what has been characterized as a "mature" perspective on life events.

Psychological Changes

With maturity comes a change in overall psychology. There is a shift from an inner-directed perspective to an outer-directed one, from self-centered to selfless, from a lower level of operations to a higher. Psychologists have delineated classic models of these transitions. Typically, we move from the younger, self-centered, possession-oriented stages of exploration and family formation, through years of self-development and career growth, to periods of community service and recognition. The highest level in Maslow's classic model is termed *self-actualization,* a state of wisdom and completeness.[4] The factors that influence cognitive changes are also operative in this realm. Environment, social roles, personal behavior, and lifestyle choices all affect psychological development.

Those who wish to communicate to older Americans must cope with a paradox. The most creative and innovative copywriters and artists tend to be in their 20s and 30s, but successful communication with the psychologically mature audience requires the guidance of older minds, those who have "been there." To illustrate, during their younger years two of the most brilliant psychologists of the 20th century, Erik Erikson and Abraham Maslow, developed theories of human maturation that were revolutionary and highly successful. However, when each of them reached his mature years, he decided to revise his theories substantially.[5] Although brilliant, the theories of their youth were not capable of encompassing the actual experiences of the elderly; their youthful insights and visualizations were inadequate to the task. Only when the two men reached the fullness of their own maturity were they able to undergo the process of aging from within and therefore describe it with authority. According to Maslow:

> The young have not yet achieved identity or autonomy, not had time enough to experience an enduring . . . post-romantic love relationship, nor have they generally found . . . the altar upon which to offer themselves, nor have they generally

acquired enough courage to be unpopular, to be unashamed about being openly virtuous.[6]

As they move into maturity, some members of the "me generation" may never attain the level of selflessness that Maslow describes. Other boomers, experienced in meditation, may have already achieved this level of maturity.

The difficulty younger writers have in writing advertisements directed toward older people appears to be innate. Many simply have not lived long enough to identify with age. Youth cannot comprehend the complex scar tissue that living for 50 years can leave upon the body and mind. It is easy to identify the physical wear and tear that occurs, and these outward effects tend to color much superficial thinking about age. Younger writers tend to err on the side of either pity or stereotype, even as younger scientists tend to test and measure attributes that are significant to youth but less relevant to maturity. Perhaps the basic lesson in all of this is that marketers should enlist older talent in preparing and evaluating ads for the elderly.

Age Cohorts

For those involved in marketing to the elderly, it is vital to be time-sensitive. Marketers should look at the dates on any statistical material they are using— the information and approach change with every passing decade. For example, this chapter was written in the late 1990s, so all the statistics presented are relative to that period. This is but one challenging aspect of the mature market that confronts marketers. For segmentation purposes, the elderly target market should be defined in two ways:

- *By their past:* This clusters seniors by the decades of their birth, or by age cohorts, which reflect the influences of their impressionable formative years.
- *By their present:* This groups seniors by the physical, cognitive, and psychological levels they have reached today, which affect their current outlooks on life.

These segmentations frequently (but not always) overlap. For instance, a marketer may want to reach men in their 60s, born in the 1930s, a cohort whose members were exposed to Depression-era thinking and the values of World War II. Some in this group will be psychologically mature or "self-realized" (see above); others will still be on the business ladder, striving for recognition or hanging on by the fingernails.

Add to these communication complexities the fact that the passage of each year changes the marketplace, on a continuing basis.

The Important Age Groups

Pragmatically, membership in the mature market comes with age, and members of each cohort or age segment are indelibly imprinted by the meaningful experiences they endured in the formative years of their youth. The following specific segments are based on birth years and are approximate:

- *Ages 70 and over (born 1929 or before):* Members of this group have lived through most of the turmoil of this century. They experienced the "Roaring 20s" of prohibition and moral rebellion, followed swiftly by the onset of the Great Depression and World War II. Traditional values are very important to this cohort.
- *Ages 50-69 (born 1930-1949):* This group was born and raised amid the deprivation, fears, and despair of the 1930s, when many Americans were unable to find work and went without food and shelter; this was followed by the stress, shortages, and rationing of World War II. Members of this group have values and needs that reflect the insecure period of their childhood. Security values are vital to this cohort.
- *Ages 30-49 (born 1950-1969):* This group includes the population of baby boomers born after World War II. Because of its size and economic impact, this enormous group has dominated marketing for its entire existence and is now approaching the maturity years. Many boomers were raised by parents who followed the permissive parenting ideology of Dr. Spock, which has been credited with fostering the self-absorbed values and rebellion of the "me generation" and the possession orientation of the "yuppies."

Conclusion

Traditional marketing thinking has always paid closer attention to young consumers than to older ones. The reason for this, presumably, is that the remaining lifetime consumption of products is greater for the young than for the old. During the past three decades, the importance of the baby boom generation has given an additional impetus to advertisers' concentration on the young.

The striking demographic change described in this chapter—the growing importance of the older age group—began to make an impression on consumer goods marketers rather late in the day. However, marketers have certainly responded strongly during the past 10 years. Their approach to older consumers has tended to be rather direct and even naive, and such attitudes have contributed to the failure of many brands directed to the older target group. As this chapter has shown, the art of communicating to the older consumer requires skills and an understanding of subtleties that are, if anything, greater than those needed for successful communication to young consumers. Marketing organizations are only slowly learning this lesson.

Notes

1. David B. Wolfe, *Serving the Ageless Market* (New York: McGraw-Hill, 1990).

2. Marion Perlmutter and Elizabeth Hall, *Adult Development and Aging* (New York: John Wiley, 1992).

3. Wolfe, *Serving the Ageless Market.*

4. Abraham Maslow, *Motivation and Personality* (New York: Harper & Row, 1970).

5. Erik Erikson, *Identity and the Life Cycle* (New York: W. W. Norton, 1967).

6. Maslow, *Motivation and Personality,* Preface to the Second Edition.

7. Delight D. Omohundro, *Nutrition Labels and Elderly Consumers* (Michigan: UMI, 1993).

Arts Organizations as Brands

The Role of Effective Direct-Response Communications

Harold F. Clark, Jr.
(from a conversation with Charles Ziff)

---

*C*harles Ziff was one of the preeminent arts marketing and advertising specialists in the United States. For more than 10 years, he headed Ziff Marketing, Inc., the country's leading arts marketing organization, where he also created memorable advertising and direct-response campaigns that are still being talked about. Ziff was a writer who thought in pictures and who believed that all writing should treat the reader as an intelligent human being. In July 1992, Charles Ziff died of AIDS.

A year earlier, on July 20, 1991, he defined his principles of persuasive writing for arts organizations; this conversation is published here for the first time. Even though Ziff was talking about a unique niche within marketing and *advertising, his principles have broad application across all forms of brand communications.*

1. Define the Essence

Whatever you write—an ad, direct mail, or a press release—you must capture the essence of what it is you are writing about. You can't even start until you know what that essence is. In marketing Shakespeare, Rembrandt, and Mozart, you learn how to deal with a product or service without the luxury of being able to redesign it. You have to get behind the obvious attributes, dig deeper, and use your intuitive ability to define the essence of a product, service, or work of art—an essence that will make the work unique in the minds of its upscale, well-educated audience.

2. Talk to the Artists

The best way to forage for the essence of a performing arts company is to insist upon time talking to the artists, the conductor, the creative director, whomever. Get them talking in a relaxed way. That's when they say something. You start the conversation and just let it ramble.

Don't ask them to tell you what ought to be in the brochure. Rather, talk about why they've chosen to do what they are doing. What are the seminal elements that first attracted them to the work? Their perceptions are often sharp and compelling. They've probably thought about it more than you. At least differently. The really juicy stuff comes when they just talk about it. I remember asking Tony Randall about *The Master Builder* once when we were in a cab going uptown; he said, "It's a play about a woman who destroys her husband just for the fun of it." That's the kind of insight I mean.

The fear of the novice is, "If I get them involved, they will take over," or "they will think I'm not doing my job." That's not the case. Many people have these kinds of conversations routinely.

3. Make Direct Mail Your Cornerstone

Once you know what the essence is, then you begin to use it in your copy. Begin with the direct-mail piece for subscription renewal. A direct mailer has two jobs:

1. to sell the tickets it is aiming to sell, and
2. to be an evocation of the personality of the place it represents and the work it is featuring.

So you need to understand two things: the essence of the company and how to sell it.

It was Danny Newman who first demonstrated the value of direct mail to arts organizations. He was a former press agent—a word man, not a picture person. He built brochures driven by superlatives in vibrant colors that yelled out at readers. These brochures generated volume because he advocated mailing to every name you could get your hands on. It worked in the early years (when there were lots of volunteers, all with their own Christmas card mailing lists).

As the market matured and institutions became bigger, several things happened:

1. The direct mail didn't always work as well as it had before.
2. The volume went up geometrically. The bizarre yelling brochure was only 1 of 25 to land in the home; as a result, its effectiveness was severely impaired.
3. There were reservations about its loud tone of voice and ugly aesthetic (versus the aesthetic on the stage).

Newman taught us the need to sell, but he didn't understand that his emphasis on superlatives failed to capture and promote the defining essence of the company. He did demonstrate that direct mail is the most efficient medium to use, especially for subscription sales. Infinitely renewable, it builds the loyalty that generates continuity of revenue.

4. Develop an Audience Service Philosophy

Arts marketing has changed fundamentally since Newman was in his heyday. Once in the caring hands of a group of well-meaning supporters who rallied their friends and neighbors to share Christmas card lists, it has now shifted to a more sophisticated, professional marketing process.

Today, the successful arts organizations have developed an audience service mentality. They understand that their existence depends on their ability to meet specific needs of their core audiences and they use every available technique to discover what those needs are. We have developed computer modeling software for direct-mail campaigns that pinpoints target markets with efficient accuracy.

At the same time, an arts organization cannot walk away from its core community, on whom it depends for donations. Raising money is getting harder to do. You have to balance local pride and heritage (the small number of "old money" people) with a whole bunch of new needs from new potential audiences (larger numbers of people with not so much money). You have to know who you are in relation to both segments.

The challenge to the arts marketer is to resolve this tension—to be true to the vision of the artistic director and the essence of the company while you simultaneously serve the needs of those people who represent your roots and origins and of those who demand that you push out the artistic edges.

5. Pick the Right Moment

To capture the essence of the work, try to envision the most exciting, touching, funny, memorable, compelling moment in each work to be sold. Does the mailing piece give you any sense of your feeling if you were there seeing it? Would it do it even if you'd already seen it? Your meaningful moment must stand on its own. The copywriter's job is to pick the right moment to show, the one that captures the essence of each piece of the work. Ask yourself when you are writing about symphony orchestras, "Do I hear the music?"

6. Create a Visual Device

There are 10 zillion ways to achieve that result. A novice would think of using a full proscenium shot of the most dramatic moment. But it may be better to evoke the essence of a work with a telling symbol or a few words. Such a device works on two levels:

1. It should be compelling, startling, and delicious on its own; and
2. it should fit, be appropriate and relevant for the work it is supposed to represent.

A good example was "No Elephants" [a headline used in a 1991 New York City Opera brochure]. The headline promised entertainment. It was likable. Then, as you read the brochure, it became a slow reveal of the special attitude

Figure 26.1. Brochure for New York City Opera

that defined the company. It contained volumes of substance about who they are and who they aren't (see Figure 26.1).

A novice might get funny and entertaining without the substance. That would be glib. You have to have something of meaning for your audience and you have to write it in a way they will want to read.

A good device has to serve a variety of publics. If you can pique their curiosity, or build audience awareness of the range of the theatrical work, then the device works. A particularly effective example is the endless variety of ways that the drawing of the little urchin promotes *Les Misérables.*

7. Try to Get a Proposition

All other things being equal, a direct-mail piece that is just an announcement works less well than one with a proposition—for example, "Buy this" by itself versus "Buy this and get . . . access to a recital or a free poster, or whatever." Ideally, there should be an "if . . . then" promise.

You don't always have to state both halves of the proposition. If you write it in such a way that the other half becomes implicit, the reader fills in the blank. A good example is a picture of a starving child with the headline "You could save this child, or you could turn the page."

8. Cut to the Quick

Simpler, bolder, singular lead lines work better. Pick the lines that draw the reader in and discard the rest. Just as you choose one piece of the work that can work as a symbol or icon, so find the words that will serve as a metaphor for all of it. In the City Opera brochure, the Pagliacci drawing gave the company a specific image, while the words "No Elephants" spoke for 13-14 other operas and gave the company a unique tone of voice.

It takes a leap of courage to do this. You have to set priorities and then have the guts to cut the other stuff out.

9. Be Somebody . . . Interesting

In your copy, it is important to establish a clear "persona" of intelligence. Know who you are and then let it out. Your readers aren't fools—particularly those readers who are apt to be reading an opera brochure. They appreciate being addressed as adults. So don't be afraid to use wit and irony; they appeal to these readers, since they honor their intelligence.

Tone of voice is important since, as in "No Elephants" for New York City Opera, it can do a lot to reveal who you are. A bland "brochure-speak" suggests to a reader that the onstage experience may not be very exciting; loud, brash superlative bragging may suggest that you will be assaulted in ways you would prefer to avoid. Be someone of intelligence: an interesting, cultured, and amusing adult your audience will want to identify with.

10. Don't Overlook the Obvious

When we did our first research for New York City Opera, I learned a trade secret I've never forgotten. On the attribute list of why people attend opera, there was one single item that went off the scale: the importance of the beauty of the human voice singing. It literally went off the charts.

Now, it is obvious, but we don't often refer to the obvious. Most creative work for opera never directly expresses the extraordinary beauty and power of hearing people sing. It's why people go to the opera in the first place: the motivator for the category. Most people talk only about the discriminators.

11. Say It More Than Once

Consumers are profoundly ignorant of many things you take for granted. And they do not always get the idea the first time. The New York City Opera has supertitles (i.e., English translations of the dialogue projected on a screen above the stage)—a fact that they have mentioned for 4 or 5 years in all their mailing and advertisements. Yet, when we did our research, we discovered that 80% of the people who had not seen supertitles had no idea what they were. After 5 years of describing them!

You cannot assume that because you say something once, people have read and understood it. You have to keep saying it again and again.

12. Strive for Order and Clarity

Any printed message, particularly in a subscription brochure, works best when the geometry or folding pattern or scheme of layout gives an order and clarity to the structure of the work that's for sale. As an example, look at Figure 26.2

[the 1990 subscription brochure for the Public Theater's New York Shakespeare Festival]. Papp had 10 plays. We have given it an orderly arrangement that holds together. We didn't have 10 panels for 11 plays, and if he had had 11 plays, we would have done something different.

In a subscription brochure, you need to make effective use of the layout to handle the tremendous volume of material. Advertisements carry one-tenth of the information required in a subscription brochure.

Whether it presents one opera, the whole season, or the performances next week, the layout has to look clean and simple. The design must be as transparent as possible and not be overladen with facts. The hard part is getting the right structure and shape to handle all the individual works in a season. It's a choice between emphasizing nothing or emphasizing everything—always difficult to sort out. Sometimes there are billing issues or contractual matters. If you have Pavarotti, you want to show him, but you don't want to suggest that he is the only thing worth seeing in the entire season.

There are no rules about how to do this—except to understand that to work, a brochure must have order and clarity.

13. Make the Order Mechanism Transparent

In any direct-response communication, both the persuasiveness and the clarity of communication must be sustained clear through to the order blank. The order mechanism must be easy and inviting to read. If it looks complicated or hard to understand, people will have an excuse to do nothing.

If you aren't certain how it is working, show it to people who aren't involved in making it and see how they do with it.

14. Tell a Story

The panels of a brochure work like the frames of a storyboard; they follow a linear sequence. Unfolding a brochure is like reading the pages of a book. As you create it, you must understand where the eyes travel and how people will in fact follow it.

The whole thing needs to tell a story. There should be a rational cogent sequence of ideas or arguments, and all the parts need to fit together logically.

Figure 26.2. Subscription Brochure for the Public Theater's New York Shakespeare Festival

Remember time and how long it will take a reader to figure out what you want him or her to read next. Take the reader by the hand and reveal your story in sequence. Build your case in a sensible, orderly, and interesting fashion. From time to time, you will have to feed juicy tidbits that make it worth the reader's while. And you will have to find a way to deal with the mandatory copy that is a distractor, competing against your story. You cannot avoid mentioning *The Nutcracker,* but that doesn't mean you jeopardize the overriding importance of *Giselle.*

You will always have to compromise, but know what you are striving for and compromises will work better.

15. Pursue Only What You Can Afford to Pursue

You can represent art directly (through photography) or through a surrogate like a metaphor. If you choose the surrogate route, it must derive from the work itself. It doesn't actually have to be a real moment in the opera, but it will have to stand for it.

You may not be able to afford the costs of creating and producing the moments you would like to use. If you cannot afford to create visuals that are as good as or better than what's happening on the stage, then stick to the stage. Cull through all the photographs to find one that most closely approximates the moment you have chosen. A mediocre photograph will always work better than a mediocre, or badly executed, illustration.

Another obvious way to extend your budget is to use media that relate to what you are presenting. If you are dealing with a musical medium (opera, symphony, or even ballet), it makes sense to feature the music in your communications. Don't rely just on print communications, but go to radio. Connect the musical sound to your key copy point and make certain that you tie the direct-mail print to your radio.

16. Beware of Structural Conveniences That Don't Sell

There is nothing wrong with exploring to see whether there is a theme in a season—or a body of work—on which to hang all the pieces. But don't push the theme to the point where it's no longer true, or relevant, or even a good marketable notion.

Let us assume that you have discovered that with just a little exaggeration, it would be possible to characterize all the operas in a season as stories of betrayal. This may be an expedient device. But it may also be awful. You need to ask yourself: Is betrayal something people are interested in buying 10 performances of? If it is only a structural convenience, then junk it.

17. Focus on How the Work Is Done More Than on What the Work Is

How we do something is often a better source for a theme than *what* we do. Particularly with works that audiences already know, how they are performed may be more motivating for sales than the familiar story of the plot. If themes that derive from the content of the work aren't part of the reason the artist chose the season, then it won't be a compelling reason for anyone to attend.

Joseph Papp's "Theater of Issues" didn't force a nonexistent affinity or similarity. Or imply there would be a sameness or repetition. The line "Public Theater: The Truth No Matter What" didn't attempt to describe the choice of plays; rather, it promised a specific point of view, an attitude that characterized the company and the promise of a provocative audience response. Ultimately, success is all about how people respond to the work.

18. Capture the Feelings

By and large, the more theatrical, narrative art forms (theater, opera, and two-thirds of dance) are at their crux a depiction of people and what happens to them. It's not about things or ideas.

In *Miss Saigon,* consider the difference between the special effect of the helicopter and the emotion on Lea's face. It will be much harder for a photographer to get the expression on Lea's face than the departing helicopter. But the home run will be Lea. It's a choice between the tangible, visible, and concrete versus something that captures the feeling.

Opera is at one end of the entertainment spectrum and drag car racing is at the other. There may be more people closer to the drag car end of the spectrum than to the opera end. Therefore, if you want more mass appeal and to affect the largest number of people, you provide the tangible stuff (the helicopter or the chandelier falling).

The more you move to the opera end of the entertainment spectrum, the more your audience will want the feeling. It is tougher for opera advertising since scenery or stage pyrotechnics are not hot buttons. You have to come up with a fresh metaphor for human emotion.

19. Remember the Ultimate Benefit

What keeps people going back to opera is that once there was a moment when singing, music, acting, dance, scenery, and costumes together created an overwhelming, emotional experience for them. It was very powerful. Operagoers return in the hope that one of those moments will happen again.

The opera brochure wants to tease you with the potential of that recurrence. All the work you do—defining the essence, understanding the artistic intentions, responding to changing market needs, developing fresh copy and a clear layout—makes this promise: The magic is possible.

In our buy-now-pay-later, money-back-guarantee society, applause comes only from those who have been touched and transported. They come because they know what it is to have an artist capture their imagination like a balloon, hold it for a moment, and then set it free again, refreshed.

20. Do It With Taste and Flair

Market research developed for one of America's major symphony orchestras suggests that most people are attracted to the symphony because it represents a personal, social achievement—something nice that they want to do for themselves. The research suggests further that how they feel about themselves can affect their expectations of, and reactions to, the performance itself.

So we market not just by showing our wares, but by addressing the buyer's needs. We must create anticipation, whet appetites, deliver audiences ready to share a beautiful work of art, an exhilarating piece of theater, or an enthralling evening of music—not only to enjoy the art, but also to enjoy themselves.

Artists free the spirit—of an individual, of an audience, or of an entire society. Our responsibility as arts marketers is to create opportunities when artists and audiences can come together. We should do our part efficiently, tastefully, and with flair. The artists will take care of the rest.

Part V

Developing an Understanding of Brands

John Philip Jones

The contributors to this book have demonstrated consistently that a brand, or at least a strong brand, provides a rich mixture of values to its users—qualities over and beyond the brand's basic ability to perform a functional task. Advertising has a good deal to do with these added values, which form part of a brand and distinguish it from its competitors. Brands are the end products of the work of scientists, manufacturers, accountants, and managers, but they are also the end products of the human imagination.

This is the context in which we should view the important topic of education for advertising. Advertising people cannot do their job of building added values if they work merely as technicians, in the way that the chemical engineers who develop the initial formula for a brand are product technicians.

Added values are psychological; they exist in the minds of consumers. As the preceding chapters have explained and illustrated, these added values stem from consumers' experiences of the brand, from the types of people who use it and are seen to use it, from the buyers' faith in the brand's effectiveness, and from the brand's appearance—the construction and in particular the design of the packaging, as an expression of the brand's intrinsic and extrinsic properties.

Added values often work at a subtle level—a reflection of the frequently unusual way in which consumers respond to brands themselves. Research has demonstrated this. When members of the public are asked to describe the personality of a brand as if it were a human being, their descriptions in most cases are a mixture of favorable and unfavorable attributes. The latter, which are occasionally more than slightly negative, are obviously unplanned by marketers. They must stem from small and half-hidden attributes and associations of the brand, or from unwelcome activities by the manufacturer who markets it.

The task of creating, building, and sustaining added values calls for practitioners who have imaginative, subtle, sensitive, and, above all, well-stocked minds. Education, reading, experience, and contemplation build an individual's intellectual depth. It is from this depth that a practitioner draws an understanding of consumers. This depth also enables or at least helps an advertiser to generate and bring to gestation the ideas that get into the consumer's mind and cause a process of resonance as brand use and added values work in harmony to foster repeat usage.

The need for intellectual depth accounts for Bruce Vanden Bergh's emphasis, in Chapter 27, on a basic liberal arts education as a foundation for advertising studies; it also accounts for the prominence Constantin Cotzias gives in Chapter 28 to the ways in which the mind must be stretched and encouraged and driven to follow sequences of idea-associations. This process, which is the real work of an advertising agency, is quite separate from the writing, graphic, and film production skills that the agency also needs, but that can be better described as applied craftsmanship.

Every advertisement, no matter how trivial its task or mundane its objective, is a creation of the human imagination. The most productive practitioners are those who have (a) the richest intellectual resources—resources that have been accumulated from experience, education, and reading; and (b) the practiced ability to sift through, recycle, and review these resources from different viewpoints. The capacity to do the latter is rather rare, although the techniques described by Cotzias in Chapter 28 can often blow on the spark to produce a flame.

It is the juxtaposition of these two things—resources and mental aptitude—that is the secret of how advertising people are able to generate the strongest ideas, create the subtlest and most durable added values, and help build significant brands for their clients.

Education for Advertising in American Universities

Bruce G. Vanden Bergh

Historical Background

Advertising education in American universities started with the beginnings of modern advertising around the early 1900s. The first courses in advertising of any kind probably were correspondence courses offered as early as 1896. The International Correspondence Schools added advertising course work to their programs of study by 1903. The Chicago College of Advertising was established in 1906.[1]

Riding the wave of new interest in professional university education at the start of the 20th century, advertising education found two existing academic partners with which it might join forces: journalism and business (marketing). To this day, most of the advertising programs in the United States are aligned

339

with journalism (or mass communications) programs rather than with business programs.

The first college-level advertising courses appeared at private universities, such as New York University (1905) and Northwestern University (1908), that were located close to centers of advertising, but they soon also appeared at large midwestern state universities such as the University of Missouri (1908), University of Kansas (1909), Indiana University (1909), Iowa State University (1910), and University of Wisconsin (1910). By 1950, 482 colleges and universities were offering some course work in advertising.

With a fairly healthy growth in advertising course work between 1905 and 1950, it was not long before advertising programs began to show up in college and university catalogs. An advertising program at the undergraduate level is typically considered to be at least a three-course sequence of advertising-titled courses. The "major" and "sequence" are the most commonly found types of programs. An advertising major leads to a bachelor's degree in the field. The first advertising programs were sequences of course work in either journalism or business programs.

The University of Missouri is credited with having established the first advertising program in 1908 as a sequence that became an advertising major in 1913. Advertising programs were also started in marketing at New York University and Marquette University (1916), Northwestern University (1917), and the University of Wisconsin (1917). The University of Oklahoma began an advertising program in journalism in 1919. Most of the growth in advertising programs took place after World War II. More than 100 of the current 148 advertising programs have come into existence since 1950.

The early development of advertising courses in colleges and universities was a result of the young advertising industry's desire to be considered a profession. Among the features that the industry believed were characteristics of a profession were a standardized curriculum of instruction and the status of an association with institutions of higher learning. The debate over what constitutes the appropriate standard curriculum for a career in advertising has never truly been reconciled.

Early disagreements over the ideal advertising curriculum arose between the "vocationalists," who resided in schools of journalism, and the "generalists," who taught in business programs. The vocationalists emphasized particularly the contribution of the human imagination to the advertising enterprise—a reflection of advertising's role in building brands (see Cotzias, Chapter 28, this volume). However, the debate concerning the best educational background for an advertising graduate has continued and has left the advertising industry without the standard core curriculum it so wanted. The lack of agreement on whether advertising education should impart primarily entry-level (first job) skills, such as copywriting, or scientifically derived principles particularly valuable to managers in client and agency organizations remains to this day.

The major growth in advertising education in the United States occurred after World War II in the large land-grant (public) universities, first in the Midwest and later in the Southeast and Southwest. The post-World War II period fueled interest in advertising education among returning veterans, who were more mature and more professionally oriented than the typical college student. They also were returning to a society that was experiencing tremendous economic growth and that had job opportunities to offer those with professional skills such as the ones learned in advertising programs.

Perhaps because of recognition of the point mentioned above—that "vocational" course work, especially that devoted to creative activities, makes a particularly important contribution to building brands—the growth of advertising education took place in schools of journalism and not colleges of business during the late 1950s and on into the 1960s. The diminution of advertising instruction in business schools was caused directly by the findings of two studies of business education published by the Ford Foundation and the Carnegie Foundation in 1959. These two influential studies recommended that business education should raise its academic and admission standards and reduce overspecialization in its course work. These recommendations had as an immediate effect the phasing out of advertising courses and programs in 13 colleges of business at major universities nationwide. Among the universities that dropped advertising from their business programs were the University of Florida, University of Washington, Columbia University, University of Minnesota, Northwestern University, Ohio State University, University of Texas, and Boston University. By 1990, 90% of all advertising programs were housed in schools, departments, or colleges of journalism, mass communications, or communication.

Advertising education maintained its well-established historical roots in journalism from the 1960s through the 1990s. Journalism and mass communications programs that had only a few freestanding advertising courses started to establish full-fledged advertising majors, and in a few cases, advertising was given department status. In the United States, the Midwest has always been the home to advertising education, with about one-fourth of all programs housed in the region. Although the roots of advertising education are in the Midwest, the growth of advertising education since the early 1960s has been firmly established in the Southeast. The number of programs in the Southeast has more than doubled since the early 1960s, when there were 13 programs in that region. The Midwest still has the most advertising programs, with about 34 being reported. The fewest advertising programs are found in the East, with just 13 reported.

Graduate education in advertising leading to a master's or doctoral degree has followed a somewhat more varied pattern of growth than that of the undergraduate programs. The total number of master's programs today is not much different from what it was in the 1960s. The trend, however, has been away from business-related programs and toward programs in journalism and mass communications. There were about 40 master's-level programs in 1965, and there are about 49 today. However, where almost 20 business-related programs existed in 1965, there are only 3 such programs today. Journalism and mass communications-related master's programs have grown from about 25 in 1965 to more than 35 today. The biggest growth in graduate programs has been at the doctoral level, as advertising education has tried to fill its own need for well-prepared college professors. Today there are about 18 doctoral programs in the journalism and mass communications area that prepare future advertising educators, with new programs being established even as this chapter is being written. There were only 4 Ph.D. programs in journalism and mass communications in 1965.

The prominent master's programs in advertising were already well established by the mid-1960s. The University of Illinois, Michigan State University, Northwestern University, and University of Texas were among the early leaders in graduate-level advertising education. These programs tended to mirror the M.B.A. degree, with an emphasis on management-oriented course work. However, these graduate programs were typically 1 year in length as opposed to the 2 years it took to earn an M.B.A. in business programs. Northwestern was, and has been, unique among advertising programs in offering only a master's degree and no baccalaureate degree in the subject.

The large master's programs at Illinois, Michigan State, Northwestern, and Texas are unique in that they lead specifically to degrees in advertising. Most master's degree programs are in journalism and mass communications, with majors, sequences, concentrations, or emphasis areas in advertising. This arrangement has something to do with size, resources, and where these programs are located. Illinois, Michigan State, Northwestern, and Texas have their own advertising departments within colleges of journalism or communication. Most of the other programs are not found in departments of advertising but in schools of journalism or departments of mass communications, which sometimes are housed in colleges of arts and sciences. The result of this arrangement is that less emphasis is given to advertising, making it only one of a number of subject-area options, along with other specialties such as journalism and telecommunication, within a mass communications program.

The growth in the number of doctoral programs that prepare students for future careers as advertising educators has been dramatic since the 1960s. There were 6 doctoral programs in existence in 1965 (4 in journalism/mass communications and 2 in business); today there are 19 doctoral programs, of which 18 are in journalism/mass communications. The University of Texas offers the only program that actually leads to a Ph.D. degree in advertising. All other journalism or communication-related doctoral programs offer degrees in journalism, communication, mass communications, or mass media.

The Advertising Curriculum

Perhaps the most controversial aspect of advertising education has been the nature of the advertising curriculum, which is part of the broader issue of whether or not advertising can be taught in the classroom. Some believe that advertising skills can best be learned on the job and that most advertising course work is too theoretical. Others feel that advertising can be taught at the university level and that an education in advertising is best supported by a broad liberal educational background. This is a point of great and persistent importance. The Accrediting Council for Education in Journalism and Mass Communication, the professional body that provides national accreditation to university schools and colleges, has always believed emphatically in the value of a broad education—a point that resonates with the role of advertising agencies in generating ideas that build the nonfunctional added values of brands (i.e., ideas outside the limits of their functional properties literally described).

Another point of controversy has been the influence of journalism education on advertising programs. For example, 30 years ago, the journalism/media influence could be seen on a typical advertising curriculum. Courses in newspaper advertising, retail advertising, radio and television advertising, and copy and layout reflected the journalistic heritage of many advertising programs.

The current curriculum model followed by most advertising programs combines a basic liberal arts education with courses in the social sciences and business. In most programs, the ratio of liberal arts course work to professional studies is approximately 3:1. The advertising core curriculum typically is some combination of courses in the principles of advertising, advertising copywriting, advertising media, advertising management, advertising campaign planning, and advertising research. A student's advertising course work is supplemented in most programs by an internship in an advertising organization.

The controversy over what constitutes the appropriate preparation for a career in advertising has not ended. The basic advertising curriculum has come under some criticism of late for not keeping pace with technological changes in the marketing communications industry. A task force made up of academicians and professionals has studied the current state of affairs regarding how best to prepare advertising and public relations professionals for the communications industry in the next century. This task force has its origins in journalism education and was born out of the interests of several key members of the Association for Education in Journalism and Mass Communication.

The task force has concluded that the pace of technological change requires that students should not be trained and educated in industry-oriented programs; rather, a unified curriculum that integrates knowledge and prepares students for careers as communicators is more appropriate. The emphasis in this new curriculum would be on the liberal arts, verbal and visual communication, business and organizational behavior, research skills, and a broad understanding of other communication disciplines beyond one's professional specialty. *Integrated marketing communications* and *integrated communications* are the common labels given to this approach. Although many academicians and professionals embrace this viewpoint, it is not clear to what extent it will alter the manner in which advertising is taught. Northwestern University's graduate program is considered to be a model for this approach to advertising education.

As university advertising programs have moved away from teaching "skills," several postgraduate professional programs have been established to fill this void. The development of these schools also has been influenced by the decline in training programs once offered by advertising agencies to entry-level employees. To fill this gap, four important schools have been established since 1979: the Portfolio Center (Atlanta), the Creative Circus (Atlanta), the Miami Ad School (Miami, Florida), and the VCU Ad Center at Virginia Commonwealth University (Richmond). The focus of these programs is on developing writers and artists who will be able to join advertising agencies in the choicest entry-level creative jobs.

It does appear that the undergraduate advertising curriculum has become less specialized and vocational over the past 30 years. The core curriculum in most advertising programs is of a "generalist" nature, with further specialization provided for by elective offerings. The deepest specialization provided for is in the creative area, with graphic design, print and broadcast production, and advanced copywriting courses found in many advertising programs. These courses are the most important ones for students to learn how to build brands.

Advertising Faculty

The number of full-time faculty teaching advertising has more than doubled since the early 1960s, growing from 135 full-time teachers in 1964 to more than 350 full-time in 1997. Two trends are apparent in the staffing of advertising programs beyond the mere growth in the number of faculty who teach advertising. First, a larger proportion of today's faculty members have earned Ph.D. degrees. Approximately 40% of those teaching advertising in 1964 had doctorates; now, close to 70% have Ph.D. degrees. The second trend, which is not necessarily unique to advertising faculty, is greater reliance on part-time faculty members, who are typically professionals from the local business community. In the mid-1990s, there were more part-time faculty teaching advertising than there were full-time faculty in some programs. Overall, there are about 160 part-time faculty teaching advertising nationally.

The combination of the growth in faculty members with Ph.D.s and reliance on part-time faculty with professional experience brings a balance of practical training and theoretical knowledge to many advertising programs. The smaller advertising programs usually have to choose between a faculty of professionals without Ph.D.s or an academically oriented faculty with doctorates. Larger programs may have more faculty slots and therefore can try to strike a skills-versus-theory balance that provides for a solid education in advertising.

The regional distribution and growth in advertising faculty follow the same pattern established by the growth of programs. The Midwest has the most faculty at about 130, whereas the Southeast has shown the most growth over the past 30 years: 18 faculty reported in 1964, increased to 104 by 1993. The East had very modest growth in advertising faculty over the same period, increasing by just 10, from 27 to 37.

Many teachers of advertising belong to the American Academy of Advertising (AAA), a professional organization that was established in the late 1950s to serve the needs and interests of a growing number of professors who were teaching advertising. Today this organization has more than 700 members from the fields of advertising and marketing. The AAA holds an annual conference each spring and publishes the conference proceedings; it also publishes one of the major advertising research publications in the field, the *Journal of Advertising*.

Student Enrollment

Student enrollment trends have been tracked annually since the 1960s by two key sources. Advertising Education Publications makes an annual inventory of advertising enrollment and reports this in its publication *Where Should I Go to Study Advertising and Public Relations?* Lee Becker at Ohio State University has continued the annual assessment of journalism enrollments started by Paul Peterson, and reports breakouts by major areas in *Journalism Educator* each year. The following enrollment figures and analysis are based on these sources.

Student enrollments in advertising programs housed in journalism and mass communications grew dramatically between the early 1960s and 1990, with some decline since 1990. Approximately 3,000 undergraduate students across the nation studied advertising in 1964. By 1990, the number had risen to more than 14,000, with a slight decline during the 1990s. In 1997, advertising enrollments rose once again to almost 16,000 students. Advertising is the second-largest major in journalism and mass communications, with public relations overtaking advertising as the largest major in the mid-1990s. Taken together, more than 36,000 students enrolled in advertising and public relations programs in 1997.

The decline in advertising enrollments in the early 1990s appears to be part of a larger trend in enrollment declines in journalism and mass communications, and also in business programs. Some of this decline can be explained by the small high school graduating classes entering colleges and universities in the early and mid-1990s. Part of the decline can be attributed to a weak national economy in the early 1990s and therefore fewer jobs being available to graduates of professionally oriented programs. In the late 1990s the trend has reversed itself, and enrollments and job prospects look strong heading toward the year 2000.

The growth in overall student enrollment (including journalism and business programs) has influenced the growth in programs and faculty on a regional basis. The Midwest has the most students studying advertising. The Southwest and Southeast, however, have experienced the greatest growth in enrollments. Each of these regions had fewer than 500 advertising students in 1964 but had experienced enrollment increases to 4,000 students in the Southwest and 5,000 in the Southeast by 1989. The Midwest's enrollment grew from a little more than 1,000 in 1964 to more than 8,000 by 1989.

Advertising has been a very popular major for college students for the past 30 years. Although there was a small percentage decline in enrollment in the early 1990s, the long-term interest among students remains strong. The public relations major appears to be following the path taken by advertising and is surpassing it in numbers of programs, faculty, and students.

The Universities

Very few studies have rated the advertising programs offered by colleges and universities. However, based on one poll published by the now-defunct magazine *Madison Avenue* and another reported in *Advertising Age,* the following are the U.S. colleges and universities most often mentioned:

University of Florida
University of Georgia
University of Illinois
Michigan State University
University of Missouri
University of North Carolina

Northwestern University
University of South Carolina
Syracuse University
University of Tennessee
University of Texas
Thunderbird School (the American Graduate School for International Management)

This list is alphabetical; it does not reflect any particular ranking. Also, programs appear on this list for different reasons. The programs have different specialties, such as graduate education, strong undergraduate creative programs, and good international programs.

Other universities with advertising programs that typically do not make the top list but fall just outside it include Boston University, University of Colorado, University of Kansas, Louisiana State University, Marquette University, University of Nebraska, University of Oklahoma, University of Oregon, Pennsylvania State University, Temple University, Virginia Commonwealth University, University of Washington, and University of Wisconsin.

Industry Involvement in Advertising Education

Most advertising programs receive both moral and financial support from their local advertising communities and alumni constituencies. In addition to this grassroots support, national organizations provide speakers, educational materials, scholarships and internships, and also sponsor student competitions. This industry involvement has grown along with the growth in programs, students, and faculty over the past 30 years. Some of the major advertising organizations and what they provide in support of advertising education are described below.

The American Advertising Federation

The American Advertising Federation (AAF) sponsors one of the more far-reaching and visible student competitions in the United States. Since 1973, the AAF has sponsored a national advertising case competition. This is invariably built around a real and major brand, with great emphasis on the brand's nonfunctional added values. The competition attracts more than 100 college and university participants every year. Each participating university competes in a regional competition to win the right to go to the national runoff, held each June at the AAF's annual national conference. The winners from the AAF's 15 regions compete at the national conference for first-, second-, third-, and fourth-place honors.

The advertising project is sponsored each year by a national advertiser such as Kodak or Saturn. The sponsor provides most of the travel funds to bring the regional winners to the national competition. Winning the AAF National Student Advertising Competition (NSAC) is considered to be one of the most prestigious accomplishments possible for a student in advertising education. The NSAC celebrated its 25th year in 1998.

The Advertising Educational Foundation

The Advertising Educational Foundation (AEF) sponsors, along with the American Academy of Advertising, a visiting professor program that places faculty members from advertising, marketing, and other academic disciplines with advertising agencies, media organizations, or advertiser companies for the purpose of gaining practical experience to bring back to the classroom. These faculty internships occur in the summer and typically are 3 weeks long.

The AEF also sponsors an "ambassador" program that brings senior advertising and marketing executives to college campuses for 2-day programs of lectures and meetings to explain to students and faculty how advertising contributes to our society. In addition, the AEF has a collection of educational materials that it makes available to college programs.

The Business Marketing Association

Formerly the Business Professional Advertising Association, the newly named Business Marketing Association (BMA) sponsors a national student competition among its member schools. The case provided for the competition is based on an industrial, professional, or business-to-business problem. The solution asked for is an advertising/marketing campaign that is videotaped by the students and submitted for national judging.

The BMA also oversees a collection of educational materials, certifies its members through examination as certified business communicators, and sponsors a back-to-school program for its members at its national conference each year.

The Direct Marketing Educational Foundation

The Direct Marketing Educational Foundation (DMEF) has a fairly broad program of support for college professors and students. For educators, the DMEF sponsors a 1-day Annual Direct Marketing Educators' Conference and a 3- to 4-day Direct Marketing Institute for Educators. The foundation awards fellowships to Direct Marketing Association (DMA) seminars and has an advanced fellowship program for educators. In addition, the DMEF produces educational materials and gives members discounts on DMA publications, which include the *Journal of Direct Marketing*. It also sponsors a student competition called ECHO.

The DMEF also offers student programs; these include a 5-day Collegiate Institute, a summer internship program, career days held in conjunction with local DMA chapters' annual conferences, and a career guidebook.

The Future of Advertising Education

Advertising education appears to be firmly established in journalism and mass communications schools nationwide. However, technological changes in the communications industry are putting pressure on educators to consider what is the appropriate curriculum with which to prepare students for this changing technological environment. Advertising course work has evolved from a skills orientation to a more theoretical approach over the past 30 years. Yet each communication specialty still provides its own professionally oriented curriculum based on the needs of the industry it serves. Critics say that this industry orientation should give way to a more integrated approach that prepares students to be communicators who can easily move across old boundaries between specialties such as advertising and public relations. The call is to look for the common corpus of knowledge that all communicators must master and to break down old artificial industry boundaries. It is yet to be seen what sort of influence these critics will have on the advertising curriculum of the future.

The growth in advertising education appears to have leveled off after two decades of rapid expansion. Some of the decline in the early 1990s was due to smaller-than-usual high school graduating classes and an economic downturn during these years. With continued improvement in the economy, and buoyancy in the numbers of university freshmen—and provided that advertising education is able to adapt to new marketplace realities—the future could be very bright. In fact, enrollments have started to increase again as we approach the year 2000. However, there are also realities on campus. Universities are suffering through some of the leanest budget years in recent memory, and consolidation of programs is one way they can deal with this problem. It is to be hoped that advertising programs will not be targeted for this type of restructuring, which could de-emphasize the importance of advertising education on campuses.

One final thought: Advertising and advertising education have been phenomenally successful during the second half of the 20th century in the United States. This success has resulted in students from all over the globe coming to the United States to study advertising. It has also resulted in the use of advertising techniques in communication areas where we had not seen their use before. The news media and entertainment media have grasped the notion that persuasive techniques as used by advertisers can work in other formats. So we have infomercials, tabloid news shows, and music videos, which are all essentially advertising. The boundaries are blurring between advertising and other forms of communication. This is the future of advertising, one in which what advertising educators have been teaching is no longer unique but pervasive. And advertising education will have to keep pace with this acceptance of techniques in fields beyond those in which these techniques originated.

Note

1. The information contained in this chapter comes from the following sources, which I also recommend as additional reading for those who would like to pursue further the topic of advertising education in the United States: Lee B. Becker and Gerald M. Kosicki, "Annual Census of Enrollment Records Fewer Undergrads," *Journalism and Mass Communication Educator,* vol. 48, no. 3, Autumn 1993, 55-65; Lee B. Becker and Gerald M. Kosicki, "Annual Survey of Enrollment

and Degrees Awarded," *Journalism and Mass Communication Educator,* vol. 52, no. 3, Autumn 1997, 63-74; Tom Duncan, Clarke Caywood, and Doug Newsom, *Preparing Advertising and Public Relations Students for the Communications Industry in the 21st Century* (Chicago: Task Force on Integrated Communications, 1993); Billy I. Ross, *The Status of Advertising Education* (Lubbock, TX: Advertising Education Publications, 1991); Billy I. Ross and Keith F. Johnson, *Where Shall I Go to Study Advertising and Public Relations?* (Lubbock, TX: Advertising Education Publications, 1998); Kim B. Rotzoll and Arnold M. Barban, "Advertising Education," in James H. Leigh and Claude R. Martin, Jr. (eds.), *Current Research and Issues in Advertising* (Ann Arbor: Division of Research, Graduate School of Business Administration, University of Michigan, 1984), 1-18.

Education for the Creative Process

Constantin G. Cotzias

Nothing in the world can take the place of persistence. Talent will not. Nothing is more common than unsuccessful men with talent. Genius will not. Unrewarded genius is almost a proverb. Education will not. The world is full of educated failures. Persistence and determination alone are omnipotent.

—Calvin Coolidge

Tenacity

Nothing scares traditionally educated, linear-thinking, anal retentive students more than having to be creative. If you ask them to regurgitate a piece of thinking from inside a textbook, reference book, or notebook, they'll do it with a smile. But if you ask them to give you an original piece of thinking

353

from inside their heads, their faces look as if they've just been stricken with polio. Eliminating the word *can't* from their vocabularies and getting them to walk with you through that dense fog known as the creative process is the first daunting task for both student and professor.

What makes those first steps a little easier is that, unbeknownst to them, they have already been practicing their creativity. One just needs to listen to the pithy one-liners they shoot at each other, the pejorative views they have about their parents, even the jokes they crack about their professors. Little do they know they have begun the process of looking at ordinary things from extraordinary points of view.

Now it is simply a process of applying that extraordinary point of view to an ordinary thing called a brand. Actually, let's scratch the word *simply,* because here is where tenacity comes in. They need to be utterly tenacious to be able to do one ad after another even if all the ads they do are horrific. It is one thing to banter well, it is another thing to apply that ability. How to keep impatient, success-driven pubescents lit is the key problem.

War stories from the business are always good, but ads that give them goose bumps are even better. Get them to develop an appetite for the award annuals. Get them to understand that 98% of the ads they see every day are pedestrian. Get them to "ooh" and "aah" over ads that are older than they are. And most important, help them understand that their success will come after a lot of failure. That is why, when taking their first creative course, they shouldn't even expect to do good ads. The only thing they should be looking to do is answer the question, Is this fun? Is the process of getting a migraine over an ad fun? If the answer is yes, then they've gotten their money's worth. If the answer is no, then they've still gotten their money's worth, because they'll know that their passions lie elsewhere.

The logic behind giving students lots of room to fail is, if it is fun, they'll ultimately succeed. They just have to keep at it long enough.

I learned persistence at the School of Visual Arts (SVA), where I took a seemingly endless series of courses while I was working in the agency business. Had someone actually discouraged me, I never would have discovered the osmosis one experiences by learning from one's mistakes. It is the kind of osmosis that seeps into every fiber of a person's being, through every pore—so that the periods between doing good ads become shorter and shorter, and one experiences the visceral thrill of coming up with a piece of thinking one knows no one else could possibly have thought of. Being allowed to fail and having the tenacity to endure it is what made my SVA experience more valuable than undergraduate and graduate schools combined. I learned to be relentless. I learned what it is to hunger for work. I learned to strive for success when no evidence of it seemed to exist. That kind of passion breeds success. All one needs is time.

Judgment

Before students can do good work, they have to know what good is. That's why the award books should become your guiding light. Serious students of advertising will learn more from the One Show, art directors' award books, and communication arts annuals than from most of their professors. There, they will learn what is good. They'll learn who's doing good work. They'll learn which agencies are good and which are dreary. And after close scrutiny, they'll learn that just because an ad won an award, that doesn't mean it's a good ad. It is at that point they'll begin to develop judgment.

To begin fostering their judgment, ask your students to go to the library and photocopy ads from the award books that knock them out—ads so good that if they did any one of them in their careers, they would retire. What students first bring to class is interesting. They usually focus on ads that use obvious wordplay put to visuals deemed "outrageous." That's when you ask the students to look at their ads from three points of view:

1. What's in it for me, a consumer?
2. What's in it for me, a client?
3. What's in it for me, a creative person?

When students look at an ad from a consumer's point of view, they begin to ask themselves such questions as "Would this ad get me to buy the brand?" "Does this brand answer a need I have?" "Does the ad give me, the consumer, enough benefit?" When they look at the ad from the point of view of a client, they ask a different set of questions: "Is this ad saying enough about my brand that it is worth hundreds of thousands of dollars to produce and run it?" "Do I own what it does say about my brand, or could any company put their name underneath?" "Is this how I want my brand represented?" Finally, when they look at an ad from a creative person's point of view, the most fun questions come to mind: "Why would I win a gold in the One Show for this?" "Would any of my advertising heroes hire me for doing this ad?" "Did the creatives get their creative rocks off coming up with this ad?"

Once they have analyzed their ads from these points of view, students realize that a vacuous play on words under a bizarre visual is, at best, self-indulgent. They also realize that doing ads that are responsible to both client and consumer requires artistry, if it is also to be done with wit. Soon, students' appreciation for irony grows, as well as their appreciation for ads that actually say something. In fact, ads that say something in a provocative way are ultimately the most appealing of all.

As students begin to form their own judgment, they begin to set benchmarks for their own work. Those students who actually find ads that make them drool are less likely to come into class with inadequate ads of their own. But, besides improving judgment, students of the annuals also learn to be original. They see that, year after year, none of the thinking in these ads is repeated. And most important, students see for themselves that, to be truly original, they first have to know what has already been done.

Research: Another Exercise in Tenacity

Before the pithy headline, before the dramatic visual, the creative process starts with research. It is impossible to do adequate advertising if one does not know the brand as well as the person who makes it. Quite simply, great facts make great ads.

I am not talking about demographics or psychographics that go into the marketing of the product. I am talking about those tangible facts that specifically answer consumers' needs. It is those facts that are the building blocks to any proposition or set of propositions that are at the heart of the advertisement. The best way for a student to obtain these facts is to call the client directly. I know my students have done a good job researching when I get calls from the company complaining about all the calls they have received.

Obviously, the key here is to ask the right questions. The way to know is to ask yourself if there is an ad in the answer to the question you are asking. As an example, let's pretend that ADT Security System is the assignment. I would call them and ask: "Is ADT used in prisons?" "Does the government use it, in the Pentagon, or the White House, or the CIA?" "Do major New York City jewelry houses use it?" "How about banks?" "How about police stations?" "Do other security companies use ADT to protect themselves?" Clearly, an affirmative answer to any one of these questions would make for a drop-dead ad. (In fact, the answer is yes to all of them.) "But isn't that the account executive's job?" ask most students. The problem is that most account executives have never written an advertisement. And most account executives try to protect their creative colleagues from what they consider superfluous information.

Once, at the large New York agency Batten, Barton, Durstine and Osborn (BBDO), I was given the assignment to do a print campaign for GE Silicone sealant, a caulk that lasts 50 years. After being briefed, I had a gut feeling there was some piece of gold I had not been given. So I called GE and pretended I was a student at SVA researching a class assignment. My jaw dropped when I asked the product manager if there had been any industrial applications of the caulk. "Well, yeah. It's used to keep the tiles up on the space shuttle."

I called the account executive. "Why in God's name didn't you tell me that this stuff was used on the space shuttle?" His response was, "Well, because I heard a couple of the tiles fell off." The first ad for GE Silicone sealant had a simple headline:

IF WE CAN KEEP 99% OF THE TILES UP ON THE SPACE SHUTTLE,
WE CAN KEEP 100% OF THE TILES DOWN ON YOUR FLOOR.

Students should always get their own information. They never know what facts they'll dig up. Once when a student researched Nicoderm as a class assignment, he came into class with no ads. When asked why, he said he came up with a fact that prevented him from doing any ads at all. Upon hearing it, I told him to use that fact and do an ad for using hypnosis to stop smoking. He did. The ad was so good I told him to produce it on a desktop publisher and run it in the local *PennySaver* newspaper, the client being Citizens for Hypnosis. The ad read:

THE ACTIVE INGREDIENT IN NICODERM MUST BE GOOD.
EXTERMINATORS HAVE BEEN USING IT FOR YEARS.

It became a finalist in the One Show. This last anecdote brings up a valuable point. The mind-set of a fact finder should be that of a mercenary. "What great facts will help me create great ads that'll make me famous?" "There's an ad in that" should become every advertising student's mantra.

The Concept: Tangents and Chains of Ideas

Students who are creating ads for the first time in their lives seem to go through the same catharsis. The first stage seems to be the relentless pursuit of the best pun, augmented with a visual deemed "wild and wacky," in a futile attempt at being funny. Once the words "wild and wacky" have been deleted from their vocabulary, the realization that advertising is still a communications business seems to dawn on most students.

The second stage then usually comes in the form of a banal statement about the product accompanied by an even duller product shot. When asked what the ad is trying to say, they inevitably refer to the squiggles at the bottom of the page representing the unwritten body copy. It is at this point that students become cognizant of the need to have a concept before they can even begin to deliberate over their witty headlines. The notion of conceiving an original thought brings the average, linear-thinking, regimented, programmed student to an abrupt halt.

Unfortunately, the traditional means of breaking through this level is trial and error. Professor and student patiently wait for that piece of provocative thinking that demonstrates some semblance of talent. The problem with trial and error is the level of frustration incurred. For every ad that even remotely possesses a piece of original thinking, the student endures the humiliating process of creating a great many vacuous ones. It is usually at this point the student throws up his or her hands, quits, and becomes an account executive.

There is, however, a technique that can totally demystify the creative process. The first step is to make the student understand that creativity is nothing more than taking something ordinary (a brand) and looking at it from an extraordinary point of view (an ad). With that as a definition, we then only need to strive to see things differently.

To exemplify this point, let's take the observation that "the sky is blue" and simply ask, What does that mean? Well, for one thing, it means it is not raining. It means the sun is out. It means we're looking up. It means there's atmosphere. And it clearly means we're not in Upstate New York. Obviously, the last of these is the most interesting point of view on the boring observation that the sky is blue.

If we break down this example, we can see that an interesting dynamic is taking place. For one thing, nothing more than sheer common sense is being used to look at this ordinary thing from a variety of points of view. The choice of "we're not in Upstate New York" as the most interesting selection is visceral, not intellectual.

Now let's take another ordinary item and try to look at it from different, extraordinary points of view in order to redefine it—let's say a piece of chalk. If we put "Chalk is:" on top of a piece of paper, we can list different ways of looking at it other than just as a piece of chalk:

- It's a toy that enables you to play hopscotch.
- It's a device that makes an annoying sound.
- It's a substance made of crushed seashells.
- It's an 18th-century computer.
- It's a tool that outlines dead bodies.

By looking at a piece of chalk from such different points of view, we've literally given it five new definitions. It's now no longer just a piece of chalk. Isn't that essentially what we do with a brand to create an ad?

These exercises can easily be elaborated into methods for creating ads for a product. As an example, let's say the assignment is Lexol leather conditioner and preservative. The first step is to define, clearly and succinctly, what this product is and does. By paraphrasing the description on the bottle, we define Lexol as "an oil preservative that can repair cracked leather." Working with a black marker on a 17-by-22-inch sheet of white drawing paper, we put what the product is and does in the middle of the page and circle it. When we apply the same method of thinking as we did for "The sky is blue" and "Chalk is:" to Lexol, five related ideas immediately come to mind, although obviously an infinite number exist. I call these ideas *tangents,* and in turn they can produce further chains of ideas.

As Figure 28.1 shows, there are five tangents leading from the basic brand description "an oil preservative that repairs cracked leather":

1. Skin cream for leather
2. Leather protector
3. Makes old leather look new
4. Heals leather like skin
5. Leather moisturizer

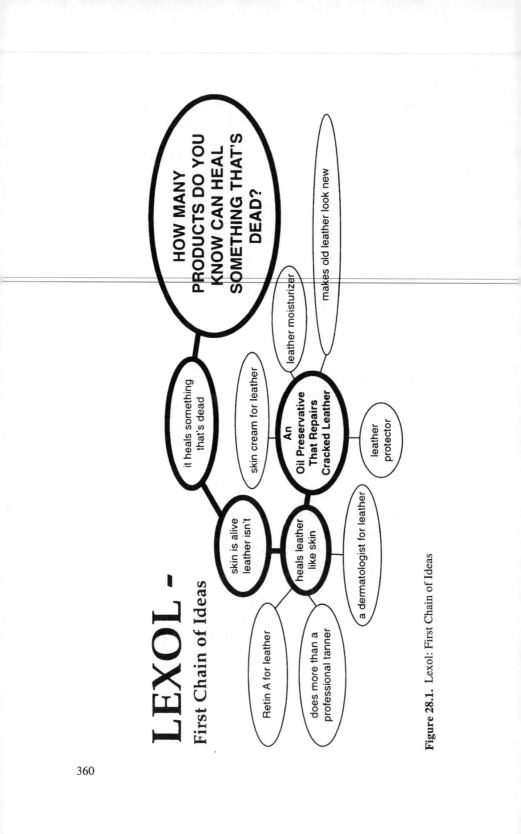

LEXOL -
First Chain of Ideas

HOW MANY PRODUCTS DO YOU KNOW CAN HEAL SOMETHING THAT'S DEAD?

it heals something that's dead

skin is alive leather isn't

skin cream for leather

leather moisturizer

makes old leather look new

An Oil Preservative That Repairs Cracked Leather

leather protector

heals leather like skin

a dermatologist for leather

Retin A for leather

does more than a professional tanner

Figure 28.1. Lexol: First Chain of Ideas

Of these five tangents, the one I would viscerally choose as the most interesting is "heals leather like skin." Once again, the same tangential thinking is applied to this point of departure. Also shown in Figure 28.1 are our four new tangents:

1. Does more than a professional tanner
2. A dermatologist for leather
3. Retin A for leather
4. Skin is alive, leather isn't

The most conceptually provocative tangent to my taste is "skin is alive, leather isn't." The logical extension, which totally redefines what Lexol is and does, is that it can heal something that is dead. Thus, if you have a tight shot of the description on the bottle where it says "repairs cracked leather" as the visual, the headline of the ad could simply be "How Many Products Do You Know Can Heal Something That's Dead?"

Let us assume for a moment that this ad is considered too cerebral, and we should look at a more direct approach. Going back to our original five tangents, we can apply our technique to, say, "leather protector." Figure 28.2 shows three simple tangents:

1. Protects leather upholstery
2. Protects leather books
3. Protects leather artifacts

If we take the first one and simply pose the question, "Is Lexol recommended by car manufacturers?" an easy phone call to local car dealers provides us with three new tangents:

1. BMW—no
2. Ferrari—yes
3. Mercedes-Benz—yes

My preference is Ferrari. The fact that Lexol leather conditioner is part of the car's maintenance lends itself immediately to the headline "The First Oil and Lube Job Ferrari Insists You Do Yourself." Let us say that this line is judged to be too glib, but we still want to do something direct, perhaps more visual. Going back to our three "leather protector" tangents, a leather artifact could

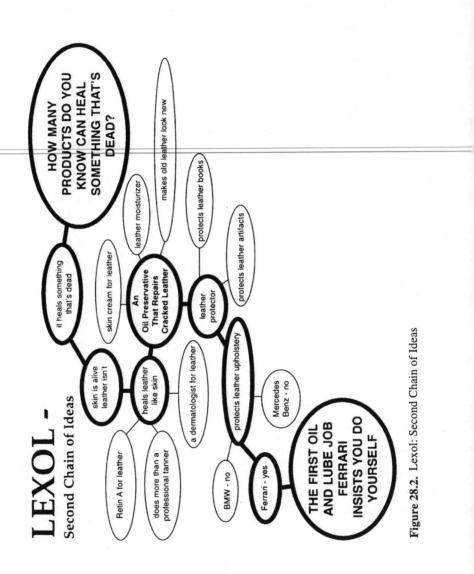

Figure 28.2. Lexol: Second Chain of Ideas

prove to be strongly visual, depending on what it is. After placing telephone calls to a variety of museums, we find Lexol is used on the following items (a train of thinking actually pursued by my students):

1. Teddy Roosevelt's riding boots at the Roosevelt Library
2. Ancient Native American leather pieces at the Museum of Natural History
3. Charles Lindbergh's leather helmet at the Smithsonian

Let us say that Lindbergh's helmet strikes our fancy the most. We apply our technique to this point of departure. As shown in Figure 28.3, three possible tangents come to mind:

1. It's in a glass case
2. It's the first piece of leather to cross the Atlantic by air
3. It's also protected by the Smithsonian's security

Because Lexol is a leather protector, the last tangent lends itself to the following ad:

Visual: Lindbergh's helmet displayed at the Smithsonian
Headline: "Protected by a $150,000 Alarm System and One Bottle of Lexol"

For the purposes of presentation, this creative approach has obviously been simplified. Here we dealt with no more than five tangents in any one level. However, because we are working with circles (as well as in them), it becomes clear that no matter how many points of view you come up with there are always others. Because a circle has 360 degrees, there are at least that many points of departure. This is a demonstration that ideas are infinite rather than finite.

The other advantage to this approach is that it *takes the fear out of a blank piece of paper.* Instead of waiting for a bolt of lightning from the heavens, the students understand that ideas are something to be pursued. With practice, this has become a proven method for a number of working professionals at New York's most creative agencies. This technique also benefits students who have yet to use it to come up with an ad. Because it is visual, it enables those who are linear in their thinking to use their minds tangentially. It helps them focus on their instinctual rather than their intellectual abilities. But most important,

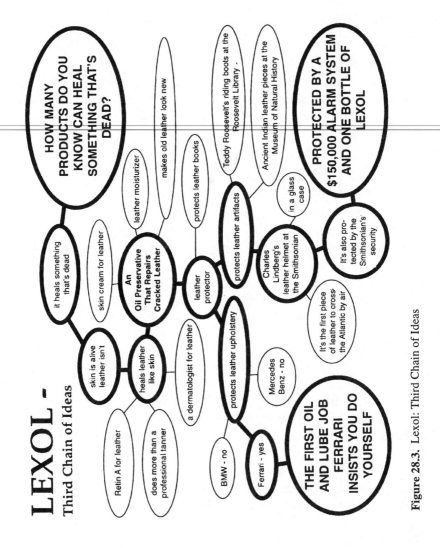

LEXOL -
Third Chain of Ideas

HOW MANY PRODUCTS DO YOU KNOW CAN HEAL SOMETHING THAT'S DEAD?

it heals something that's dead

skin is alive leather isn't

skin cream for leather

leather moisturizer

makes old leather look new

An Oil Preservative That Repairs Cracked Leather

heals leather like skin

a dermatologist for leather

Retin A for leather

does more than a professional tanner

protects leather books

leather protector

protects leather artifacts

protects leather upholstery

Mercedes Benz - no

BMW - no

Ferrari - yes

THE FIRST OIL AND LUBE JOB FERRARI INSISTS YOU DO YOURSELF

Charles Lindberg's leather helmet at the Smithsonian

in a glass case

Teddy Roosevelt's riding boots at the Roosevelt Library

Ancient Indian leather pieces at the Museum of Natural History

It's the first piece of leather to cross the Atlantic by air

It's also protected by the Smithsonian's security

PROTECTED BY A $150,000 ALARM SYSTEM AND ONE BOTTLE OF LEXOL

Figure 28.3. Lexol: Third Chain of Ideas

it teaches them that thinking of an idea can be just as much fun as executing one.

For those students who jump into execution too quickly, this method immediately slams the brakes on them. An appreciation for *ideas* is created, instead of just pithy lines. It also fosters curiosity, because it forces the students to question the object they're looking at. Soon they're able to regress to the mental age of a 4-year-old child who is constantly asking, "What if?" or "Why?" How many times as adults have we been stumped by the questions of 4-year-olds like "Why is the sky blue?" "Well, the sky is blue because . . . Oh . . . why is the sky blue?" By bringing back this kind of curiosity, old things look new again, which helps us look at things from new points of view. When a student uses this technique faithfully, his or her creative method begins to take shape. Soon what follows is the development of that individual's voice and creative style. It is then that the student can realize the single most coveted ability in advertising: consistency.

As students start to get an understanding of what ideas are and how to use them, they can begin to employ a more sophisticated method to help generate ads.

The Concept: Generating and Organizing Tag Lines

A good tag line is the campaign idea articulated in one sentence and used to tie together the ads in a series.

- "Suburu. Inexpensive and built to stay that way" has a depth of thinking that gives direction to at least 2 years' worth of executions.
- "Perdue. It takes a tough man to make a tender chicken" is a line that allows for ad after ad featuring a very driven and single-minded character doing everything he can to make his chickens tender.
- "Volvo. The car for people who think" conjures up intelligent ads about a car that is bought by intelligent people.

Each of these classic tag lines carried its respective campaign for years if not decades.

For an exercise in producing tag lines, the best place to start is with a 4-by-4-inch pad of paper and one very long blank wall. As students come up with tag lines for a product, each is written on a sheet of paper and taped up on the wall. They don't have to be tightly written lines, but they must be tightly thought-out ideas. Soon, it becomes clear that these ideas reflect a variety of different creative positionings for our brand. We start by organizing them horizontally across the wall, reflecting the different viewpoints on this product. It soon becomes apparent that a number of lines are mere rephrasings of the same thoughts. We put those up vertically, with the line we feel has the most depth on top.

When we step back and look at our wall, we can begin to see that our thinking has been organized in an interesting way. The horizontal lines represent campaign ideas, whereas the vertical lines represent ideas for individual ads under one campaign.

The use of this technique requires students to be comfortable writing lines. They literally "shotgun" line after line on pieces of paper with little thought to the phrasing. When a particular line strikes our interest, we go back and rewrite it as tightly as possible until we feel comfortable with it as an ad.

Although writer-driven, this technique invariably conjures up images. Notations about the image should be written in parentheses under each respective line. The interesting thing about this technique is that we may never come up with the tag line, but we're sure to come up with ads that have evolved out of a focused piece of thinking. In fact, that's what this technique is designed to do: make the students focus on what they are trying to say. In a sense, this is much like the tangent/chain technique; it just organizes thinking with lines instead. Obviously the tangent/chain technique can be used to generate the lines put up on the wall. But whichever technique is used, this exercise is an excellent way to make thinking fun and a method of creating conceptual advertising without getting a cerebral hemorrhage.

Execution

If you watch consumers flipping through magazines, you will see that few will spend even 3 seconds looking at an ad. The problem for most students and creative beginners is that creative directors will spend even less time looking at the students' ads when flipping through their portfolios (usually referred to as their books). To say an ad has to be as clear as a bell is an understatement. It may have the wittiest, pithiest piece of thinking ever conceived, but if a creative director does not get it in 3 seconds, it is nothing but air.

At one of the agencies where I worked, I had a secretary who had the IQ of a kitchen sink. When my creative director asked me if I wanted to get rid of her, I said absolutely not. To me she was a piece of gold. After every ad I wrote, I would show it to her and ask, "Do you get it?"

"Well, I really don't like this ad because . . . "

"No, no, no. I don't want to know if you like it, I want to know if you get it."

"Oh, I get it."

Bingo. The dumbest human being on earth got this ad. Perfect. Idiots are invaluable. Every junior should find one. The next problem most juniors face is making their work provocative.

When a creative director has a job vacancy, his or her office turns into a sea of black portfolio cases. If you calculate that there are an average of 25 ads per book, that is an enormous amount of clutter for a beginner's work to cut through just to get noticed.

"Attitude"

One surefire way for a junior to get his or her ads noticed is to give the ads as much "attitude" as possible. If you study Ed McCabe's work during the Scali heyday, you'll see that he built an entire agency with smart pieces of communication said in the most provocative, "attitudinal" way possible. In fact, you could put the word *schmuck* at the end of each of his lines:

- Perdue: "My chickens eat better than you do," schmuck.
- Horn and Hardarts: "You can't eat atmosphere," schmuck.
- Public service: "Your lungs are as dirty as your window sill," schmuck.

Headlines

The same applies to headlines. If a student finds him- or herself hankering to put an exclamation point at the end of a line, then the message has definitely not been delivered in the most provocative way possible. The interesting thing about exclamation points on headlines is that you never see them in the award books, only in hack newspaper ads.

Puns

Virtually anybody can write a pun—even a good pun. But puns usually don't have ideas behind them. They're nothing but wordplay that inspires nothing more than a "yuk, yuk" poke in the ribs with an elbow.

Strong Ending to the Headline

If a line feels dull, look to see if your student hasn't buried the most provocative word in the middle of the line. Rodney Dangerfield, in my view, would have made an outstanding copywriter. He is a master of the one-liner. Analyze his work, such as this line: "I went to tell my son about the birds and the bees, and he told me about my wife and the mailman." If you put the word *mailman* anywhere else in that line, it falls flat on its face.

The Visual

The most obvious way to make any ad provocative, however, is with the visual. I strongly recommend that students stay away from product shots as visuals. For all intents and purposes, it is a waste. The best way to assess whether a visual is provocative is to ask yourself if this is a shoot you would want to go to. If you are merely shooting a product, all you have to look forward to are the bagels served at every shoot. Students are putting together speculative portfolios ("spec books"). There are no cost limitations to producing their ads. Their visuals can cost as much as they want. A visual book is as important for a writer as it is for an art director. By the same token, a well-written book is just as vital for an art director as for a writer.

Words and Pictures Working Together

The most important thing a well-written line and a provocative visual have to do is work together. Ideally, I should not be able to understand one without the other. Neil Drossman once did an ad that had a man in a wheelchair fiddling around with the back of a television set. The headline was "What You're Seeing Is a TV Repairing a Man." The ironic twist of the ad is strengthened because of how the visual and the line work together. If one is covered up, you don't understand the other. Neither is redundant. Here, the studying of comic scripts like Gary Larson's "The Far Side" helps. Rarely do you see one of his cartoons that doesn't turn the visual or the line into a straight man.

Tension Between Words and Pictures

This brings us to creating tension between line and visual. A British radio station once ran an ad to get advertisers to advertise on radio. The picture showed Adolf Hitler with a contorted face screaming into a microphone. The headline was simply "Radio Works." The secret of the advertisement was the complementarity between the headline and the visual. One was a set up for the other, giving both line and visual enormous punch.

One of the best examples of tension in an ad is the now-classic Maxell audiotape poster in which a man is blasted by a pair of stereo speakers and his hair, drink, and furniture are flying. The line to that ad is incredibly dull. It simply says, "After 500 plays our high fidelity tape still plays high fidelity." The lesson here is which sets up which. If the line had been on the bottom, the ad would not come close to having the punch it has. It would have left the reader with a dull line instead of a bizarre visual.

Which Is Read First—Headline or Visual?

In art directing their ads, students have to be sensitive to which they want to be read first, the line or the visual. Once that is decided, then the element to be read first has to be made dominant in the layout of the ad.

Believability

The final point in executing any ad is believability. More important than a speculative ad's being true is it's being believable. This I learned with an actual advertisement I wrote. The ad was for Clorox Soft Scrub. Visually, the line was all scratched up; it said: "One Can of Comet Will Do More Damage to Your Bathroom Than 15 Years of Use." Upon seeing that ad, Joe O'Neill, a senior colleague, said, "Before you engrave this, change 15 years to 5." "Why?" I asked. "The truth is it's 15 years." O'Neill said, "It doesn't matter. I don't believe 15 years. I believe 5 years. If you reduce the years you're still telling the truth, but now I believe you."

This is a particularly valuable lesson for students. Because their ads are speculative, I have less reason to believe a fact or even a dramatic visual—unlike a real advertisement for a real brand, it does not have to be truthful. That's why, when it comes to speculative work, believability is much more important than truth.

Again the Concept

In an era when execution reigns, my advice is still to concentrate on concept. Once a truly provocative concept is attained, an equally provocative execution will evolve. That is why I used to run Sunday-night creative workshops for my students. There they worked in teams for a couple of hours on an assignment that never went to execution. They just thought of ideas. I would go from team to team and simply critique their thinking. The logic is, once you have an idea that is focused, clear, and provocative, lines and visuals will just drop right into your lap.

The methods I have described in this chapter are highly pragmatic. But I can attest to their effectiveness and have practiced them for many years. They are a result of accrued knowledge attained from taking and teaching a multitude of courses, as well as 15 years' writing experience at five significant New York advertising agencies.

Index

About the Contributors

Alexander L. Biel is a distinguished international market research and marketing consultant, as well as an acknowledged expert on brand equity and advertising evaluation. He was educated at the University of Chicago and Columbia University. After serving as Associate Director of Research at Leo Burnett, he held a series of senior posts at Ogilvy & Mather in Europe and North America. He was Executive Director of David Ogilvy's Center for Research & Development (later the WPP Center for R&D). He is the author of more than 70 articles and papers on marketing topics, and his 1993 book *Brand Equity and Advertising* (with David Aaker) is in its fourth printing. He is a nonexecutive director of Research International and President of Alexander L. Biel & Associates in San Francisco, California.

Harold F. Clark, Jr., is president of Smith Clark Associates, a communications and marketing consulting firm in Amenia, New York. Among his clients are Johnson & Johnson, the Bechtel Corporation, the American Association of Advertising Agencies, J. Walter Thompson, and the American Soybean Association. He spent 28 years at J. Walter Thompson, from which he retired in 1988 as Executive Vice President and member of the board of directors, responsible for advertising standards and training and development worldwide. He is a graduate of Amherst College (B.A.), Stanford University (M.A.), and Columbia University (Ph.D.).

John Dalla Costa is a Canadian advertising practitioner and consultant. He was former President/CEO of Miller, Myers, Bruce, Dalla Costa Inc., a prominent marketing and advertising consultancy. He completed the Owner/President Program at the Harvard Business School. He is currently President of Catalysis Consulting, Inc., in Toronto, working with senior executives from blue-chip companies on organizational renewal, brand equity planning, and relationship management. He is the author of three books, including *The Ethical Imperative: Why Moral Leadership Is Good Business.* He is a regular columnist for the *Financial Post* magazine and *Marketing* magazine. He is also an instructor in the Executive Education Marketing Program at Queen's School of Business, Queen's University, Kingston, Ontario, and founder of the Centre for Ethical Orientation, working with academic and business leaders to foster "a global ethic for the global economy."

Constantin G. Cotzias received his B.A. from Gettysburg College and his M.B.A. from New York University. He spent 15 years as a copywriter at a number of agencies, including Ammirati Puris; Scali McCabe Sloves; Levine, Huntley, Schmidt, & Beaver; BBDO; and Messner Vetere. He has been the recipient of many major advertising awards, including One Show, Andy, Clio, and the International Film Festival. His students have won numerous student awards, including two silvers and two bronzes in the One Show. He is currently an Associate Professor at the VCU Adcenter (Virginia Commonwealth University) in Richmond, Virginia.

Janet DiLorenzo earned her M.B.A. in marketing from Hofstra University and her doctorate in business from Columbia University. She is currently Professor of Marketing in Fordham University's College of Business. In addition, she is Coordinator of and Adviser to the Marketing Internship Program for undergraduate business students. She has taught a variety of marketing courses, including courses in international marketing, entrepreneurship, advertising, marketing internship, and consumer behavior. She has been the recipient of the Dean's Award for Teaching Excellence at Fordham University. Previously, she has worked full-time for such organizations as Lord and Taylor and Mobil Oil Corporation. In addition, she has worked as a consultant in strategic planning and promotion for Canon, MCI, and Polo/Ralph Lauren. Her research interests are in the areas of marketing education, advertising, international marketing, and service marketing. She has published articles in such journals as the *Journal of Marketing for Higher Education, Psychology & Marketing,* and *Multinational Business Review.*

Andy Farr is Group Research and Development Director for the Millward Brown Group, based in the United Kingdom, where he is responsible for the development of new techniques in the areas of brand, advertising, and media research. He joined Millward Brown in 1985 and has worked in a wide range of markets, including packaged goods, media, and automotive, specializing in advertising research. In 1990 he moved to become U.K. Research & Development Director, working with Gordon Brown, the company's founder. With Brown, he has jointly published papers on the relationship between the immediate and longer-term effects of advertising, winning the WPP Atticus award for original thinking in marketing services. In 1994 he was a founding member of Millward Brown's global R&D team, working on the development and enhancement of Millward Brown's portfolio of research products. In 1996 he was responsible for the creation of Millward Brown's successful brand equity evaluation system, BrandDynamics™, and in 1998 worked with the advertising and media group WPP to develop and launch the WPP BRANDZ™ study, a global monitor of brand equity covering 3,500 brands based on the BrandDynamics methodology. He has published a wide range of papers relating to advertising effectiveness and brand building, print media effectiveness, and effective frequency. He was a judge for the 1998 Institute of Practitioners in Advertising (IPA) Advertising Effectiveness Awards in the United Kingdom.

Paul Feldwick, a graduate of Oxford University, is a leading British advertising analyst and planner. He is currently Executive Planning Director at BMP DDB, London (the agency where Stanley Pollitt pioneered the account planning concept in the 1960s), and he also has global responsibilities with DDB Needham Worldwide. He is a key participant in the Institute of Practitioners in Advertising (IPA) Advertising Effectiveness Awards and editor of two volumes of the collected prize-winning papers, *Advertising Works 5* and *Advertising Works 6.* A Fellow of the IPA and of the Market Research Society, he is a well-known writer and speaker on advertising and research topics.

David Haigh read English at Bristol University before qualifying as a Chartered Accountant with Price Waterhouse in London. He worked in international financial management then moved into the marketing services sector, first as Financial Director of the Creative Business and then as Financial Director of WCRS & Partners. He left to set up a financial marketing consultancy, which was later acquired by Publicis, the pan-European marketing services group, where he worked as a Director for 5 years. He moved to Interbrand as Director of Brand Valuation in its London-based global brand valuation practice, leaving in 1996 to launch Brand Finance Limited, where he is Managing Director. He is a Fellow of the U.K. Chartered Institute of Marketing and a member of the Institute of Practitioners in Advertising (IPA) Advertising Effectiveness Awards judging panel. He is the author of several books on brand valuation, and has written extensively for the financial and marketing press on the same subject, including articles for *The Times, Journal of Brand Management, Brand Strategy, Marketing Business,* and *Admap.*

John Philip Jones is a British-born American academic and a graduate of Cambridge University (B.A. with honors and M.A. in economics). He spent 27 years in the advertising agency business, including 25 years with J. Walter Thompson in Britain, Holland, and Scandinavia, managing the advertising for a wide range of major brands of repeat-purchase packaged goods. In 1981, he joined the faculty of the S. I. Newhouse School of Public Communications, Syracuse University, where he is now a tenured full Professor and former Chairman of the Advertising Department. He is also Adjunct Professor at the Royal Melbourne Institute of Technology, Australia. His published works include six books and more than 70 journal articles. He specializes in the measurement of advertising effects, and is an active consultant to many advertisers and advertising agencies in the United States and overseas. He has been the recipient of a number of professional awards, and is currently a member of the (U.S.) National Advertising Review Board.

Mary Baumgartner Jones was born in Indiana but grew up in Europe, New York, and Georgia. She received a B.A. in international relations from Mount Holyoke College. She began her career as a Management Consultant with R. S. Carmichael and Company, a firm specializing in new product development and marketing for financial services companies. From there she moved to Grey Direct to learn the discipline of direct marketing, and then on to Ross Roy Communications/NY to head that agency's account services department.

She currently works at Home Box Office (HBO), where she has spent time working in advertising and new product development; she holds the position of Director of Field Marketing and Promotion.

Judie Lannon is a distinguished qualitative researcher and marketing communications strategist based in the United Kingdom. After graduating in psychology from the University of Michigan, she began her career with Leo Burnett in Chicago. She then spent 20 years with J. Walter Thompson in London, becoming Research and Development Director for J. Walter Thompson Europe. Currently she manages her own consultancy. Her expertise is in developing local and international communication strategies for British and international clients as well as running courses in research and marketing communications. She has published many papers on research, branding, and integrated communications and is a frequent speaker at international conferences and business schools. She is editor of the prestigious journal of the Marketing Society in Britain, *Market Leader,* features editor for the *International Journal of Advertising,* and a member of the judging panel of the Market Research Society (U.K.). She is active in promoting closer relationships between academia and the practitioner world.

Carla V. Lloyd is a tenured Associate Professor at the S. I. Newhouse School of Public Communications, Syracuse University, and former Chair of the Advertising Department there. She holds a B.A. from the University of Utah; an M.A. from the Medill School of Journalism, Northwestern University; and a Ph.D. in sociology from the Maxwell School of Citizenship and Public Affairs, Syracuse University. As a widely recognized teacher who specializes in advertising media planning, she has won a number of awards and has professional experience in publishing, retailing, and newspaper sales. Before joining the Syracuse University faculty, she was an Instructor at the University of Miami, Oxford, Ohio. She has copublished articles with Dr. Dennis Martin (author of the best-selling media workbook *The Media Flight Plan*).

Richard E. Mathisen is Professor of Marketing at Coles College of Business, Kennesaw State University, Georgia. He is a specialist in the increasingly important field of green marketing.

Delight L. Omohundro was National Merit Scholar in creative writing at Cornell and has an M.S. in nutritional biology. She received her Ph.D. from

Syracuse University with a dissertation on the use of food labels by the elderly. During her advertising career she has worked with William Bernbach and Mary Wells, at Caldor's and Warner's, and for clients such as Chevrolet, Velcro, *Playboy,* and J. L. Hudson, the world's largest department store. She has also won Addy awards for consumer and business advertising. She is the author of *How to Win the Grocery Game,* which is still used as a consumer text, and she spent 2 years as an editor at *Consumer Digest.* She has taught advertising, copywriting, and media at the S. I. Newhouse School of Public Communications at Syracuse University, and she is currently President of Megafax Research Inc., which specializes in the measurement of customer satisfaction for large corporations.

Filip Palda is Associate Professor of Economics at the National School of Public Administration in Montreal, Canada. He received his Ph.D. in economics from the University of Chicago in 1989. He has written five books, edited five books, and published numerous articles in learned journals on political phenomena and on the interaction of the tax system with the underground economy.

Kristian Palda is Professor at the Queen's University School of Business in Canada. He received his Ph.D. in business from the University of Chicago in 1963, where his doctoral dissertation, "The Measurement of Cumulative Advertising Effects," won the Ford Foundation Doctoral Dissertation Prize. His research covers marketing, political advertising, and research and development policy. He is the author of eight books and numerous academic publications in such periodicals as the *Journal of Business, Journal of Marketing Research,* and *Journal of Law and Economics.* His current research is on the history of political terror.

Jan S. Slater, Ph.D., is Assistant Professor of Advertising in the E. W. Scripps School of Journalism at Ohio University in Athens, Ohio. Prior to her appointment at Ohio University, she was Assistant Professor and Coordinator of the Advertising Major at Xavier University in Cincinnati, Ohio, and an Instructor in Advertising at the S. I. Newhouse School of Public Communications at Syracuse University, as well as at the University of Nebraska in Omaha. In addition to her 10 years of teaching experience, she has 20 years' experience in the advertising industry, having worked in both private industry and advertising agencies. Until 1990, she owned her own agency, J. Slater &

Associates, in Omaha, Nebraska. She earned her B.A. from Hastings College, Hastings, Nebraska; an M.S. in advertising from the University of Illinois, Champaign-Urbana; and a Ph.D. in mass communications from Syracuse University.

Mark Stockdale holds a bachelor's degree in economics and statistics and a master's degree (with commendation) in marketing. He worked for a number of years in marketing and account planning in three major London agencies: Allen Brady & Marsh, J. Walter Thompson, and Leagas Delaney. He joined Leo Burnett London in 1992 as Brand Planning Director and was promoted in 1996 to Executive Planning Director. He is also a member of the agency's management group. He sits on the (British) Institute of Practitioners in Advertising (IPA) Value of Advertising Committee and is the author of the IPA's Guide to Producing Effective Financial Services Advertising; he is also a member of the (British) Account Planning Group Executive. He is a regular speaker at conferences and the author of numerous journal articles.

Bruce G. Vanden Bergh, Ph.D., is Professor in the Department of Advertising at Michigan State University, where he has been on the faculty since 1978. During his time there, he has been Chair of the Graduate Affairs Committee and Chair of the Department of Advertising. He was President of the American Academy of Advertising in 1995 and has been appointed to the Academic Division of the American Advertising Federation (AAF). He has published widely in academic journals and has coauthored two books in the field: *Advertising Campaign Strategy* and *Advertising Principles.* He has also served on the editorial advisory boards of the *Journal of Advertising* and *Journalism & Mass Communication Quarterly.* He has been the recipient of several honors, including the AAF's Distinguished Educator Award in 1996 and the Distinguished Alumni Award from the College of Communications at the University of Tennessee in 1994. His specialties are in the areas of advertising creativity, campaign development, and consumer behavior.

Roderick White graduated from Cambridge University and spent more than 35 years in advertising, with J. Walter Thompson and Lansdown Conquest, as planner, researcher, and marketing consultant. During this time, he has worked in a very wide range of markets, both in the United Kingdom and internationally, for clients that range from major multinationals such as Unilever, Nestlé, Kodak, Ford, and Kellogg's to trade associations, government departments, and agencies of the United Nations. In recent years he has concentrated on financial services markets and on the application of theories of consumer goods marketing and branding in this field. He is the author of two books and numerous articles in the marketing and advertising press. He is the editor of *Admap,* an established British monthly magazine providing a practitioner's view of developments in communications, marketing, and the media.

Charles Ziff was a graduate of Wesleyan University. He was founder of Ziff Marketing, specializing in marketing and advertising services for arts organizations. He served as Marketing Specialist in the Ford Foundation Office on the Arts, as Vice President for promotion at the Brooklyn Academy of Music, as Managing Director of the Nicolais-Louis Foundation for Dance, and as Director of the American Arts Alliance. He taught at New York University and at the City University of New York. He died in 1992.